SERIES 79
EXAM STUDY GUIDE
2025 + TEST BANK

SECURITIES INSTITUTE
SECURITIES LICENSING SERIES

The Securities Institute of America proudly publishes world class textbooks, test banks and video training classes for the following Financial Services exams:

Securities Industry Essentials exam / SIE exam
Series 3 exam
Series 4 exam
Series 6 exam
Series 7 exam
Series 9 exam
Series 10 exam
Series 22 exam
Series 24 exam
Series 26 exam
Series 39 exam
Series 57 exam
Series 63 exam
Series 65 exam
Series 66 exam
Series 79 exam
Series 99 exam

For more information, visit us at www.securitiesCE.com.

SERIES 79 EXAM STUDY GUIDE 2025 + TEST BANK

Investment Banking Representative Exam

The Securities Institute of America, Inc.

Copyright © by The Securities Institute of America, Inc. All rights reserved.

Published by The Securities Institute of America, Inc.

No part of this publication may be reproduced, stored in a retrieval system, or transmitted in any form or by any means, electronic, mechanical, photocopying, recording, scanning, or otherwise, except as permitted under Section 107 or 108 of the 1976 United States Copyright Act, without either the prior written permission of The Securities Institute of America, Inc.

Limit of Liability/Disclaimer of Warranty: While the publisher and author have used their best efforts in preparing this book, they make no representations or warranties with respect to the accuracy or completeness of the contents of this book and specifically disclaim any implied warranties of merchantability or fitness for a particular purpose. No warranty may be created or extended by sales representatives or written sales materials. The advice and strategies contained herein may not be suitable for your situation. You should consult with a professional where appropriate. Neither the publisher nor author shall be liable for any loss of profit or any other commercial damages, including but not limited to special, incidental, consequential, or other damages.

ISBN: (Paperback) 978-1-959462-31-6

Printed in the United States of America.

10 9 8 7 6 5 4 3 2 1

Contents

ABOUT THE SERIES 79 EXAM	XI
ABOUT THIS BOOK	XV
ABOUT THE TEST BANK	XVII
ABOUT THE SECURITIES INSTITUTE OF AMERICA	XIX

CHAPTER 1
EQUITY AND DEBT SECURITIES — 1

What Is a Security?	1
Common Stock	2
Preferred Stock	7
Types of Dividends	10
Rights	11
Warrants	12
Options	14
Futures and Forwards	14
American Depositary Receipts (ADRs)/American Depositary Shares (ADSs)	15
General partnership	16
Grantor Trust	17
Joint venture	17
Limited Liability Company	17
Limited Liability Partnership	18
Limited Partnership	18
General Partner	18
Limited Partner	19
Master limited partnership	20
Subchapter S Corporation	20
C corporations	20
Debt Securities/Bonds	21
Institutional investors and Investment Strategies	32

Delta Neutral / Market Neutral	34
Short Sales	34
High Frequency and Algorithmic Trading	35
Momentum Trading	35
Arbitrage	35
Broker Dealer Operations	36
Pretest	39

CHAPTER 2
SEC REPORTING, RULES AND REGULATIONS — 43

The Securities Exchange Act of 1934	43
The Securities and Exchange Commission (SEC)	44
Proxies	44
Preliminary and Special Proxies	45
Extension of Credit	46
Trading Suspensions	46
SEC Reporting	47
Rule 135 and Rule 165	49
SEC Form 13D, 13G and 13F	50
The Insider Trading and Securities Fraud Enforcement Act of 1988	51
Firewall	52
The Trust Indenture Act of 1939	52
Sarbanes-Oxley Act	53
SEC Regulation S-K	54
SEC Regulation M-A	56
The Hart-Scott-Rodino Act	58
FINRA Rule 5150 (Fairness Opinion)	59
SEC Regulation S-X	59
Audit Committee	61
Pretest	63

CHAPTER 3
MERGERS AND ACQUISITIONS — 67

Mergers and acquisitions / M&A	67
Sellers and sell-side bankers	69
Buyers and buy-side bankers	70
Strategic Buyers and Financial buyers	71

Management-led buyout	73
Bilateral Negotiation	73
Public and controlled auctions	74
The Auction Process	75
identifying prospective buyers	76
Developing the business profile	76
Drafting confidentiality agreements	76
Compiling the confidential information memorandum (CIM)	77
Creating the bidding procedure letter	77
Creating the data room	77
Accepting indications of Interest	78
Delivering management presentations	78
Bid evaluation	78
Receiving letters of intent	79
Distributing a final bid letter	79
Receiving final bids	80
Selecting the final buyer	80
Executing definitive purchase agreement	80
Obtaining a Fairness Opinion	81
Closing of the acquisition	82
Other M & A Transactions	82
Reverse mergers	83
Consolidations	83
Forward triangular mergers	83
Reverse triangular merger	84
Split offs	84
Spin offs	84
Valuation	85
The structure of the transaction	87
Cash and Stock Transactions	88
International Implications	90
Protective Measures and Takeover Defenses	91
Pretest	93

CHAPTER 4
TENDER OFFERS AND FINANCIAL RESTRUCTURING 97

- Tender Offers 97
- Issuer Buybacks and Going Private Transactions 102
- The Two Step Merger 103
- Financial restructuring 104
- Filing Chapter 11 Bankruptcy 104
- Estate Operation and Payment Priorities 106
- Filing Chapter 7 Bankruptcy 109
- Distressed Asset Sales 109
- Pretest 111

CHAPTER 5
ISSUING CORPORATE SECURITIES 115

- The Prospectus 116
- The Final Prospectus 117
- Free Writing Prospectus 117
- Providing the Prospectus to Aftermarket Purchasers 118
- SEC Disclaimer 118
- Misrepresentations 119
- Tombstone Ads 120
- Free Riding and Withholding/FINRA Rule 5130 120
- Underwriting Corporate Securities 122
- Types of Underwriting Commitments 123
- Types of Offerings 125
- Awarding the Issue 126
- The Underwriting Syndicate 126
- Selling Group 127
- Underwriter's Compensation 127
- Underwriting Spread 128
- Factors That Determine the Size of the Underwriting Spread 129
- Review of Underwriting Agreements by FINRA 129
- Underwriter's Compensation 129
- Unreasonable Compensation 130
- Offering of Securities by FINRA Members and Other Conflicts 132
- Syndicate Operations 134

Syndicate Short Positions	136
Exempt Securities	136
Exempt Transactions	137
Rule 144	139
Broker Transactions Under Rule 144	140
Registration Rights and Lock up Agreements	142
Regulation S Offerings	143
Regulation A Offerings	144
Crowdfunding	144
Rule 145	145
Rule 147 Intrastate Offering	146
Research Reports	147
Rule 137 Nonparticipants	151
Rule 138 Nonequivalent Securities	151
Rule 139 Issuing Research Reports	152
Rule 415 Shelf Registration	153
SEC Rule 405	153
ADDITIONAL COMMUNICATION RULES	155
DPP Roll-UP Transactions	156
Nasdaq Listing Standards	157
Listing Requirements for the NYSE	158
Market Making During Syndication	158
Regulation M, Rule 101	159
Penalty Bids	159
Regulation M, Rule 102	160
Regulation M, Rule 103	160
Passive Market Makers' Daily Purchase Limit	161
Regulation M, Rule 104	161
Regulation M, Rule 105	162
Pretest	165

CHAPTER 6
FINANCIAL ANALYSIS

	167
GAAP Accounting and Reporting	167
The Balance Sheet	168
Capitalization	172

Changes in the Balance Sheet 172
The Income Statement 175
Statement of cash flows 177
The Impact of Converting Bonds 181
Refunding Debt 183
Stock Splits and Stock Dividends 184
Retained earnings 185
Pro Forma Financial Statements 186
Inventory Valuation and Accounting 186
comparative financial analysis 192
Accounting Challenges 194
Deferred Tax Issues 196
Depreciation and amortization 199
Fixed and variable costs 200
Restructuring charges 201
Market Capitalization 202
Pretest 205

CHAPTER 7
VALUATION 209

Price to Earnings Valuation 209
Earnings Yield 213
PEG Ratio 214
Enterprise value 217
Free Cash flow 222
Price to free cash flow 225
Price to Book 226
Price to sales 227
Weighted average cost of capital 227
Levered and Unlevered Beta 232
Cost of Equity Based on Issuance of New Common Shares 233
Cost of Equity Based on Retained Earnings 234
Dividend Valuation Models 238
Sum of the Parts (SOTP) Valuation 241
Discounted Cash flow 242
Economic Value Added 249
Pretest 253

CHAPTER 8
M & A ANALYSIS 257
    How to Determine the Offering Price In M & A 257
    Accretive and Dilutive Transactions 260
    Cash and stock transactions 264
    Determining the Combined Enterprise Value 268
    How to Build an LBO Model 269
    Employee Stock Options 271
    The Creation of Goodwill 273
    Cross Border Complications 274
    Pretest 277

ANSWER KEYS 281

About the Series 79 Exam

Congratulations! You are on your way to becoming a registered investment banking professional, licensed to perform a variety of investment banking functions for a broker dealer. The Series 79 exam will be presented in a 75-question multiple-choice format. Each candidate will have 2 hours and 30 minutes to complete the exam. A score of 73% or higher is required to pass. Your training materials from The Securities Institute will make sure that you have the required knowledge to pass the Series 79 and that you are confident in the application of that knowledge during the exam.

> **IMPORTANT EXAM NOTE**
>
> Candidates who wish to take the Series 79 exam must also successfully complete the SIE exam to become fully registered.

TAKING THE SERIES 79 EXAM

The Series 79 exam is presented in multiple-choice format on a touch-screen computer known as the PROCTOR system. No computer skills are required, and candidates will find that the test screen works in the same way as an ordinary ATM. Each test is made up of 75 questions that are randomly chosen from a test bank of several thousand questions. The test has a time limit of 2 hours and 30 minutes, which is designed to provide enough time for all candidates to complete the exam. Each Series 79 exam will comprise questions that focus on the following areas:

Collection, Analysis and Evaluation of Data	37
Underwriting / New financing transactions and Registration of Securities	20
Mergers and Acquisitions, Tender offers and Financial Restructuring	18
TOTAL	**75 questions**

HOW TO PREPARE FOR THE SERIES 79 EXAM

For most candidates, the combination of reading the textbook, watching the video class lectures and taking practice questions proves to be sufficient to successfully complete the exam. It is recommended that candidates spend at least 70 to 80 hours preparing for the exam by reading the textbook, underlining key points, and answering as many practice questions as possible. We recommend that candidates schedule their exam no more than 1 week after finishing their Series 79 preparation.

Test-Taking Tips

- Read the full question before answering.
- Identify what the question is asking.
- Identify key words and phrases.
- Watch out for hedge clauses, such as *except* and *not*.
- Eliminate wrong answers.
- Identify synonymous terms.
- Be wary of changing answers.

WHAT TYPE OF TRANSACTIONS MAY A SERIES 79 INVESTMENT BANKING REPRESENTATIVE ENGAGE IN ?

A Series 79 registered investment banking professional may advise on or facilitate a variety of offerings and transactions including:

- Debt and equity offerings (private placement or public offering)
- Mergers and acquisitions
- Tender offers
- Financial restructurings
- Asset sales
- Divestitures or other corporate reorganizations
- Business combination transactions

WHAT SCORE IS NEEDED TO PASS THE EXAM?

A score of 73% or higher is needed to pass the Series 79 exam.

ARE THERE ANY PREREQUISITES FOR THE SERIES 79?

Candidates who wish to take the Series 79 exam must also successfully complete the SIE exam to become fully registered.

HOW DO I SCHEDULE AN EXAM?

Ask your firm's compliance department to schedule the exam for you or to provide a list of test centers in your area. You must be sponsored by a FINRA member firm prior to making an appointment. The Series 79 exam may be taken any day that the exam center is open.

WHAT MUST I TAKE TO THE EXAM CENTER?

A picture ID is required. All other materials will be provided, including a calculator and scratch paper.

HOW SOON WILL I RECEIVE RESULTS OF THE EXAM?

The exam will be graded as soon as you answer your final question and hit the Submit for Grading button. It will take only a few minutes to get your results. Your grade will appear on the computer screen, and you will be given a paper copy at the exam center.

If you do not pass the test, you will need to wait 30 days before taking it again. If you do not pass on the second try, you will need to wait another 30 days. If you do not pass on the third try, you must wait 6 months to take the test again.

About This Book

The writers and instructors at The Securities Institute have developed the Series 79 textbook, exam prep software, and videos to ensure that you have the knowledge required to pass the test and that you are confident in the application of that knowledge during the exam. The writers and instructors at The Securities Institute are subject-matter experts as well as Series 79 test experts. We understand how the test is written, and our proven test-taking techniques can dramatically improve your results.

Each chapter includes notes, tips, examples, and case studies with key information, hints for taking the exam, and additional insight into the topics. Each chapter ends with a practice test to ensure that you have mastered the concepts before moving on to the next topic.

About the Test Bank

This book is accompanied by a test bank of hundreds of questions to further reinforce the concepts and information presented here. The test bank is provided to help students who have purchased our book from a traditional bookstore or from an online retailer such as Amazon. If you have purchased this textbook as part of a package from our website containing the full version of the software, you are all set and simply need to use the login instructions that were emailed to you at the time of purchase. Otherwise to access the test bank please email your purchase receipt to sales@securitiesce.com and we will activate your account. This test bank provides a small sample of the questions and features that are contained in the full version of the exam prep software.

If you have not purchased the full version of the exam prep software with this book, we highly recommend it to ensure that you have mastered the knowledge required for your exam. To purchase the exam prep software for this exam, visit The Securities Institute of America online at: www.securitiesce.com or call 877-218-1776.

About The Securities Institute of America

The Securities Institute of America, Inc. Helps thousands of securities and insurance professionals build successful careers in the financial services industry every year. In more than 25 years we have helped students pass more than 400,000 exams. Our securities training options include:

- Classroom training
- Private tutoring
- Interactive online video training classes
- State-of-the-art exam prep test banks
- Printed textbooks
- ebooks
- Real-time tracking and reporting for managers and training directors

As a result, you can choose a securities training solution that matches your skill level, learning style, and schedule. Regardless of the format you choose, you can be sure that our securities training courses are relevant, tested, and designed to help you succeed. It is the experience of our instructors and the quality of our materials that make our courses requested by name at some of the largest financial services firms in the world.

To contact The Securities Institute of America, visit us on the Web at: www.securitiesce.com or call 877-218-1776.

CHAPTER 1

Equity and Debt Securities

> **INTRODUCTION**
>
> The first chapter will lay the foundation on which the rest of the text is built. A thorough understanding of this material will be necessary in order to successfully complete the Series 79 exam. Because Series 79 investment banking professionals advise on the issuance and the valuation of equity, debt, and derivative securities, it is an important starting point.

WHAT IS A SECURITY?

A security is any investment product that can be exchanged for value and involves risk. In order for an investment to be considered a security, it must be readily transferable between two parties and the owner must be subject to the loss of some or all of their invested principal. If the product is not transferable or does not contain risk, then it is not a security.

Securities are broken up into two major categories for the Series 79: equity and debt. Let's begin by comparing the two different types of securities:

EQUITY = STOCK

The term *equity* is synonymous with the term *stock*. Throughout your preparation for this exam, as well as on the exam itself, you will find many terms that are used interchangeably. Equity or stock creates an ownership relationship with the issuing company. Once an investor has purchased stock in a corporation, he or she becomes an owner of that corporation. The corporation sells off pieces of itself to investors in the form of shares in an effort to raise working capital. Equity is perpetual, meaning there is no maturity date for the shares and investors may own the shares until they decide to sell them. Most corporations use the sale of equity as their main source of business capital.

DEBT = BONDS

A bond, or any other debt instrument, is actually a loan to the issuer. By purchasing a bond, the investor has made a loan to the corporation and becomes a creditor of the issuing company.

Debt instruments, unlike their equity counterparts, have a time frame or maturity date associated with them. Whether it is 1 year, 5 years, or 30 years, at some point the issue will mature, and the investor will receive his or her principal back and will cease to be a creditor of the corporation. We will examine how investors may purchase stocks and bonds, but first we must look at how the corporation uses the sale of these securities to meet its organizational goals.

COMMON STOCK

There are thousands of companies whose stock trades publicly and that have used the sale of equity as a source of raising business capital. All publicly traded companies must issue common stock before they may issue any other type of equity security. The two types of equity securities are common stock and preferred stock. Although all publicly traded companies must have sold or issued common stock, not all companies may want to issue or sell preferred stock. Let's take a look at the creation of a company and how common stock is created.

Authorized Stock

Authorized stock is the maximum number of shares that a company may sell to the investing public in an effort to raise cash to meet the organization's goals. The number of authorized shares is determined arbitrarily and is set at the time of incorporation. A corporation may sell all or part of its authorized stock. If the corporation wants to sell more shares than it is authorized to sell, the shareholders must approve an increase in the number of authorized shares.

Issued Stock

Issued stock is stock that has been authorized for sale and has actually been sold to the investing public. The total number of authorized shares typically exceeds the total number of issued shares so that the corporation may sell additional shares in the future to meet its needs. Once shares have been sold to the investing public, they will always be counted as issued shares regardless of their ownership or subsequent repurchase by the corporation. It is important to note that the total number of issued shares may never exceed the total number of authorized shares.

Additional authorized shares may be issued in the future to:

- Pay a stock dividend.
- Expand current operations.
- Exchange common shares for convertible preferred or convertible bonds.
- Satisfy obligations under employee stock options or purchase plans.

Outstanding Stock

Outstanding stock is stock that has been sold or issued to the investing public and that actually remains in the hands of the investing public.

Treasury Stock

Treasury stock is stock that has been sold to the investing public and that has subsequently been repurchased by the corporation. The corporation may elect to reissue the shares or it may retire the shares that it holds in treasury stock. Treasury stock does not receive dividends nor does it vote.

A corporation may elect to repurchase its own shares to:

- Maintain control of the company.
- Increase earnings per share.
- Fund employee stock purchase plans.
- Use shares to pay for a merger or acquisition.

To determine the amount of treasury stock, use the following formula:

issued stock − outstanding stock = treasury stock

VALUES OF COMMON STOCK

The market value of a common stock is determined by supply and demand and may or may not have any real relationship to what the shares are actually worth. The market value of common stock is affected by the current and future expectations for the company.

Book Value

The book value of a corporation is the theoretical liquidation value of the company. It is calculated by taking all of the company's assets and subtracting all of its liabilities. To determine the book value per share, divide the total book value by the total number of outstanding common shares.

Because intangible assets such as goodwill, patents and copyrights are difficult to value, investors will sometimes exclude them from the assets and calculate the company's tangible book value. The tangible book value represents a more conservative valuation which may be substantially lower than the book value if the company is carrying a large amount of intangible assets on its balance sheet.

Par Value

Par value, in a discussion regarding common stock, is only important if you are an accountant looking at the balance sheet. For investors, it has no relationship to any measure of value that may otherwise be employed.

RIGHTS OF COMMON STOCKHOLDERS

As an owner of common stock, investors are owners of the corporation. As such, investors have certain rights that are granted to all common stockholders.

Preemptive Rights

As a stockholder, an investor has the right to maintain a percentage interest in the company. This is known as a preemptive right. Should the company wish to sell additional shares to raise new capital, it must first offer the new shares to existing shareholders. If the existing shareholders decide not to purchase the new shares, they may be offered to the general public.

A shareholder's preemptive right is ensured through a rights offering. The existing shareholders will have the right to purchase the new shares at a discount to the current market value for 45 days. This is known as the subscription price. Once the subscription price is set, it remains constant for 45 days, while the price of the stock is moving up and down in the marketplace. The three possible outcomes for a right are that it is exercised or sold or that it expires.

Exercised

The investor decides to purchase the additional shares and sends in the money as well as the rights to receive the additional shares.

Sold

The rights have value, and if the investor does not want to purchase the additional shares they may be sold to another investor who would like to purchase the shares.

Expire

CHAPTER 1 Equity and Debt Securities

The rights will expire if no one wants to purchase the stock. This will only occur when the market price of the share has fallen below the subscription price of the right and the 45 days have elapsed.

VOTING

A common stockholder has the right to vote on major issues facing the corporation. Common stockholders are part owners of the company and, as a result, have the right to say how the company is run. The biggest emphasis is placed on the election of the board of directors.

Common stockholders may also vote on:
- The issuance of bonds or additional common shares.
- Stock splits.
- Mergers and acquisitions.
- Major changes in corporate policy.

Methods of Voting

There are two methods by which the voting process may be conducted: the statutory and cumulative methods. A stockholder may cast one vote for each share of stock owned, and the statutory or cumulative method will determine how those votes are cast. The test focuses on the election of the board of directors, so we will use that in our example.

EXAMPLE

An investor owns 200 shares of XYZ. There are two board members to be elected and there are four people running in the election. Under both the statutory and cumulative methods of voting, the number of votes the shareholder has is decided by multiplying the number of shares owned by the number of people to be elected. In this case, 200 shares × 2 = 400 votes. The cumulative or statutory methods dictate how those votes may be cast.

Candidate	Statutory	Cumulative
1	200 votes	400 votes
2		
3		
4	200 votes	

The statutory method requires that the votes be distributed evenly among the candidates the investor wishes to vote for.

The cumulative method allows the shareholder to cast all of their votes in favor of one candidate if they so choose. The cumulative method is said to favor smaller investors for this reason.

LIMITED LIABILITY

Stockholders' liability is limited to the amount of money they have invested in the stock. They cannot be held liable for any amount that exceeds their invested capital.

INSPECTION OF BOOKS AND RECORDS

All stockholders have the right to inspect the company's books and records. For most shareholders, this right is ensured through the company's filing of quarterly and annual reports. Stockholders also have the right to obtain a list of shareholders, but they do not have the right to review other corporate financial data that the corporation may deem confidential.

RESIDUAL CLAIM TO ASSETS

In the event of a company's bankruptcy or liquidation, common stockholders have the right to receive their proportional interest in residual assets. After all other security holders, as well as all creditors of the corporation, have been paid, common stockholders may claim the residual assets. For this reason, common stock is the most junior security.

WHY DO PEOPLE BUY COMMON STOCK?

Capital Appreciation/Growth

The main reason people invest in common stock is for capital appreciation. They want their money to grow in value over time. An investor in common stock hopes to buy the stock at a low price and sell it at a higher price at some point in the future.

EXAMPLE An investor purchases 100 shares of XYZ at $20 per share on March 15, On April 30, of the following year, the investor sells 100 shares of XYZ for $30 per share, realizing a profit of $10 per share, or $1,000 on the 100 shares.

Income

Many corporations distribute a portion of their earnings to their investors in the form of dividends. This distribution of earnings creates income for the investor. Investors in common stock generally receive dividends quarterly.

EXAMPLE

ABC pays a $.50 quarterly dividend to its shareholders. The stock is currently trading at $20 per share. What is its current yield (also known as the dividend yield)?

$$\text{annual income/current market price} = \text{current yield}$$
$$\$.50 \times 4 \text{ quarters} = \$2.00$$
$$\$2/\$20 = 10\%$$

The investor in this example is receiving 10% of the purchase price of the stock each year in the form of dividends.

WHAT ARE THE RISKS OF OWNING COMMON STOCK?

The major risk in owning common stock is that the stock may fall in value. There are no sure things in the stock market, and even if a company seems great, an investor may end up losing money.

Dividends May Be Stopped or Reduced

Common stockholders are not entitled to receive dividends just because they own part of the company. It is up to the company to elect to pay a dividend. The corporation is in no way obligated to pay common shareholders a dividend.

Junior Claim on Corporate Assets

A common stockholder is the last person to get paid if the company is liquidated. It is very possible that after all creditors and other investors are paid there will be little or no money left for the common stockholder.

PREFERRED STOCK

Preferred stock is an equity security with a fixed-income component. Like a common stockholder, the preferred stockholder is an owner of the company. However, the preferred stockholder is investing in the stock for the fixed income that the preferred shares generate through their semiannual dividends. Preferred stock has a stated dividend rate, or a fixed rate, that the corporation must pay to its preferred shareholders. Growth is generally not achieved through investing in preferred shares.

FEATURES OF PREFERRED STOCK

Par Value

Par value on preferred stock is very important because it is what the dividend is based on. Par value for preferred shares is $100. Companies generally express the dividend as a percentage of par value for preferred stock.

> **EXAMPLE**
>
> An investor buys 100 shares of TWT 9% preferred. How much would the investor receive in annual income from the investment?
>
> **$100 × .09 = $9 per share × 100 = $900**

PAYMENT OF DIVIDENDS

The dividend on preferred shares must be paid before any dividends are paid to common shareholders. This gives the preferred shareholder a priority claim on the corporation's distribution of earnings.

Distribution of Assets

If a corporation liquidates or declares bankruptcy, the preferred shareholders are paid prior to any common shareholder, giving the preferred shareholders a higher claim on the corporation's assets.

Perpetual

Preferred stock, unlike bonds, is perpetual, with no maturity date. Investors may hold shares for as long as they wish or until they are called in by the company under a call feature.

Nonvoting

Most preferred stock is nonvoting. Occasionally, if the company has been in financial difficulty and has missed preferred dividend payments for an extended period of time, preferred shareholders may receive the right to vote.

Interest Rate Sensitive

Because of the fixed income generated by preferred shares, their price will be more sensitive to a change in interest rates than the price of their common stock counterparts. As interest rates decline, the value of preferred shares

CHAPTER 1 Equity and Debt Securities

tends to increase. When interest rates rise, the value of the preferred shares tends to fall. This is known as an inverse relationship.

TYPES OF PREFERRED STOCK

Preferred stock has more features associated with it than common stock. Most of the features are designed to make the issue more attractive to investors.

Straight/Noncumulative Preferred

Straight, or noncumulative, preferred stock has no additional features. The holder is entitled to the stated dividend rate and nothing else. If the corporation is unable to pay the dividend, it is not owed to the investor.

Cumulative Preferred

A cumulative feature protects the investor in cases when a corporation is having financial difficulties and cannot pay the dividend. Dividends on cumulative preferred stock accumulate in arrears until the corporation is able to pay them. If the dividend on a cumulative preferred stock is missed, it is still owed to the holder. Dividends in arrears on cumulative issues are always the first dividends to be paid. If the company wants to pay a dividend to common shareholders, it must first pay the dividends in arrears as well as the stated preferred dividend before common shareholders receive anything.

> **TEST FOCUS!**
>
> GNR has an 8% cumulative preferred stock outstanding. It has not paid the dividend this year or for the prior 3 years. How much must the holders of GNR cumulative preferred be paid per share before the common stockholders are paid a dividend?
>
> The dividend has not been paid this year nor for the previous 3 years, so the holders are owed 4 years worth of dividends or
>
> **4 × $8 = $32 per share**

Participating Preferred

Holders of participating preferred stock are entitled to receive the stated preferred rate as well as additional common dividends. The holder of participating preferred stock receives the dividend payable to the common stockholders over and above the stated preferred dividend.

Convertible Preferred

A convertible feature allows the preferred stockholder to convert or exchange their preferred shares for common shares at a fixed price known as the conversion price.

> **EXAMPLE**
>
> TRW has issued a 4% convertible preferred stock, which may be converted into TRW common stock at $20 per share. How many shares may the preferred stockholder receive upon conversion?
>
> **par value/conversion price = number of shares**
>
> $100/$20 = $5
>
> The investor may receive five common shares for every preferred share.

Callable Preferred

A call feature is the only feature that benefits the company and not the investor. A call feature allows the corporation to call in or redeem the preferred shares at its discretion or after some period of time has expired. Most preferred stock that is callable cannot be called in the first few years after its issuance. This is known as call protection. Many callable preferred shares will be called at a premium price above par. For example, a $100 par preferred stock may be called at $103. The main reasons a company would call in its preferred shares would be to eliminate the fixed dividend payment or to sell a new preferred stock with a lower dividend rate when interest rates decline. Preferred stock is more likely to be called by the corporation during a decline in interest rates.

TYPES OF DIVIDENDS

CASH

A cash dividend is the most common form of dividend, and it is one that the test focuses on. With a cash dividend, a corporation will send out a cash payment in the form of a check directly to the stockholders. For those stockholders who have their stock held in the name of the brokerage firm, a check will be sent to the brokerage firm, and the money will be credited to the investor's account. Securities held in the name of the brokerage firm are said to be held in street name. To determine the amount that an investor will receive, simply multiply the amount of the dividend to be paid by the number of shares.

EXAMPLE   JPF pays a $.10 dividend to shareholders. An investor who owns 1,000 shares of JPF will receive $100:

1,000 shares × $.10 = $100

STOCK

A corporation that wants to reward its shareholders, but also wants to conserve cash for other business purposes may elect to pay a stock dividend to its shareholders. With a stock dividend, investors will receive an additional number of shares based on the number of shares that they own. The market price of the stock will decline after the stock dividend has been distributed to reflect that there are now more shares outstanding, but the total market value of the company will remain the same.

EXAMPLE   If HRT pays a 5% stock dividend to its shareholders, an investor with 500 shares will receive an additional 25 shares. This is determined by multiplying the number of shares owned by the amount of the dividend to be paid:

500 × 5% = 25

PROPERTY/PRODUCT

A corporation may send out to its shareholders samples of its products or portions of its property. This is the least likely way in which a corporation would pay a dividend, but it is a permissible dividend distribution.

RIGHTS

A right is issued to existing shareholders by a corporation that wants to sell additional common shares to raise new capital. All common stockholders have a preemptive right to maintain the proportional ownership in the company. If the corporation were allowed to sell additional shares to the general public, the existing shareholders' interest in the company would be diluted. As a result, any new offering of additional common shares first must be made to the existing shareholders. Common shareholders will receive a notice of their right to purchase the new shares. They will be offered the opportunity to purchase the new shares at a price that is below the current market value of the stock. This is known as the subscription price. The shareholder will have the right to purchase the new shares for 45 days.

POSSIBLE OUTCOMES FOR A RIGHT

Exercised

The shareholder may elect to purchase the additional shares. This is known as exercising the right. The investor sends in the rights as well as a check for the total purchase price to the rights agent, and the additional shares are issued to the investor.

Sold

The investor may not want to purchase the additional shares and may elect to sell the rights to another investor. The investor who purchases the right will then have the opportunity to purchase the stock at the subscription price for the duration of the original 45-day period.

Expire

The right to purchase the additional shares will expire at the end of the 45-day period if no one has elected to purchase the shares. A right will only expire if the stock's market price has fallen below the subscription price of the right. While market price of the stock is fluctuating during the 45-day period, the subscription price of the right remains fixed.

TERMS

The particular terms of the rights will be printed on the right certificate, and each share of outstanding stock will be issued one right. The terms will include the subscription price, the final date for exercising the right, the number of rights required to purchase additional shares, and the date that the new shares will be issued.

STANDBY UNDERWRITING

A corporation may retain a brokerage firm to purchase any shares that existing shareholders do not purchase. This is known as a standby underwriter. The brokerage firm will purchase the shares that were not bought by the existing shareholders and resell them to the investing public.

WARRANTS

A warrant is a security that gives the holder the opportunity to purchase common stock. Like a right, the warrant has a subscription price; however, the subscription price is always above the current market value of the common stock when the warrant is originally issued. A warrant has a much longer life than a right—the holder of a warrant may have up to 10 years to purchase the stock at the subscription price. The long life is what makes the warrant valuable, even though the subscription price is higher than the market price of the common stock when the warrant is issued.

HOW DO PEOPLE GET WARRANTS?

Units

Oftentimes companies will issue warrants to people who purchased their common stock during its initial public offering (IPO). A common share, which comes with a warrant attached to purchase an additional common share, is known as a unit.

Attached to Bonds

Many times companies will attach warrants to their bond offerings as a "sweetener" to help market the bond offering. The warrant to purchase the common stock makes the bond more attractive to the investor and may allow the company to issue the bonds with a lower coupon rate.

Secondary Market

Warrants will often trade in the secondary market just like the common stock. An investor who wishes to participate in the potential price appreciation of the common stock may elect to purchase the corporation's warrant instead of its common shares.

POSSIBLE OUTCOMES OF A WARRANT

A warrant, like a right, may be exercised or sold by the investor. A warrant also may expire if the stock price is below the warrant's subscription price at its expiration.

RIGHTS VS. WARRANTS

Rights		Warrants
Up to 45 days	**Term**	Up to 10 years
Below the market	**Subscription price**	Above the market
May trade with or without common stock	**Trading**	May trade with or without common stock or bonds
Issued to existing shareholders to ensure preemptive rights	**Who**	Offered as a sweetener to make securities more attractive

OPTIONS

An option is a contract between two parties, the buyer and the seller, that determines the time and price at which a security may be bought or sold. The buyer of the option pays money, known as the option's premium, to the seller. For this premium, the buyer obtains a right to buy or sell the security, depending on what type of option is involved in the transaction. The seller, because he or she received the premium from the buyer, now has an obligation to perform under that contract. Depending on the type of option involved, the seller may have an obligation to buy or sell the security.

CALLS

A call option gives the buyer the right to buy, or to "call," the security from the option seller at a specific price for a certain period of time. The sale of a call option obligates the seller to deliver or sell that security to the buyer at that specific price for a certain period of time.

PUTS

A put option gives the buyer the right to sell, or to "put," the security to the seller at a specific price for a certain period of time. The sale of a put option obligates the seller to buy the security from the buyer at that specific price for a certain period of time.

FUTURES AND FORWARDS

Futures, like options, are a two-party contract. Many future contracts are an agreement for the delivery of a specific amount of a commodity at a specific place and time. Futures began to trade for commodities such as wheat and gold and over the years have expanded to include financial futures such as on Treasury securities and, most recently, single stock futures. The specific terms and conditions of the contracts are standardized and set by the exchanges on which they trade. The contract amount, delivery date, and type of settlement vary between the different futures contracts. Most investors will use futures as a hedge or to speculate on the value of the underlying commodity or instrument. Forwards are privately negotiated contracts for the purchase and sale of a commodity or financial instrument. Forwards often are used in the currency markets by corporations and banks doing business internationally. If a corporation knows that it needs to make a payment for a purchase in foreign currency three months from now, the corporation can arrange to purchase the currency from a bank the day before the payment is due. The big drawback with forwards is that there is no secondary market for the contracts. All of the terms and conditions relating to the forward contract are customized and set by the two parties. As a result, there is substantial counterparty risk. If one party fails to perform, the other party may suffer substantial losses as a result.

AMERICAN DEPOSITARY RECEIPTS (ADRS)/ AMERICAN DEPOSITARY SHARES (ADSS)

American depositary receipts (ADRs) facilitate the trading of foreign securities in the U.S. markets. An ADR is a receipt that represents the ownership of the foreign shares that are being held abroad in a branch of a United States bank. Each ADR represents ownership of between 1 and 10 shares of the foreign stock, and the holder of the ADR may request the delivery of the foreign shares. Holders of ADRs also have the right to vote and the right to receive dividends that the foreign corporation declares for payment to shareholders.

CURRENCY RISKS

The owner of an ADR has currency risk along with the normal risks associated with the ownership of the stock. Should the currency of the country decline relative to the U.S. dollar, the holder of the ADR will receive fewer U.S. dollars when a dividend is paid and fewer U.S. dollars when the security is sold. It is important to note that the dividend on the ADR is paid by the corporation in the foreign currency and is converted so that the dividend is received by the holder of the ADR in U.S. dollars.

REAL ESTATE INVESTMENT TRUSTS (REITS)

A real estate investment trust, or REIT, is a special type of equity security. REITs are organized for the specific purpose of buying, developing, or managing a portfolio of real estate. REITs are organized as a corporation or as a trust, and publicly traded REITs will trade on the exchanges or in the over-the-counter market just like other stocks. A REIT is organized as a conduit for the investment income generated by the portfolio of real estate. REITs are entitled to special tax treatment under Internal Revenue Code subchapter M. A REIT will not pay taxes at the corporate level so long as:

- It receives 75% of its income from real estate.
- It distributes at least 90% of its taxable income to shareholders.

So long as the REIT meets the above requirements, the income will be allowed to flow through to the shareholders and will be taxed at their rate. Dividends received by REIT shareholders will continue to be taxed as ordinary income.

NON-TRADED REITS

Non-traded real estate investment trust or REITs lack liquidity, have high fees, and can be difficult to value. The fees for investing in a non-traded REIT may be as much as 15% of the per shares price. These fees include commissions and expenses which cannot exceed 10% of the offering price. Investors are often attracted to the high yields offered by these investments. Firms who conduct business in these products must conduct ongoing suitability determination on the REITs they recommend. Firms must react to red flags in the financial statements and from the REIT's management and adjust the recommendation process accordingly or stop recommending if material changes take place that would make the REIT unsuitable. Holding periods can be 8 years or more and the opportunities to liquidate the investments may be very limited. Furthermore the distributions from the REITs themselves may be based on the use of borrowed funds and may include a return of principal which may be adversely impacted and cause the distributions to be vulnerable to being significantly reduced or stopped altogether. Distributions may exceed cash flow and the amount of the distributions in any are at the discretion of the Board of Directors Non-traded REITs like exchange-traded REITs must distribute 90% of the income to shareholders and must file 10-Ks and 10-Qs with the SEC. Broker dealers who sell non-traded REITs must provide investors with a valuation of the REIT within 18 months of the closing of the offering of shares.

GENERAL PARTNERSHIP

A general partnership is a venture between one or more parties and allows all partners to make management decisions and to enter into legally binding contracts on behalf of the partnership. All General partners are jointly and severally liable for all of the obligations of the partnership unless otherwise stated in the partnership agreement. All of the income will be distributed to the partners and the partners will pay taxes on their individual return.

GRANTOR TRUST

With a grantor trust, the creator of the trust retains control of the assets in the trust. Grantor trusts may be set up as revocable or irrevocable trusts. In the case of a revocable grantor trust, the creator of the trust is deemed to be the owner of the assets and will report the income on his / her tax return. A revocable trust will also be deemed to be part of the grantor's estate at the time the grantor passes away. Should the grantor trust be established as an irrevocable trust, the grantor may retain the ability to pass income through to his / her own tax return and the assets will not be deemed to be part of the grantor's estate, provided the grantor meets certain minimum IRS requirements. the establishment of the irrevocable grantor Trust which allows the grantor to retain the income and the assets to be seen as separate from the grantor are sometimes referred to as intentionally defective grantor trusts. the type of grantor trust established will be set forth in the trust instrument or trust deed.

JOINT VENTURE

A joint venture is a business entity that has been created by two or more parties. The parties to the joint venture share in the ownership, management, returns, and risks of the operation or entity. A joint venture may be an incorporated or unincorporated entity and are usually designed to carry out a particular business goal. Joint ventures are organized on a temporary basis and will terminate upon the completion of the objective or upon agreement of the owners

LIMITED LIABILITY COMPANY

A limited liability company is a hybrid entity that allows for the flow through of taxes and significant flexibility for the members of the limited liability company. Unlike a limited partnership, where the limited partners are precluded from exercising any management control over the partnership, limited liability company members may operate, manage or control the limited liability company and still enjoy asset protection. the financial and management Arrangements agreed to by the members of a limited liability company will be set forth in the operating agreement. the terms and conditions spelled out in the operating agreement are of particular importance to investors who are considering becoming a member of the limited liability company. These financial and management aspects are of particular importance when determining suitability.

LIMITED LIABILITY PARTNERSHIP

A limited liability partnership as the name implies affords the partners protection from liabilities of the limited liability partnership. However, this form of business structure may only be used by professional organizations such as accountants, attorneys, architects and physicians.

LIMITED PARTNERSHIP

A limited partnership is a type of unincorporated direct participation program created through the association of limited partners and one or more General partners. The limited partnership must conform with the state regulations where the partnership is organized as well as a revised uniform limited partnership Act

GENERAL PARTNER

The general partner of a limited partnership is the individual or entity who provides management expertise and is responsible for the day-to-day operations of the limited partnership. While the general partner may be a natural person, more often than not the general partner is a corporation or other legal entity that is designed to provide a level of legal protection to the natural persons who operate the partnership

LIMITED PARTNER

A limited partner is an investor in a limited partnership who has provided Capital to the partnership in exchange for an economic interest in the partnership. A limited partner's liability is generally limited to the amount of the partner's investment. A limited partner may not exercise any management over the partnership operations, nor may they seek to control the actions of the general partner. If a limited partner exercises management over the partnership's operations or controls the general partner, the limited partner will lose their classification as a limited partner and will be deemed to be a general partner of the partnership.

LIMITED PARTNERSHIP AGREEMENT

The limited partnership agreement is the foundation for the limited partnership. It spells out the business purpose of the partnership and all of the terms under which the partnership will operate. The agreement will be signed by both the general and limited partners to ensure all parties understand their rights and responsibilities. The partnership agreement will state The terms and conditions for the following:

1. the acceptance of limited partners
2. the acceptance of substitute limited partners or additional limited partners
3. the withdraw a capital by a limited partner
4. the allocation of profits and losses
5. how distributions to the limited partners will be made
6. any priority among partners
7. the powers of the general partner to manage and control the partnership
8. the powers of the general partner to acquire and sell property on behalf of the partnership
9. the voting rights of the limited partners
10. the requirement of the general partner to maintain books and Records for the partnership
11. the requirement of the general partner to provide periodic performance reports to the limited partners
12. the amount of time required to be committed by the general partner to the management of the partnership

13. the compensation to be paid to the general partner for its Management Services
14. The acceptance of a substitute General partner or the assignment of the general Partner's interest in the partnership

MASTER LIMITED PARTNERSHIP

A master limited partnership combines the tax benefits of a partnership with liquidity provided by the public exchanges. The mlp's must receive at least 90% of their revenue from production, processing, storage, or transportation of Natural Resources such as oil and gas. An MLP will also qualify if it owns real property designed to produce rental income, or in some cases, if it provides financial management services. Master limited partnerships are required to make quarterly distributions to limited partners in the form of dividends.

SUBCHAPTER S CORPORATION

A company organized as an S corporation allows for the flow through of income to the shareholders. the income distributed to the shareholders will be taxed as ordinary income to the recipient. interest in an S corporation may be distributed as part of a direct participation program. Ownership in an S corporation is limited to 100 shareholders and the S corporation must be organized as a domestic corporation within that state.

C CORPORATIONS

Most corporations whose stock trade in the market are organized as C corporations. One of the advantages of a C corp is that there is no limit to how many shareholders may own the corporation. It provides full asset protection to shareholders and shareholder liability is limited to the amount paid for the shares. For tax purposes a C corporation reports income on its own corporate return and will pay taxes at the corporate rate. The C corporations may elect to distribute a portion of its after tax income to shareholders in the form of a dividend. Shareholders who receive dividends will pay taxes on the income at a rate determined by the IRS. The drawback for the C corporation is the fact that the income is subject to double taxation.

DEBT SECURITIES/BONDS

Many different types of entities issue bonds in an effort to raise working capital. Corporations and municipalities as well as the U.S. government and U.S. government agencies issue bonds in order to meet their capital needs. A bond represents a loan to the issuer in exchange for a promise to repay the face amount of the bond, known as the principal amount at maturity. On most bonds, the investor receives semiannual interest payments, during the bond's term. These semiannual interest payments, as well as any capital appreciation or depreciation at maturity, represent the investor's return. A bondholder invests primarily for the interest income that will be generated during the bond's term.

CORPORATE BONDS

Corporations will issue bonds in an effort to raise working capital to build and expand their business. Corporate bondholders are not owners of the corporation; they are creditors of the company. Corporate debt financing is known as leverage financing because the company pays interest only on the loan until maturity. Bondholders do not have voting rights as long as the company pays the interest and principal payments in a timely fashion. If the company defaults, the bondholders may be able to use their position as creditors to gain a voice in the company's management. Bondholders will always be paid before preferred and common stockholders in the event of liquidation. Interest income received by investors on corporate bonds is taxable at all levels: federal, state, and local.

THE U.S. GOVERNMENT

The U.S. government is the largest issuer of debt. It is also the issuer with the least amount of default risk. Default risk is also known as credit risk, which is the risk that the issuer will not be able to meet its obligations under the terms of the bond in a timely fashion. The U.S. government issues debt securities with maturities ranging from 3 months to 30 years. The Treasury Department issues the securities on behalf of the federal government, and they are a legally binding obligation of the federal government. Interest earned by the investors from U.S. government securities is only taxed at the federal level. State and local governments do not tax the interest income.

U.S. GOVERNMENT AGENCIES

The U.S. government has many agencies that operate to provide financial and other assistance to American businesses and families. These agencies also must raise capital to operate, and much of the money is raised through the sale of agency securities. These debt instruments have only a slightly higher risk of default than the direct government obligations. As a result of the small increase in risk, the interest rate earned by investors will, in most cases, only be slightly higher than those on Treasury securities. Interest income earned by investors on agency securities is taxable at all levels: federal, state, and local.

MUNICIPAL BONDS

Both state and local governments will issue debt securities to meet their goals. Municipal bonds are issued to meet a variety of needs, from working capital to bridge and tunnel projects. Once bonds have been issued, they become a legally binding obligation of the state or municipality. Interest earned by investors will be free from federal taxes and may be free from state and local taxes if the investor purchases a municipal bond issued by the state in which he or she resides.

TYPES OF BOND ISSUANCE

Bearer Bonds

Bonds that are issued in coupon or bearer form do not record the owner's information with the issuer, and the bond certificate does not have the legal owner's name printed on it. As a result, anyone who possesses the bond is entitled to receive the interest payment by clipping the coupons attached to the bond and depositing them in a bank or trust company for payment. Additionally, the bearer is entitled to receive the principal payment at the bond's maturity. Bearer bonds are no longer issued within the United States; however, they are still issued outside the United States.

Registered Bonds

Most bonds are now issued in registered form. Bonds that have been issued in registered form have the owner's name recorded in the books of the issuer, and the buyer's name will appear on the bond certificate.

Principal-Only Registration

Bonds that have been registered as principal only have the owner's name printed on the bond certificate. The issuer knows who owns the bond and who is entitled to receive the principal payment at maturity. However, the bondholder will still be required to clip the coupons to receive the semiannual interest payments.

Fully Registered

Bonds that have been issued in fully registered form have the owner's name recorded for both the interest and principal payments. The owner is not required to clip coupons, and the issuer will send out the interest payments directly to the holder on a semiannual basis. The issuer also will send the principal payment as well as the last semiannual interest payment directly to the owner at maturity. Most bonds in the United States are issued in fully registered form.

Book Entry/Journal Entry

Bonds that have been issued in book entry or journal entry form have no physical certificate issued to the holder as evidence of ownership. The bonds are fully registered, and the issuer knows who is entitled to receive the semiannual interest payments and the principal payment at maturity. The investor's only evidence of ownership is the trade confirmation, which is generated by the brokerage firm when the purchase order has been executed.

BOND CERTIFICATE

If a bond certificate is issued, it must include:

- Name of issuer.
- Principal amount.
- Issuing date.
- Maturity date.
- Interest payment dates.
- Place where interest is payable (paying agent).
- Type of bond.
- Interest rate.
- Call feature (if any or noncallable).
- Reference to the trust indenture.

BOND PRICING

Once issued, bonds trade in the secondary market between investors similar to the way equity securities do. The price of bonds in the secondary market depends on the following:

- Rating
- Interest rates
- Term
- Coupon rate
- Type of bond
- Issuer
- Supply and demand
- Other features (e.g., callable, convertible)

Bonds are always priced as a percentage of par. Par value for all bonds is $1,000.

Par Value

The par value of a bond is equal to the amount that the investor has loaned to the issuer. The terms par value, face value, and principal amount are all synonymous and always equal $1,000. The principal amount is the amount that will be received by the investor at maturity, regardless of the price the investor paid for the bond. An investor who purchases a bond in the secondary market for $1,000 is said to have paid par for the bond.

Discount

In the secondary market, many different factors affect the price of the bond. It is not unusual for an investor to purchase a bond at a price that is below the bond's par value. Anytime an investor buys a bond at a price that is below the par value, they are said to be buying the bond at a discount.

Premium

Oftentimes market conditions will cause the price of existing bonds to rise, making it attractive for investors to purchase a bond at a price that is greater than its par value. When an investor buys a bond at a price that exceeds its par value, the investor is said to have paid a premium.

Corporate Bond Pricing

All corporate bonds are priced as a percentage of par in fractions of a percent. For example, a quote for a corporate bond reading 95 actually translates into:

CHAPTER 1 Equity and Debt Securities

95% × $1,000 = $950

A quote for a corporate bond of 97.25 translates into:
97.25% × $1,000 = $972.50

Treasury Bond and Note Pricing

Treasury notes and bonds are also quoted as a percentage of par. However, unlike their corporate counterparts, Treasury notes and bonds are quoted as a percentage of par down to 32nds of 1%. For example, a bond quote of 92.02 translates into:
92-2/32% × $1,000 = $920.625

A quote of 98.04 translates into:
98.125% × $1,000 = $981.25

It is important to remember that the number after the decimal points represents 32nds of a percent.

Treasury Bill Pricing

Treasury bills do not pay semiannual interest and are issued at a discount from par. The bill's appreciation up to par at maturity represents the investor's interest. Treasury bills are quoted on a discounted yield basis. Series 79 candidates are unlikely to see a Treasury bill quote on the exam.

Municipal Bond Pricing

Most municipal bonds are also quoted on a yield basis; however, they are quoted on a yield-to-maturity basis. Some municipal bonds are quoted as a percentage of par, just like corporate bonds, and they are known as dollar bonds.

BOND YIELDS

A bond's yield is the investor's return for holding the bond. Many factors affect the yield an investor will receive from a bond, such as:

- Current interest rates
- Term of the bond
- Credit quality of the issuer
- Type of collateral
- Convertible or callable
- Purchase price

An investor who is considering investing in a bond needs to be familiar with the bond's nominal yield, current yield, and yield to maturity.

Nominal Yield

A bond's nominal yield is the interest rate that is printed, or named, on the bond. The nominal yield is always stated as a percentage of par. It is fixed at the time of the bond's issuance and never changes. The nominal yield may also be called the coupon rate. For example, a corporate bond with a coupon rate of 8% will pay the holder $80 per year in interest:

8% × $1,000 = $80

Thus, the nominal yield is 8%.

Current Yield

The current yield is a relationship between the annual interest generated by the bond and the bond's current market price. To find any investment's current yield use the following formula:

annual income/current market price

For example, let's take the same 8% corporate bond we used in the previous example on nominal yield and see what its current yield would be if we paid $1,100 for the bond:

annual income = 8% × $1,000 = $80
current market price = 110% × $1,000 = $1,100
current yield = $80/$1,100 = 7.27%

In this example we have purchased the bond at a premium or a price that is higher than par, and we see that the current yield on the bond is lower than the nominal yield.

Let's take a look at the current yield on the same bond if we were to purchase the bond at a discount, or a price that is lower than par. Let's see what the current yield for the bond would be if we paid $900 for the bond:

annual income = 8% × $1,000 = $80
current market price = 90% × $1,000 = $900
current yield = $80/$900 = 8.89%

In this example, the current yield is higher than the nominal yield. By showing examples calculating the current yield for the same bond purchased at a premium and at a discount, we have demonstrated the inverse relationship between prices and yields. That is to say that prices and yields on income-producing investments move in the opposite direction. As the price of an investment rises, the investment's yield will fall. Conversely, as the price of the investment falls, the investment's yield will rise.

Yield to Maturity

The yield to maturity of a bond is the investor's total annualized return for investing in the bond. A bond's yield to maturity takes into consideration the annual income received by the investor as well as any difference between the price the investor paid for the bond and the par value that will be received at maturity. The yield to maturity is the most important yield for an investor who purchases the bond.

Yield to Maturity: Premium Bond

The yield to maturity for a bond purchased at a premium will be the lowest of all the investor's yields. Although an investor may purchase a bond at a price that exceeds the par value of the bond, the issuer is only obligated to pay the bondholder the par value upon maturity. For example: An investor, who purchases a bond at 110, or for $1,100, will receive only $1,000 at maturity and therefore will lose $100. This loss is what causes the yield to maturity to be the lowest of the three yields for an investor who purchases a bond at a premium.

Yield to Maturity: Discount Bond

The yield to maturity for a bond purchased at a discount will be the highest of the investor's yields. In this case, the investor has purchased the bond at a price that is less than the par value of the bond. In this example, even though the investor paid less than the par value for the bond, the issuer is still obligated to pay the full par value of the bond at maturity, or the full $1,000. For example: An investor who purchases a bond at 90, or for $900, will still be entitled to receive the full par amount of $1,000 at maturity, therefore gaining $100. This gain is what causes the yield to maturity to be the highest of the three yields for an investor who purchases a bond at a discount.

The following illustration demonstrates the inverse relationship between prices and yields.

A corporation will issue or sell bonds as a means to borrow money to help the organization meet its goals. Corporate bonds are divided into two main categories: secured and unsecured.

SECURED BONDS

A secured bond is one that is backed by a specific pledge of assets. The assets that have been pledged become known as collateral for the bond issue or the loan. A trustee will hold the title to the collateral, and in the event of default the bondholders may claim the assets that have been pledged. The trustee will then attempt to sell off the assets in an effort to pay off the bondholders.

Mortgage Bonds

A mortgage bond is a bond that has been backed by a pledge of real property. The corporation will issue bonds to investors and will pledge real estate owned by the company as collateral. A mortgage bond works in a similar fashion to a residential mortgage. In the event of default, the bondholders take the property.

Equipment Trust Certificates

An equipment trust certificate is backed by a pledge of large equipment that the corporation owns. Airlines, railroads, and large shipping companies will often borrow money to purchase the equipment that they need through the sale of equipment trust certificates. Airplanes, railroad cars, and ships are all good examples of the types of assets that might be pledged as collateral. In the event of default, the equipment will be liquidated by the trustee in an effort to pay off the bondholders.

Collateral Trust Certificates

A collateral trust certificate is a bond that has been backed by a pledge of securities that the issuer has purchased for investment purposes or by shares of a wholly owned subsidiary. Both stocks and bonds are acceptable forms of collateral as long as they have been issued by another issuer. Securities that have been pledged as collateral are generally required to be held by the trustee for safekeeping. In the event of a default, the trustee will attempt to liquidate the securities that have been pledged as collateral and divide the proceeds among the bondholders.

It is important to note that while having a specific claim against an asset that has been pledged as collateral benefits the bondholder, bondholders do not want to take title to the collateral. Bondholders invest for the semiannual interest payments and the return of their principal at maturity.

UNSECURED BONDS

Unsecured bonds are known as debentures and have no specific asset pledged as collateral for the loan. Debentures are only backed by the good faith and credit of the issuer. In the event of a default, the holder of a debenture is treated like a general creditor.

Subordinated Debentures

A subordinated debenture is an unsecured loan to the issuer that has a junior claim on the issuer in the event of default relative to the straight debenture. Should the issuer default, the holders of the debentures and other general creditors will be paid before the holders of the subordinated debentures.

Income/Adjustment Bonds

Corporations, usually those in severe financial difficulty, issue income or adjustment bonds. The bond is unsecured, and the investor is only promised to be paid interest if the corporation has enough income to do so. As a result of the large risk that the investor is taking, the interest rate is very high, and the bonds are issued at a deep discount to par. An income bond is never an appropriate recommendation for an investor seeking income or safety of principal.

Zero-Coupon Bonds

A zero-coupon bond is a bond that pays no semiannual interest. It is issued at a deep discount from the par value and appreciates up to par at maturity. This appreciation represents the investor's interest for purchasing the bond. Corporations, the U.S. government, and municipalities will all issue zero-coupon bonds in an effort to finance their activities. An investor might be able to purchase the $1,000 principal payment in 20 years for as little as $300 today. Because the zero-coupon bonds pay no semiannual interest and the price is so deeply discounted from par, the price of the bond will be the most sensitive to a change in the interest rates. Both corporate and U.S. government zero-coupon bonds subject the investor to federal income taxes on the annual appreciation of the bond. This is known as phantom income.

Convertible Bonds

A convertible bond is a corporate bond that may be converted or exchanged for common shares of the corporation at a predetermined price, known as the conversion price. Convertible bonds have benefits to both the issuer and the investor. Because the bond is convertible, it usually will pay a lower rate of interest than nonconvertible bonds. This lower interest rate can save the corporation an enormous amount of money in interest expense over the life of the issue. The convertible feature will also benefit the investor if the common stock does well. If the shares of the underlying common stock appreciate, the investor could realize significant capital appreciation in the price of the bond and may also elect to convert the bond into common stock in the hopes of realizing additional appreciation. As an investor in the bond, the investor maintains a senior position as a creditor while enjoying the potential for capital appreciation.

Converting Bonds into Common Stock

All Series 79 candidates must be able to perform the conversion calculations for both convertible bonds and preferred stock. It is essential that prospective representatives are able to determine the following:

Number of shares: To determine the number of shares that can be received upon conversion use the following formula:

par value/conversion price

> **EXAMPLE**
>
> XYZ has a 7% subordinated debenture trading in the marketplace at 120. The bonds are convertible into XYZ common stock at $25 per share. How many shares can the investor receive upon conversion?
>
> $1,000/$25 = 40 shares

The investor is entitled to receive 40 shares of XYZ common stock for each bond owned.

Parity Price

A stock's parity price determines the value at which the stock must be priced in order for the value of the common stock to be equal to the value of the bond that the investor already owns. The value of the stock that can be received by the investor upon conversion must be equal to or at parity with the value of the bond, otherwise converting the bonds into common stock would not make economic sense. Determining the parity price is a two-step process. First, the number of shares that can be received must be determined by using the formula: par value/conversion price. Then it is necessary to calculate the price of each share at the parity price. To determine the parity price, use the following formula:

$$\frac{\textbf{current market value of the convertible}}{\textbf{number of shares to be received}}$$

In the above example, the convertible bond was quoted at 120, which equals a dollar price of $1,200. We determined that the investor could receive 40 shares of stock for each bond, so the parity price equals:

$1,200/40 = $30

If the question is looking for the number of shares or the parity price for a convertible preferred stock, the formulas are the same; the only thing that changes is the par value. Par value for all preferred stocks is $100, instead of $1,000 par value for bonds.

TREASURY BILLS, NOTES, AND BONDS

Treasury Security	Type of Interest	Term	Priced
Bill	None	4, 13, 26, 52 weeks 1, 3, 6, 12 months	At a discount from par
Note	Semiannual	1–10 years	As a percentage of par to 32nds of 1%
Bond	Semiannual	10–30 years	As a percentage of par to 32nds of 1%

The minimum denomination for purchasing a Treasury bill, note, or bond through TreasuryDirect.gov is $100.

Purchasing Treasury Bills

Treasury bills range in maturity from 4 to 52 weeks and are auctioned off by the Treasury Department through a weekly competitive auction. Large banks and broker dealers, known as primary dealers, submit competitive bids or tenders for the bills being sold. The Treasury awards the bills to the bidders who submitted the highest bid and work their way down to lower bids until all of the bills are sold. Treasury bills pay no semiannual interest and are

 TAKE NOTE!

The Treasury does not currently sell 1-year bills. However this is a policy decision; the Treasury may at any time elect to issue 1-year bills, just as it recently decided to reissue 30-year bonds.

issued at a discount from par. The bill appreciates up to par at maturity and the appreciation represents the investor's interest. Because bills are priced at a discount from par, a higher dollar price represents a lower interest rate for the purchaser. All noncompetitive tenders are filled before any competitive tenders are filled. A bidder who submits a noncompetitive tender agrees to accept the average of all the yields accepted by the Treasury and does not try to get the best yield. All competitive tenders are limited to a maximum amount of $500,000. All bids that are accepted and filled by the Treasury are settled in fed funds. Treasury bills range in denominations from $100 up to $1,000,000.

> **TAKE NOTE!**
>
> A quote for a Treasury bill has a bid that appears to be higher than the offer. But remember that the bills are quoted on a discounted yield basis. The higher bid actually represents a lower dollar price than the offer.

EXAMPLE

Bid	Ask
2.91	2.75

INSTITUTIONAL INVESTORS AND INVESTMENT STRATEGIES

Institutional investors have large amounts of capital, are extremely sophisticated and employ investment strategies that are not normally available to individual investors. Institutional investors include:

- Private Equity
- Hedge Funds
- Venture capital
- Broker dealers
- Investment Banks
- Registered Investment Companies
- Banks and savings institutions
- Insurance companies
- Employee benefit plans
- Government agencies and subdivisions
- Qualified institutional buyers (QIBs) with $100 million in assets
- Any entity or individual with $50 million in assets

Many of these institutional investors will seek to invest in the markets and companies in accordance with their investment policies. Each will have its own set of criteria for the method it uses to evaluate and select companies for potential investments. Value, distressed and growth oriented investment objectives are frequently at the center of the investment policy for hedge funds, private equity and venture capital investors.

Value investing - is a method of selecting companies whose assets or stock price are undervalued in relation to their intrinsic value. For public companies fundamental analysis will reveal low price to earnings ratios, low price to book ratios and high dividend yields

Distressed investing - Distressed investors seek to acquire the debt securities of companies who are in the process of restructuring due to default or bankruptcy. These investors will often acquire the bonds of the target companies for pennies on the dollar in the hope that they will be able to realize a substantial return on their investment once the company restructures its debt and or exits bankruptcy

Growth investing - Investors who are seeking capital appreciation over time will invest in the stock of companies that have earnings that are projected to increase faster than other more mature companies. Growth companies tend to pay no dividends as the earnings are reinvested in the business and used to further accelerate growth. A fundamental analysis of these companies will tend to show relatively high price to earnings ratios. A variation of growth investing is an approach called growth at a reasonable price (GARP). This approach combines both the growth and value approach and measures the company's price earning ratio relative to its growth rate. This approach allows an investor to determine an appropriate value to pay for the growth of the company. This measurement known as the PEG ratio can make what appears to be an incredibly inflated valuation on a price to earnings basis look more reasonable as it relates to the rapid growth of the company's earnings. It is important to note that the PEG ratio may differ significantly from one analyst to another if their projected growth rates for the company are materially different. The lower the PEG ratio the more attractive the investment is to a GARP investor. These concepts will be discussed in much greater detail later in this book.

In addition to investing in the securities of target companies institutional investors may deploy a variety of trading strategies. Some of the strategies include

- Indexing
- Delta / Market neutral
- Short sales
- High frequency trading
- Momentum trading

- Arbitrage

Index investing is designed to mirror the performance of a large market index such as the S&P 500 or the Dow Jones Industrial Average. An index investor will create a portfolio composed of the stocks that are included in the index that the investor is seeking to track. The investor does not actively seek out which stocks to buy or sell, making index investing a passive asset management strategy. If the stock is in the index, it will usually be in the portfolio. Portfolio turnover for index investors is generally low, which helps keep the expenses down and taxable events at a minimum.

DELTA NEUTRAL / MARKET NEUTRAL

Delta is the rate of change in the price of an investment. When an investor owns a security the security position creates positive delta and when an investor is short a security, that position creates negative delta. With a delta neutral or market neutral strategy the investor will establish both long and short positions in an effort to earn excess returns while reducing risk. Delta neutral strategies usually include offsetting positions using options and derivatives. (Long calls and short puts create positive delta. Long puts and short calls create negative delta.) While market neutral strategies tend to focus on establishing long positions in undervalued securities and offsetting short positions in overvalued positions.

SHORT SALES

An investor who believes that a stock price has appreciated too far and is likely to decline may profit from this belief by selling the stock short. In a short sale, the customer borrows the security in order to complete delivery to the buying party. The investor sells the stock high hoping that it can be bought back and replaced at a cheaper price. It is a perfectly legitimate investment strategy. The investor's first transaction is a sell. The investor exits the position by repurchasing the stock. The short sale of stock has unlimited risk because there is no limit to how high the stock price may go. The investor will lose money if the stock appreciates past the sales price.

HIGH FREQUENCY AND ALGORITHMIC TRADING

Many sophisticated institutions invest significant amounts of money in the development of proprietary computerized trading models. These trading models are often driven by the use of sophisticated algorithms. An algorithm is a set of mathematical procedures and instructions that are designed to execute orders based on many variables. These computerized trading models are able to take advantage of trading opportunities that last only nanoseconds. The trading algorithms are the basis of the high frequency trading module, which route and display a substantial amount of orders for execution based on market conditions that may only last a nanosecond. If the orders are not executed the orders may be immediately canceled by the trading program. The constant routing and canceling of orders can result in flickering quotes. A firm that executes a customer order at an inferior price due to a flickering quote in another market will not have committed a violation due to the extremely temporary nature of the flickering quote.

MOMENTUM TRADING

This type of trading strategy is used by investors to follow a market trend which is confirmed by substantial volume. The trend in the market or security is confirmed and is said to have substantial momentum when the volume of trading is significantly higher than average. The greater the amount of volume, the stronger the trend and the greater the momentum. Momentum trading is used to establish positions on the same side of the market and to ride the trend. Parabolic moves in the market or in a security trend to pick up strength as the trend continues sending the price almost straight up. When the volume dries up, the momentum loses steam. Momentum traders are not concerned with the direction of the move and are focused on the strength of the move up or down.

ARBITRAGE

Arbitrage is an investment strategy used to take advantage of market inefficiencies and to profit from the price discrepancies that result from those inefficiencies. There are three types of arbitrage. They are:

1. Market arbitrage

2. Security arbitrage
3. Risk arbitrage

Market Arbitrage: Securities that trade in more than one market will sometimes be quoted and traded at different prices. Market arbitrage consists of the simultaneous purchase and sale of the same security in two different markets to take advantage of the price discrepancy.

Security Arbitrage: Securities that give the holder the right to convert or exercise the security into the underlying stock may be purchased or sold to take advantage of price discrepancies between that security and the underlying common stock. Securities arbitrage consists of the purchase or sale of one security and the simultaneous purchase or sale of the underlying security.

Risk Arbitrage: Risk arbitrage tries to take advantage of the price discrepancies that come about as a result of a takeover. A risk arbitrageur will short the stock of the acquiring company and purchase the stock of the company being acquired.

BROKER DEALER OPERATIONS

Most large broker dealers are made up of specialized departments designed to perform a specific function for the firm. Every major operation performed by the firm has its own department. It is important to have an understanding of the business operations of a broker dealer. The process of executing a customer's order lies in the operational procedures that route the order to the markets and handle trade input functions for the order once it has been executed. The brokerage firm assigns specific departments to handle all of the important functions of trade execution and input. The departments are:

- Sales department.
- Order room/wire room.
- Purchase and sales department.
- Margin department.
- Cashiering department.
- Custody department.
- Corporate action department

SALES DEPARTMENT

The sales department is where registered representatives interact with the investing public. Representatives work with individual and institutional investors, manage portfolios, make recommendations, and accept orders.

ORDER ROOM/WIRE ROOM

Once a representative has received an order from a client, the representative must present the order for execution to the order room. The order room will promptly route the order to the appropriate market for execution. Once the order has been executed, the order room will forward a confirmation of the execution to the registered representative and to the purchase and sales department.

PURCHASE AND SALES DEPARTMENT

Once the order has been executed, the purchase and sales department inputs the transaction to the customer's account. The purchase and sales department, sometimes called P&S, is also responsible for mailing confirmations to the customer and for all billing.

MARGIN DEPARTMENT

All transactions, regardless of the type of account, are sent through the margin department. The margin or credit department calculates the amount of money owed by the customer and the date when the money is due. The margin department will also calculate any amount due to a customer.

CASHIERING DEPARTMENT

The cashiering department handles all receipts and distributions of cash and securities. All securities and payments delivered from clients to the firm are processed by the cashiering department. The cashiering department will also issue checks to customers and, at the request of the margin department, forward certificates to the transfer agent.

CUSTODY DEPARTMENT

The custody department maintains physical control of customer and firm assets. The custody department, sometimes referred as the "cage," safeguards the physical securities in the firm's possession. Employees in the custody department will create stock records for each security in the firm's control and will record which securities belong to the firm and which securities belong to customers. The box count of physical securities will take place in the custody department, and any long or short differences in securities positions will be investigated by members of the custody department.

CORPORATE ACTION DEPARTMENT

The corporate action department handles communications between the investors and the issuers of securities. The corporate action department will mail proxies and prospectuses to beneficial owners of securities and handles mergers, reorganizations, and name changes relating to issuers. The corporate action department also manages the collection of interest and dividend payments.

CHAPTER 1

Pretest

EQUITY AND DEBT SECURITIES

1. Which of the following is NOT a right of common stockholders?
    A. Right to elect the board of directors
    B. Right to vote for executive compensation
    C. Right to vote for a stock split
    D. Right to maintain their percentage of ownership in the company

2. Which of the following is NOT true regarding ADRs?
    A. They are receipts of ownership of foreign shares being held abroad in a U.S. bank.
    B. Each ADR represents 100 shares of foreign stock, and the ADR holder may request delivery of the foreign shares.
    C. ADR holders have the right to vote and receive dividends that the foreign corporation declares for shareholders.
    D. The foreign country may issue restrictions on the foreign ownership of stock.

3. Which of the following is NOT true of authorized stock?
    A. It is the maximum number of shares a company may sell.
    B. It is arbitrarily determined at the time of incorporation and may not be changed.
    C. It may be sold in total or in part when the company goes public.
    D. It may be sold to investors to raise operating capital for the company.

4. Which of the following issues standardized options?
   A. The exchanges
   B. The OCC
   C. The company
   D. Nasdaq

5. Common stockholders do not have the right to vote on which of the following issues?
   A. Election of the board of directors
   B. Stock splits
   C. Issuance of additional common shares
   D. Bankruptcy

6. Which type of bond requires the investor to deposit coupons to receive interest payments but have the owner's name recorded on the books of the issuer?
   A. Registered bonds
   B. Bearer bonds
   C. Book entry/journal entry bonds
   D. Principal-only bonds

7. Which bonds are issued as a physical certificate without the owner's name on them and require whoever possesses these bonds to clip the coupons to receive their interest payments and to surrender the bond at maturity in order to receive the principal payment?
   A. Registered bonds
   B. Book entry/journal entry bonds
   C. Principal-only registered bonds
   D. Bearer bonds

8. In a DPP all of the following may be depreciated, EXCEPT:
   A. buildings.
   B. machinery.
   C. equipment.
   D. raw land.

CHAPTER 1 Pretest   41

9. Which of the following are true about an option?
   A. It is a contract between two parties that determines the time and place at which a security may be bought or sold.
   B. The two parties are known as the buyer and the seller. The money paid by the buyer of the option is known as the option's premium.
   C. The buyer has bought the right to buy or sell the security depending on the type of option.
   D. The seller has an obligation to perform under the contract, possibly to buy or sell the stock depending on the option involved.
      a. II, III, and IV
      b. I, II, III, and IV
      c. I, II, and III
      d. III and IV

10. Which of the following are bearish?
    A. Call seller
    B. Put seller
    C. Call buyer
    D. Put buyer
       a. II and III
       b. II and IV
       c. I and IV
       d. I and II

CHAPTER 2

SEC Reporting, Rules and Regulations

> **INTRODUCTION**
>
> The SEC as the ultimate securities industry regulator requires issuers of securities to disclose financial performance, to solicit votes from shareholders and to publicly disclose material events. In addition, the SEC requires large investors and insiders to disclose their ownership stake and transactions by filing a notice with the SEC. In this chapter we will review the rules and regulations you will be required to master in order to pass the series 79 exam. Many of the filings in this chapter are part of the data collection process.

THE SECURITIES EXCHANGE ACT OF 1934

The Securities Exchange Act of 1934 was the second major piece of legislation that resulted from the market crash of 1929. The Securities Exchange Act regulates the secondary market that consists of investor-to-investor transactions. All transactions between two investors that are executed on any of the exchanges or in the over-the-counter (OTC) market are secondary market transactions. In a secondary market transaction, the selling security holder receives the money, not the issuing corporation. The Securities Exchange Act of 1934 also regulates all individuals and firms that conduct business in the securities industry. The Securities Exchange Act of 1934:

- Created the Securities and Exchange Commission (SEC).
- Requires the registration of broker dealers and agents.
- Regulates the exchanges and FINRA.
- Requires net capital for broker dealers.
- Regulates short sales.

- Regulates insider transactions.
- Requires public companies to solicit proxies.
- Requires segregation of customer and firm assets.
- Authorized the Federal Reserve Board to regulate the extension of credit for securities purchases under Regulation T.
- Regulates the handling of client accounts.
- Regulates interstate securities transactions.

THE SECURITIES AND EXCHANGE COMMISSION (SEC)

One of the biggest components of the Securities Exchange Act of 1934 was the creation of the SEC. The SEC is the ultimate securities industry authority and is a direct government body. Five commissioners are appointed to five-year terms by the president, and each must be approved by the Senate. No more than three members may be from any one political party. During their term as a commissioner, individuals may only act as a commissioner and may not engage in any outside employment. The SEC is not a self-regulatory organization (SRO) or a designated examining authority (DEA). An SRO is an organization that regulates its own members, such as the NYSE or FINRA. A DEA is an entity that inspects a broker dealer's books and records, and it can also be the NYSE or FINRA. All broker dealers, exchanges, agents, and securities must register with the SEC. All exchanges are required to file a registration statement with the SEC that includes the exchange's articles of incorporation, bylaws, and constitution. All new rules and regulations adopted by an exchange must be disclosed to the SEC as soon as they are enacted. Issuers of securities with more than 500 shareholders and with assets exceeding $10,000,000 or issuers whose securities are traded on an exchange or Nasdaq must register with the SEC, file quarterly (10-Q) and annual (10-K) reports, and follow certain rules relating to the solicitation of proxies from stockholders. The issuer must file the proxy with the SEC, and the proxy must be in the required form and must be accompanied by certain information.

PROXIES

Common stockholders have the right to vote on major corporate issues. Most stockholders, however, do not have the time to attend the meetings and must therefore vote using an absentee ballot, known as a proxy. The Securities

Exchange Act of 1934 requires that all corporations that distribute proxies solicit votes from their shareholders. The corporation will send proxies to the shareholders of record. Stockholders who have their securities held in street name will have the proxies forwarded to them by the brokerage firm. The brokerage firm will then cast the beneficial shareholder's votes as indicated on the proxy as the shareholder of record. Proxies that have been signed and returned without indicating how to vote must be voted in accordance with the issuer's management's recommendation. If a shareholder fails to return the proxy to the member at least 10 days prior to the annual meeting, the member may vote the shares as it sees fit, as long as the matter is not of major importance. If the vote concerns a major issue, such as a merger, the member may never cast the votes. Member firms are required to forward proxies and other corporate communications, such as annual and quarterly reports, to the beneficial owner and the issuer is required to reimburse the member for reasonable expenses. Annual proxy statements must be sent to shareholders at least 20 days prior to the annual meeting. Alternatively, if the issuer is notifying shareholders electronically, the notification must be sent at least 40 days prior to the annual meeting and will notify shareholders how to obtain proxy materials free of charge. The annual proxy statement includes:

- Executive compensation including stock options and stock grants
- A list of board members
- Name of the independent accounting firm who audits the corporation's financial information
- A list of 5 percent owners who have submitted 13D and 13 G filings
- Shareholder proposals and Board of Directors' response

Minutes of board meetings, results of board votes and the voting records of the Board of Directors are not included as part of the annual proxy statement

PRELIMINARY AND SPECIAL PROXIES

If a reporting issuer finds it necessary to solicit votes from shareholders as a result of an unscheduled material event suchs as a merger, acquisition or spin off, the company will be required to file both a preliminary and definitive (special) proxy statement with the SEC on Form 14A. The preliminary proxy must be filed with the SEC at least 10 days prior to the date the definitive proxy is sent to shareholders. The preliminary proxy is submitted to the SEC to notify the Commission that a material event has taken place requiring shareholder approval. The preliminary proxy contains a draft of the information to be included in the definitive proxy that is sent to shareholders. The unscheduled material event will require the issuer to hold a special meeting to allow shareholders to vote on the matter. The issuer must file the definitive proxy with the SEC on the day the proxy is sent to shareholders. With an annual proxy, issuers are not required to file a preliminary proxy with the SEC and will only file the definitive proxy at the time it is sent to shareholders.

EXTENSION OF CREDIT

The Securities Act of 1934 gave the authority to the Federal Reserve Board to regulate the extension of credit by broker dealers for the purchase of securities by their customers. The following is a list of the regulations of the different lenders and the regulations that gave the Federal Reserve Board the authority to govern their activities:

- Regulation T: Broker dealers
- Regulation U: Banks
- Regulation G: All other financial institutions

> **TAKE NOTE!**
>
> Exempt securities issued by the U.S. government and municipal governments are exempt from most of the conditions of the Securities Exchange Act of 1934, including Regulation T, proxy requirements, and insider reporting.

TRADING SUSPENSIONS

The SEC may impose trading suspensions in nonexempt securities or on an exchange or Nasdaq if certain emergency conditions exist. In the case of significant and excessive price fluctuations, or the prospect of significant and excessive price fluctuations that would disrupt the orderly operation of the security or market, the SEC may suspend trading in the security or in the market as a whole. The SEC may suspend the trading in a security for up to 10 business days, including any extension of the order. The SEC may suspend the trading on an exchange or in a market as a whole for up to 90 days. In the case of a market-wide suspension, the SEC must notify the president of the United States, and he or she must not disapprove the suspension.

SEC REPORTING

The Securities Exchange Act requires most publicly traded companies to file financial reports with the SEC at least 4 times per year. All companies whose securities trade on a national exchange such as the NYSE or NASDAQ or who meet the following conditions are required to become reporting issuers:

- Corporate assets exceed $10 million

And;

- The issuer's securities are owned by more than 500 non accredited investors

Or;

- The issuer's securities are owned by more than 2,000 investors

Both publicly traded non-public companies who meet the above requirements are required to file 3 quarterly reports, 10Qs and 1 annual report, 10K with the SEC. Form 10K is filled for the corporation's full fiscal year and includes the company's fourth quarter. The reports are required to ensure financial results are reported to both the SEC and investors. The information submitted on form 10K includes the following important disclosures:

- Audited financial statements
- 2 year balance sheet
- 3 year income statement and cash flow statement
- Financial footnotes attached to financial statements
- Management statement regarding financial performance and condition
- Any substantial risk factors that may impact the business
- Disclosure statement regarding legal or regulatory actions
- List of corporate executives and compensation including stock options and grants
- Marketplace for securities and outstanding shares
- Signatures of CEO, CFO, Controller and majority of the board members.

The information submitted on form 10-K is disclosed to the SEC in the format prescribed by the SEC. The information on form 10-K is used to generate the annual report which is sent to shareholders. While the terms 10K and annual report are very often used interchangeably, it is important to be aware of the subtle difference.

The time when reporting companies are required to file 10Qs and 10Ks is set by the SEC based on the size of the issuer. The timing requirements are as follows:

- Non accelerated files are companies whose public float is less than $75 million. Non accelerated filers must file 10Qs within 45 days of the end of the quarter and 10Ks must be filed within 90 days of fiscal year end
- Accelerated filers are companies who have a public float between $75 -$700 million who have filed at least 1 form 10K and who have been a reporting issuer for at least 12 months. Accelerated filers must file 10Qs within 40 days of the end of the quarter and 10Ks must be filed within 75 days of fiscal year end
- Large Accelerated filers are companies that have a public float greater than $700 million, who have filed at least 1 form 10K and who have been a reporting issuer for at least 12 months. Large accelerated filers must file 10Qs within 40 days of the end of the quarter and 10Ks must be filed within 60 days of fiscal year end

The 10Ks and 10Qs are great sources for financial information which can be used by analysts and investment bankers to calculate important financial ratios. It is important to remember that only the financial data in the 10K is audited and that the 10K provides more historical financial data than the information contained in the 10Qs. Additionally, the 10Q does not include information regarding shareholders and the 10Q is only required to be signed by one principal officer.

Further, non-scheduled material events must also be reported to the SEC through the submission of form 8-K. Events that may be reported on Form 8-K include:

- Management changes including senior officers and board of directors
- Changes in corporate governance
- Corporate developments (regulatory approvals, gain or loss of a substantial contract)
- The issuance of certain securities
- Disclosures required to be made under regulation FD
- Asset sales, off-balance-sheet transactions
- Asset write-downs and impairments
- Change in accounting firms
- Notices received from Securities markets such as notice of delisting

- Financial statements and exhibits attached to corporate earnings announcements
- Bankruptcy declaration
- Notices of default or failing to make required distributions to securities holders or creditors

Investors who are interested in reviewing corporate filings may access all reports electronically through the SEC's Electronic Data Gathering Analysis and Retrieval (EDGAR) system.

RULE 135 AND RULE 165

Under SEC Rule 135, an issuer of securities who has a class of securities in registration will not be deemed to be making an offer of those securities as a result of a public announcement, as long as certain conditions are met. The announcement may come in the form of a press release or other similar announcements. The announcement must state that an offer may only be made by prospectus and must be limited to factual information such as :

- The issuer's name
- The type and class of securities being issued
- Purpose or the offering
- Anticipated offering date
- Any additional information or disclosures required by state or federal law or regulatory authority

SEC Rule 165 requires the issuer to file certain communications with the SEC. The issuer must file any written statement distributed between the time the issuer announces its intent to issue securities and the time the registration statement is filed by the issuer. These communications are known in the industry as Form 425 filings. The issue may file these disclosures on form 8K provided the issuer indicates the filing is being made based on "written communications pursuant to Rule 425 under the Securities Act" . It is important to note that even though these written communications are required to be filed with the SEC, there is no requirement that they be sent to shareholders. Press releases and emails to employees regarding the transaction are all examples of written communications required to be filed.

SEC FORM 13D, 13G AND 13F

Individuals, entities or groups of investors working in concert who acquire 5 percent or more of an issuer's equity securities must file Form 13D with the SEC within 10 days of reaching the 5 percent stake. Rule 13D requires that the SEC, the exchange where the securities are listed, and the issuer be informed of the size of the investor's holdings (percent ownership and number of shares) . The acquirer must also state the purpose for the investment and the source of funds used to purchase the stake. Form 13D requires the purchaser to disclose any agreements in place that pertain to the purchase of the issuer's securities. For example, if the filer and the issuer were in the process of negotiating an acquisition, the parties may have entered into a standstill agreement in which the purchaser agrees not to acquire more than a stated percentage of the company's outstanding stock. An amended 13D must be filed if the reporting party increases or decreases its ownership by 1% or more. Rule 13D does not require that the stockholders be informed directly by the investor. An entity may acquire more than 5 percent of the issuer's securities for investment purposes, for control, or for acquisition.

Other entities must also disclose their holdings in an issuer's securities. Investment companies who acquire 5 percent or more of an issuer must file a notice of their ownership on Form 13G within 45 days of its year end. If an investment company's ownership exceeds 10 percent, the investment company would be required to file form 13G within 10 days of the end of the month in which its ownership first exceeded 10 percent. Investment advisers who have discretion over $100 million or more in assets must disclose all of their holdings without regard to the amount within 45 days of the end of each calendar quarter on Form 13F. For example, If a large investment advisor who has discretion over more than $100 million owns 1 share of XYZ, the adviser would be required to include that position on its 13F filing. 13 D, 13 G and 13F filings are great sources of information for investment bankers who may wish to approach large shareholders on behalf of a buy-side client to gauge their interest in supporting an acquisition.

Certain market participants who directly or indirectly exercise investment discretion over one or more accounts are required to register as large traders with the SEC. These large traders will be assigned a large trader ID (LTID). The large trader is required to provide its LTID to each broker dealer that executes orders for the large trader. The executing broker dealer is required to record all transactions executed for the large trader and the LTID and time must be noted on each order. The large trader must file form 13H with the SEC within 45 days of the end of each calendar year. A large trader is defined as an entity that:

- Executes a trade or trades in an NMS security of 2 million shares or greater, or with a value of $20 million or greater on a single day; or
- Executes a trade or trades in an NMS security of 20 million shares or greater or with a value of $200 million or greater in a calendar quarter; or
- Executes a trade or trades in options that meet the daily or quarterly limits above based on the value or number of the underlying shares covered by the option contracts

Certain officers, directors and insiders who own shares of the company he / she work for must file form 3 within 10 days of the date the shares are initially purchased or received from the company. If the officer or director buys or sells shares he / she is required to file form 4 within 2 days of the transaction. Additionally, these subject parties are required to annually disclose any gifting of shares on Form 5.

THE INSIDER TRADING AND SECURITIES FRAUD ENFORCEMENT ACT OF 1988

The Insider Trading and Securities Fraud Enforcement Act of 1988 set forth guidelines and controls for the use and dissemination of nonpublic material information. Nonpublic information is information that is not known by people outside of the company. Material information is information regarding a situation or development that will materially affect the company in the present or in the future. It is not only just for insiders to have this type of information, but it is required in order for them to do their jobs effectively. It is, however, unlawful for an insider to use this information to profit from a forthcoming move in the stock price. An insider is defined as any officer, director, 10 percent stockholder, or anyone who is in possession of nonpublic material information, as well as the spouse of any such person. Additionally, it is unlawful for the insider to divulge any of this information to any outside party. Trading on inside information has always been a violation of the Securities Exchange Act of 1934, and the Insider Trading Act prescribed penalties for violators, which include:

- A fine of the greater of 300 percent of the amount of the gain or 300 percent of the amount of the loss avoided or $1,000,000 for the person who acts on the information.

- A fine of up to $1,000,000 for the person who divulges the information.
- Insider traders may be sued by the affected parties.
- Criminal prosecutions.

Information becomes public information once it has been disseminated over public media. The SEC will pay a reward of up to 10 percent to informants who turn in individuals who trade on inside information. In addition to the insiders already listed, the following are also considered insiders:

- Accountants
- Attorneys
- Investment bankers

FIREWALL

Broker dealers that act as underwriters and investment bankers for corporate clients must have access to information regarding the company in order to advise the company properly. The broker dealer must ensure that no inside information is passed between its investment banking department and its retail trading departments. The broker dealer is required to physically separate these divisions by a firewall. The broker dealer must maintain written supervisory procedures to adequately guard against the wrongful use or dissemination of inside information.

THE TRUST INDENTURE ACT OF 1939

The Trust Indenture Act of 1939 requires that corporate bond issues in excess of $10,000,000 dollars that are to be repaid during a term in excess of one year, sold interstate, issue a trust indenture for the issue. The trust indenture is a contract between the issuer and the trustee. The trustee acts on behalf of all of the bondholders and ensures that the issuer is in compliance with all of the promises and covenants made to the bondholders. The trustee is appointed by the corporation and is usually a bank or a trust company. If the issuer defaults the trustee will take possession of the collateral pledged if any and liquidate it in an effort to repay bondholders. The Trust Indenture Act of 1939 only applies to corporate issuers. Both federal and municipal issuers are exempt.

SARBANES-OXLEY ACT

The Sarbanes-Oxley Act, also known as the Public Company Accounting Reform and Investor Protection Act of 2002, or SARBOX, was enacted to help restore confidence in the financial reports and accounting standards of publicly traded companies. The act created the Public Company Accounting Oversight Board to oversee, regulate, and discipline accounting firms' activities when performing auditing functions for publicly traded companies. Section 302 of the Sarbanes-Oxley Act requires the management of publicly traded companies to affirm the accuracy of the company's financial reports and to accept responsibility for the content of the reports by signing all annual and quarterly reports filed under the Securities Exchange Act of 1934. The principal executive officer (CEO) as well as the principal financial officer (CFO) must:

- Sign an acknowledgment that they have read the report.
- Certify to their knowledge that the financial reports do not contain any untrue or misleading statements.
- Certify that to their knowledge the reports do not omit any material fact and accurately represent the company's financial condition for the period covered by the report.
- Establish internal controls to ensure the accurate reporting of all of the issuer's subsidiaries.
- Evaluate the effectiveness of the internal controls within 90 days prior to the filing of the report and file a report relating to the effectiveness of the internal controls.
- Disclose to the audit committee and the board of directors any deficiencies with internal controls, any act of fraud involving management, or any employee significantly involved in the company's internal controls.
- Disclose any material changes to the internal controls or any weaknesses or corrective actions taken.

Section 401 of the Sarbanes-Oxley Act requires financial reports to contain detailed information regarding any off-balance-sheet transactions, obligations, and liabilities the company may have engaged in or have outstanding. The statement may not contain any false or misleading information.

Section 402 of the Sarbanes-Oxley Act enhanced conflict of interest rules regarding loans made by the company to any officer. Section 402 of the act made it unlawful for any company to extend or maintain personal loans either directly or indirectly through a subsidiary to or for any officer of the company. An exception to this rule is for executives of banks who may obtain a mortgage or credit card through their employer. Additionally, officers of brokerage firms may receive margin loans from the employing broker dealer.

Section 403 of the Sarbanes-Oxley Act requires that the company's management as well as any owner of 10 percent or more of the company's securities file reports regarding holdings and transactions in the company's securities. These reports must be filed within 10 days of the person becoming an officer or a 10 percent holder. If any person subject to the reporting requirements of Section 403 purchases or sells the company's securities or enters into a security-based swap agreement a report of the transaction must be filed within two business days. Such reports may be filed electronically and the information must be posted to the company's website.

Section 404 of the Sarbanes-Oxley Act requires that management file with the annual report a report detailing the company's internal controls over financial reporting. The internal controls are designed as a stress test to ensure accuracy of the company's financial reporting . The company's independent auditor is required to certify management's report regarding its internal controls.

Additionally, Sarbanes- Oxley requires the company to establish a code of ethics for its principal officers. The code of ethics is created to further ensure that the principal officers conduct themselves with professional and personal integrity. This code will often list actions that will result in the termination and loss of benefits if the executive is found to have violated the ethics code. If the company fails to comply with this requirement, it must disclose that it has not established a code of ethics in its annual report to shareholders. While the Sarbanes - Oxley Act requires companies to establish a code of ethics or to disclose that they have not established a code, all companies whose stock is listed on the NYSE or NASDAQ must establish a code of ethics as part of the listing criteria.

SEC REGULATION S-K

SEC Regulation S-K details the form and layout an issuer is required to follow when submitting information to the SEC. Regulation S-K applies to the filing of registration statements, proxy statements, annual reports and tender offer statements. Regulation S-K is particularly concerned with projections that are included in a registration statement or as part of other forms or statements filed with the SEC (including proxy statements, annual reports and tender offer statements). Projections regarding the issuer's earnings, revenue and income must all be based on management's reasonable belief based on historical trends for the business and for a specific period of time. When management develops forward looking projections it must ensure that the projections are reasonable and include disclosures of all material facts that may positively or negatively impact the issuer's ability to meet the projections. Management must also consider including previous projections to allow investors to have a better understanding of its current projections. A company's management is not required to provide projections and a disclosure statement stating that management may discontinue or initiate making projections as it sees fit or as business conditions allow must be included. In order to ensure that its projections are reasonable, management may elect to have the projections reviewed by outside experts. If the projections are reviewed, the extent of the review, the qualifications of the reviewing party and the relationship between the reviewer and issuer must all be disclosed. In addition to setting standards for financial projections, Regulation S-K requires financial reports and projections to be submitted using generally accepted account principles (GAAP). There are times when the management of certain types of businesses feel that non-GAAP measures more actually represent the financial performance of the company. In these cases, the issuer must include a statement detailing the reason for using non-GAAP accounting methods and must provide a report comparing its non-GAAP and GAAP financial performance. Non-GAAP accounting methods tend to exclude items that are traditionally included in GAAP accounting. Financial performance as measured by free cash flow, core earnings or EBITDA are all non-GAAP accounting measurements. It is difficult to compare non-GAAP earnings because there are no standard methods employed among companies. Issuers in certain cases may wish to incorporate reference materials or ratings information as part of the registration statement submitted to the SEC. If an issuer wants to include reference material, that material must be on file with the SEC. The issuer may not include reference material that has been on file with the SEC for more than 5 years. If the issuer is submitting a registration statement for convertible bonds, non-convertible debt or preferred stock, the issuer may elect to include ratings information as prepared by a nationally recognized ratings agency such as S & P or Moodys. Should the issuer submit a rating that is substantially different or should the ratings agency change its rating, the issuer must amend the prospectus to reflect the rating issued by the ratings organization. Regulation S-K also sets reporting requirements regarding transactions with an issuer's related persons, promoters, and certain control people, as well as with their immediate family members. Regulation S-K defines an immediate family member as any of the following individuals:

- Spouse
- Parents
- Mother-in-law/father-in-law
- Brother/sister
- Brother-in-law/sister-in-law
- Children/stepchildren/children-in-law

Any transaction entered into with the above identified parties with a value exceeding $120,000 during the issuer's fiscal year must be reported. The issuer is also required to maintain policies for the review, approval, and ratification of related party transactions and is required to disclose such policies even if the issuer has no related parties transactions to report.

TAKE NOTE!

The review and disclosure requirements only relate to relationships that are current at the time the transaction occurs. Should a relationship terminate due to divorce prior to the transaction, the transaction is not subject to the disclosure requirements of Regulation S-K.

In addition to disclosing related transactions, Regulation S-K requires issuers to disclose the performance of the company's Board of Directors. The issuer is required to disclose the name and role of each board member, a list of directors who attended at least 75% of the board meetings in the previous fiscal year and the number of meetings held.

SEC REGULATION M-A

SEC Regulation M-A is a subsection of Regulation S-K and was designed to simplify the reporting, communication, and filing requirements and procedures relating to mergers and acquisitions. Regulation M-A requires that a "plain English" term sheet be filed relating to any merger, acquisition, or going-private transaction. This plain English term sheet is designed to clearly communicate with existing shareholders so they may easily understand the terms of the proposed transaction, such as:

- Who is offering to buy my securities?
- What are the types and amounts of securities subject to the offer?
- How much is being offered and what is the form of payment?
- Does the bidder have the ability to make the payment?
- How long do I have to tender my securities?
- Can the offer be changed or extended, and under what circumstances?
- How will I be notified if the offer is changed or extended?
- What are the conditions to the offer?
- How do I tender into the offer?
- How long do I have to withdraw previously tendered shares?
- What steps do I need to take to withdraw previously tendered shares?
- If the transaction is negotiated, is the board of directors for or against the offer?
- Is this the first step in a going-private transaction?
- Will the tender offer be followed by a merger if all the company's shares are not tendered in the offer?
- What will happen if I decide not to tender my shares?
- What is the market value (if traded) or the net asset or liquidation value (if not traded) of my shares as of a recent date?
- Who can I speak to if I have questions about the tender offer?

Regulation M-A also allows additional types of communication with shareholders regarding proposed transactions and allows certain communications to be made or filed electronically.

Regulation M-A permits:

- The dissemination of more information on a timely basis, so long as the written communications are filed on the date of first use.
- More communications before the filing of a registration statement in connection with either a stock tender offer or a stock merger transaction.
- More communications before the filing of a proxy statement (whether or not a business combination transaction is involved).
- More communications regarding a proposed tender offer without commencing the offer and requiring the filing and dissemination of specified information.

- Harmonizing the various communications principles applicable to business combinations under the Securities Act, tender offer rules, and proxy rules.
- Elimination of the confidential treatment currently available for merger proxy statements, except when communications made outside the proxy statement are limited to those specified in Rule 135.
- Combining the existing schedules for issuer and third-party tender offers into one schedule available for all tender offers, entitled Schedule TO.

THE HART-SCOTT-RODINO ACT

The Hart-Scott-Rodino Act requires both parties in certain mergers and acquisitions to file notification of the transaction with the Federal Trade Commission (FTC) and with the Department of Justice (DOJ). Parties required to file pre merger notifications may file electronically with the appropriate departments and must wait until a 30-day waiting period expires prior to closing the transaction (15 days for all cash offers). The waiting period begins on the date the notification is first filed and allows the FTC and DOJ to review any anticompetitive or antitrust impact the transaction may have on the economy. Any party required to file may request that the waiting period be terminated before the statutory period expires. A request for early termination may be granted only after compliance with the rules and if both the FTC and DOJ Antitrust Division have completed their review and determined not to take any enforcement action during the waiting period. If after a request for additional information has been issued the agency determines that no further action is necessary, the waiting period may be terminated before full compliance with the second request is made.

Exempt from the filing requirements of the act are things such as:

- Acquisition of real estate.
- Purchase of interests in oil reserves less than $500,000,000.
- Purchase of durable goods.

FINRA RULE 5150 (FAIRNESS OPINION)

Any member who issues a fairness opinion to shareholders in connection with a proposed transaction must establish and maintain procedures under which fairness opinions may be issued. Members must establish a fairness committee and outline the qualifications required for committee members. The processes and methods for evaluating the fairness of any proposed transaction and the type of transactions it reviews must also be detailed in the procedures. Members issuing fairness options must also disclose any potential conflicts of interest the member may have in connection with the opinion. Members that issue fairness opinions must disclose:

- If the member acted as a financial adviser to either party.
- If the opinion is contingent upon the successful completion of the transaction.
- If the member has received or will receive compensation from either party.
- Any material relationship with either party in the last two years.
- The categories of information used to evaluate the fairness of the transaction.
- Procedures used to establish the opinion.
- If the opinion includes a fairness review of the compensation to be received by insiders if different than that received by shareholders
- If information used to prepare the opinion was provided by the requesting party and if an independent verification was conducted
- If the opinion was approved by the fairness committee.

A broker dealer who produces a fairness opinion may rely on the information provided by the requesting party and is not required to verify the information. If the information provided by the requesting party is found to be inaccurate, misleading or fraudulent, the broker dealer will not be deemed to be liable for any resulting inaccuracies based on the information supplied by the requesting party.

SEC REGULATION S-X

SEC Regulation S-X sets forth guidelines for how issuers that file reports under the Securities Act of 1933 or the Securities Exchange Act of 1934 submit financial information and how issuers account for certain assets that appear on their balance sheets. Regulation S-X requires that an independent accounting firm submit a report attesting to whether or not are any material weaknesses or misstatements have been identified. The attestation report must also include a statement that any material misstatements included within the report may not be discovered in a timely manner. An issuer who files a registration statement for securities must use current financial statements and may not include "stale" financial data. The longer it takes for a registration statement to become effective, the greater the chance that the financial information incorporated in the filing will become stale and unusable. In the case of an IPO, the useful life of the financial data for registration purposes expires at 135 days. For series 79 test purposes, financial data may be used for up to 134 days from its creation. For accelerated filers such as well known and seasoned issuers, the useful life for the financial data expires at 130 days. Issuers that normally would account for the value of assets under an equity method may account for the value of the asset under a fair value method. The value of the asset will be reported on the balance sheet at its fair value, with changes in the asset's value between reporting periods being reported on the issuer's income statement. Under the equity method, issuers will no longer report its share of income or loss from the investment on its income statement. Issuers of securities whose investment in a subsidiary or entity is equal to 50 percent or less of the subsidiary or entity, and when the income of the subsidiary or entity is 20 percent or more of the issuer's income, are required to file separate financial statements for that subsidiary or entity in connection with the issuer's financial statements. If the income generated by the subsidiary or entity is 10 percent or less of the issuer's income, the issuer may consolidate the income from the investment on its balance sheet and income statements. Regulation S-X regulates the submission of the following:

- Employee stock grants, options and savings plans
- Consolidated or combined financial statements
- Pro-Forma financial statements
- Interim financial statements
- Reports to be submitted by accountants
- Accountant qualifications
- Form and data submitted on SEC schedules and filings

A credit default swap (CDS) is a derivative security that is used to transfer the risk of default from the holder of a credit instrument to the seller of the CDS. The buyer of the CDS makes payments to the seller of the contract, much like the premium on an insurance policy. The CDS is based on a notational or stated amount of value of a particular reference issue or issues not on an actual bond. The seller of the CDS will be required to make a payment to the buyer if certain stipulated credit events take place, such as a default or a credit rating downgrade by a nationally recognized statistical rating organization.

A CDS can also be used by speculators to bet on the creditworthiness of the reference issues. Credit default swaps have margin requirements that are based on the contract's term and the interest rate or basis point spread above the London Interbank Offered Rate or LIBOR and based on whether the account holder is long or short the CDS. The contract requirement for an account short a CDS is anywhere from 1 to 50 percent of the notional amount, while the margin requirement for buyers of CDS are usually half that of the seller's margin requirement.

AUDIT COMMITTEE

Sarbanes-Oxley, Regulation S-K as well as the NYSE and NASDAQ require reporting issuers to maintain an audit committee to ensure the accuracy of the financial statements and reports released by the company. SARBOX requires that each member of the audit committee serve as an independent member of the issuer's board of directors. Regulation S-K and the exchanges have all set requirements regarding financial experts serving as a member of the audit committee. The exchanges require that at least one member of the audit committee be qualified as a financial expert, while Regulation S-K merely requires the issuer to disclose if a member of the audit committee is a financial expert. If a member of the audit committee is deemed to be a financial expert Regulation S-K requires that the identity of the individual be reported to investors. A financial expert is an individual who:

- Has substantial audit experience
- Is well versed in GAAP
- Can evaluate financial statements
- Understands the function of the audit committee
- Can evaluate internal controls and reporting procedures

The audit committee provides oversight for the company's internal control systems as well as for the independent auditors. If the independent auditors uncover fraud or any illegal act, the auditor will first report the act to the audit committee.

CHAPTER 2

Pretest

SEC REPORTING, RULES AND REGULATIONS

1. XYZ industries is a manufacturing company whose public float is valued at $60 million. XYZ is approaching the end of its fiscal year. Which of the following is correct ?
   A. XYZ must file its 10K within 60 days of its fiscal year end
   B. XYZ must file its 10K within 45 days of its fiscal year end
   C. XYZ must file its 10K within 40 days of its fiscal year end
   D. XYZ must file its 10K within 90 days of its fiscal year end

2. As an investment banker you are reviewing the annual and quarterly reports for QWER Micro, a manufacturer of computer chips. Which of the following pieces of information would be found in the 10 K but not in the 10Q?
   A. Stockholder information and audited financial data
   B. Financial data and footnotes
   C. Annual results and financial data
   D. Income statements and balance sheets

3. JKL manufacturing has been enduring a long period of challenging economic conditions. The CFO has determined that the value of its inventory assets have declined substantially and the company will be taking a substantial write down. JKL would be required to:
   A. File an impairment notification in line with generally accepted accounting principles.
   B. File a asset write down notification with the principal exchange where its securities are listed
   C. Accelerate the filing of its quarterly report to within 15 days of the end of its quarter
   D. File a notice of a non scheduled material event

4. A large venture capital firm has joined together with an activist hedge fund to acquire a large state in a publicly traded company. As it relates to the filing of form 13 D, which of the following is not correct?
   A. If the parties increase or decrease their holdings by more than 1 percent, form 13 D must be amended
   B. Any negotiations between the acquiring parties and the company are strictly confidential
   C. Form 13 D need not be sent directly to the stockholders
   D. Form 13 D must be sent to the exchange where the securities are listed

5. Smart Money has discretionary authority over $475 million which of the following accurately describes its obligations to file form 13F?
   A. Form 13 F must be filed within 30 days of the end of each quarter for positions exceeding 1 percent of the fund's assets
   B. Form 13 F must be filed within 30 days of the end of each quarter for all positions regardless of size
   C. Form 13 F must be filed within 45 days of the end of each quarter for positions exceeding 1 percent of the fund's assets
   D. Form 13 F must be filed within 45 days of the end of each quarter for all positions regardless of size

6. Issuers of publicly traded securities must follow certain guidelines under Regulation S-K. Which of the following is not part of the requirements of Regulation S-K?
   A. Reporting financial results using measures such as free cash flow and core earnings is strictly prohibited
   B. Issuers may cite or include reference materials so long as the material is on file with the SEC and is not more than 5 years old
   C. Insurers who register debt or preferred stock may cite the ratings of nationally recognized rating agencies
   D. Regulation S-K requires issuers to provide attendance records for the members of its board of directors

7. SEC Regulation M-A is designed to ensure timely and effective communication between a company and its shareholders in the event of certain transactions. Which of the following is not part of the communication process regulated under SEC Regulation M-A?
   A. Information regarding the person or persons who are offering to purchase the securities
   B. Information regarding the purchaser's ability to make the payment offered
   C. Information regarding the terms and conditions of the offer and the circumstances under which the conditions may be changed, if any.
   D. Information, regarding the fairness opinion issued in connection with the offer and the reasonableness of the compensation to be paid.

CHAPTER 2 Pretest **65**

8. GoodAdvice broker dealers have been retained by TragetCo to provide a fairness opinion regarding an acquisition offer it has received from a larger company looking to expand. TargetCo has provided all of its confidential financial information to GoodAdvice to use as the basis for its opinion. Which of the following is correct?
    A. If the information provided to GoodAdvice was false and misleading both GoodAdvce and TargetCo are liable for any negative consequences suffered based on the fairness opinion
    B. If the information provided to GoodAdvice was false and misleading only GoodAdvce is liable for any negative consequences suffered based on the fairness opinion it prepared
    C. GoodAdvice is not responsible for verifying the accuracy of the information and will not be liable for any negative consequences suffered as a result of the fairness opinion
    D. GoodAdvice is responsible for verifying the accuracy of the information prior to developing and distributing the fairness opinion.

9. Regulation S-X sets requirements for issuers who file reports pursuant to The Securities Exchange act of 1934. Under the terms of an IPO, financial data may be used as part of the registration process for:
    A. 130 days
    B. 134 days
    C. 135 days
    D. 136 days

10. As it relates to requirements regarding financial experts serving on the board of publicly traded companies, which of the following is correct?
    A. All members of the audit committee are required to be financial experts and to serve as independent members of the board of directors.
    B. All members of the audit committee are required to be financial experts and one member is required to serve as an independent member of the board of directors.
    C. At least one member of the audit committee must be a financial expert and all members of the audit committee must serve as independent members of the board of directors.
    D. The identity of the financial experts serving on the audit committee must be disclosed, but there is no requirement to serve on the board of directors.

CHAPTER 3

Mergers and Acquisitions

> **INTRODUCTION**
>
> In this chapter we will review the various types of corporate transactions that commonly fall under the broad heading of mergers and acquisitions. Being able to identify the key elements to these transactions as well as the advantages and disadvantages to all parties is an integral part of the Series 79 exam. The information contained in this chapter is part of Section 3 of The Series 79 exam.

MERGERS AND ACQUISITIONS / M&A

While the terms merger and acquisitions generally appear together, the transactions are actually substantially different. In a merger two companies combine in whole or in part to join together to form a larger entity. The stockholders from both companies surrender their shares and are issued shares in the new combined entity. When corporations merge, the management teams believe that the synergies that exist between the two companies will lead to increased operational efficiency, economies of scale and cost savings. These synergies will allow the new combined company to be more profitable and as a result will be more valuable than the companies were when operating independently. Further, when two corporations are combined, the new entity is able to eliminate duplication of effort and reduce the costs associated with similar departments, technologies and services that were being used by each party prior to the merger. If the synergies exist and the integration of the two businesses is effective, the merger will be seen as successful. However, as is the case in the real world, not everything always goes as planned. If the integration of the two companies proves to be more difficult than expected or the synergies are less than anticipated, the combined entity may end up being less profitable and as a result, less valuable than the companies were when they were independent.

EXAMPLE: ABC Manufacturing Inc. has entered into a merger agreement with XYZ Manufacturing Inc. The terms of the merger are that shareholders of ABC will receive a 60% ownership interest and shareholders of XYZ will own a 40% interest in the new entity known as DEF Manufacturing Corporation. DEF Manufacturing will be issuing 100 million shares of common stock upon the completion of the merger. 60 million shares in DEF Manufacturing will be issued to the shareholders of ABC in exchange for their holdings in ABC. While shareholders of XYZ Manufacturing will surrender their ownership in XYZ for 40 million shares of DEF Manufacturing

In an acquisition a corporation will purchase an existing company in order to expand its operations, its product line or to vertically integrate its business. The acquiring party may offer cash, stock or a combination of the two to shareholders of the target organization. Once completed, the target company will effectively cease to exist and will become a part of the acquirer's organization.

EXAMPLE Build Right Home Developers, a large homebuilder in the Northeast, is seeking to expand its footprint and to enter the homebuilding market in Florida. Build Right's stock is trading in the marketplace at $70 per share. Sunnyside Builders is a regional builder in Florida whose stock is trading at $12 per share. When evaluating the best way to enter the homebuilding market in Florida, the management team at Build Right determines that it is easier and cheaper to try to acquire Sunnyside Builders rather than starting up its own operations in Florida. Build Right acquires Sunnyside Builders for $21 in cash. Upon completion of the acquisition, the entity known as Sunnyside ceases to exist and becomes a division of Build Right Home Developers. Alternatively, Build Rite could have offered to acquire Sunnyside by offering the equivalent of $21 in stock by offering to exchange each share of Sunnyside for .3 shares of Build Right. We will review the risks and benefits associated with making an acquisition for stock later in this chapter.

Both mergers and acquisitions are complicated transactions. In addition to combining the operational and financial performance of more than one entity, the personalities and emotions of management and employees can further complicate matters. The leaders of large corporations often have egos and an emotional investment in the business. Sometimes, to get a deal done, a transaction that would be seen as a takeover or acquisition of one company is billed as a merger of equals so that the management team of the smaller entity feels as if they and their employees are at the same level as the management and employees of the larger entity.

SELLERS AND SELL-SIDE BANKERS

When an individual, family, group of partners or board of directors make the decision to sell a business, the seller must go through a long process. Having elected to sell the business, the timing and method of sale need to be selected. In addition to the operational aspects, the seller must understand how to value the business and the market conditions impacting the value of the business. Other important factors include:

- Tax implications of sale
- If any owners of the business object to the sale
- If any owners wish to continue to work
- If any owners wish to exit completely
- Acceptable forms of payment including cash or, stock
- Acceptable timing of the payments such as an earn-out

Due to the complicated nature of selling a business, many sellers will make the decision to engage a sell-side banker. The role of the sell-side banker is not unlike the role of a real estate broker who helps a homeowner market and sell a home. The sell-side banker will advise the owners on the best way to prepare the business for sale, to value and to market the business. During the review process the bankers may identify opportunities for improvement that can help the seller obtain a higher price. For example, paying down debt or improving payment collection on accounts receivable may improve the balance sheet and make the business more attractive to a buyer. The bankers will also advise the owners as to the best method of sale. For example, should the business be widely advertised, offered for sale through private negotiations or sold through an open auction. It is not unusual for a business owner to have a perceived value of the business that differs substantially from the market value. The banker will advise and educate the owners as to the true value of the business based on the current market conditions. Owners who have a perceived value that is lower than the actual value of the business, may be pleasantly surprised. While owners who have an inflated estimated value for the business, may need to lower their expectations in order to finalize a sale. If a business owner feels that the value of the business is substantially higher than its actual value, the banker must help the owner become more realistic about the value. Many sellers of private businesses have an emotional and sentimental attachment to the business that does not always translate into increased value for the buyer. The sell-side banker will also:

- Perform due diligence on the business (review financials, speak to management, employees and customers)
- Determine if sale will be stock sale or asset sale
- Evaluate competitive advantages and weaknesses
- In the case of a spin off or split off (divestiture) identify assets / divisions
- Write a fairness opinion regarding valuation
- Create a data room for potential buyers to review the listing
- Identify qualified potential buyers
- Market the business to qualified buyers
- Evaluate buyers' financial strength and ability to close
- Advise buyers on the best way to finance acquisition if needed
- Provide prepackaged financing to buyer if desiderd
- If seller is a large player in its industry, evaluate any antitrust issues

BUYERS AND BUY-SIDE BANKERS

Just like sellers, buyers of a business come in all shapes and sizes. The buyer's motivation to acquire a business may range from expanding its current operations, to building a portfolio of companies in a similar industry or to turn around a struggling business to increase its value and to sell to the ultimate buyer. Identifying and approaching potential targets for acquisition can be a daunting task. Many buyers will engage the assistance of a buy- side investment banker to assist with identifying and approaching potential target companies for acquisition . The method used to identify potential targets by the buy-side investment banker will depend upon the size and ownership structure of potential target companies. For example, smaller acquisitions of private companies may require specialized industry knowledge and information regarding potential willing sellers. In the case of an acquisition of a larger public company, more data is readily available and the buy-side investment banker may find it easier to contact management to ascertain their willingness to be acquired. Another method the buy-side investment banker can use when approaching a publicly traded company, is reviewing the SEC filings detailing the corporation's large shareholders. By reviewing the 13 D, 13 G and 13 F filings the buy-side investment banker may be able to approach the large shareholders to evaluate their willingness to support the acquisition of the company and to understand a value at which they would be willing to sell the substantial stake in the company. While identifying private companies to acquire may be more difficult, the ability to negotiate with a very small shareholder group may make it easier to acquire than a large public company with a massive shareholder base. Additionally, the acquisition of a smaller private company is usually completed in a shorter period of time and without substantial regulatory concerns. As part of its services to its clients, the buy-side investment banker will:

- Review acquisition strategy
- Review valuation of target company
- Perform due diligence on target companies
- Evaluate the potential post-acquisition financial performance of the company and create a pro forma balance sheet
- Perform accretion / dilution analysis
- Evaluate any potential risks such as potential lawsuits, off-balance-sheet liabilities, unfunded pensions, golden parachutes or patent expirations
- Evaluate any takeover defense such as a staggered board of directors, shareholder rights plans or other poison pills
- Assist buyer with preparing and developing a bid
- Prepare a fairness opinion
- Evaluate and arrange financing options

STRATEGIC BUYERS AND FINANCIAL BUYERS

Most strategic buyers are operating a business and looking to expand the business through acquisition. The strategic buyer traditionally seeks to acquire other businesses within its own industry or in one that complements its existing operations. The ability to integrate the target company into its existing business and the synergies between the two companies are the most important aspects for a strategic buyer. Upon completion, a strategic buyer will eliminate personnel and operations of the acquired company to realize cost savings and to increase performance. A strategic buyer is often willing to place a higher valuation on a target company than a financial buyer in order to grow its business. Increased distribution, geographic footprint, cross-selling opportunities, patents, and research and development are all reasons why a strategic buyer will seek to grow through acquisition.

Financial buyers include private equity and leveraged buyout firms. These financial buyers are more interested in the return that they can earn on their capital than they are with operating a business. Financial buyers generally leave a company's management in place to run the business while seeking to improve its financial performance with the ultimate goal of increasing the value and selling the company.

Private equity firms will seek to acquire a majority stake in a company by using a combination of cash and financing obtained from a bank or other lending partner. This type of transaction is typically referred to as a recapitalization. The owners of the enterprise are able to realize a liquidity event while maintaining an equity interest in the company. The private-equity majority owners will work closely with existing management in an effort to grow the business. If successful, the increased revenue will be used to pay down debt to increase the value of the equity. Private equity firms will also use financial engineering, restructuring or additional acquisitions tactics to increase the value of the company. Once the value of the business has increased to a level that would provide the private equity firm with its desired rate of return, the business can then be sold. The private-equity firm may seek to exit by selling the company to a strategic buyer, another private equity firm or potentially through an initial public offering. Since the original owners maintained an equity interest in the company at the time of the recapitalization, the original owners will participate in the sale. In lieu of a sale, a private equity firm may seek to access additional liquidity from the company through a transaction known as a dividend recapitalization. With a dividend recapitalization the company borrows money through the sale of debt and uses the proceeds of the offering to pay a dividend to shareholders. Since the private equity firm is the majority shareholder, the company is increasing its debt to pay private equity (and other shareholders) a dividend. This type of transaction is generally seen as negative for the company as the company may have trouble servicing the increased debt.

TAKE NOTE:

> A minority recapitalization would occur when the private-equity buyer acquires less than 50% of a company. A minority recapitalization may be used to buy out or to provide liquidity to a specified group of owners.

Leveraged buyout / LBO firms seek to acquire companies through the use of borrowed funds. Once a target company has been identified LBO firms will often borrow up to 90% of the purchase price from banks and other lending partners The assets of the target company are pledged as collateral to the lenders. The LBO firm will then use the cash flow generated by the business to service the substantial amount of debt issued to complete the transaction. Leveraged buyouts place a significant debt burden on the corporation. As such, targets for leveraged buyouts must have solid balance sheets and significant cash flow in order to absorb the debt burden placed upon it by the leveraged buyout.

MANAGEMENT-LED BUYOUT

There are times when a management team will seek to purchase the company it is operating, this is known as a management-led buyout or MBO. A management-led buyout may seek to gain the ownership of a public or private corporation. Because the management team currently operates the business, it has an in-depth understanding of the operations and value of the company. As a result, the due diligence process for an MBO tends to be substantially shorter than for other types of buyouts. In the case of a publicly traded company, the management team will often seek to take the company private. Whereas with an MBO of a private company, the management team is generally seeking to buy the business from its founders. Depending on the size and complexity of the transaction, the management team may partner with a private equity firm or with banks to obtain the financing to complete the purchase. If the MBO is for a private company, the owners may assist with the financing or help determine the type of financing used to complete the transaction.

BILATERAL NEGOTIATION

When contemplating a merger or acquisition, a buyer and seller may engage in direct negotiations. Direct negotiations would usually be initiated when the two parties already have business dealings together or when one party approaches the other directly. In many ways bilateral negotiations are the simplest way to get a deal done. These bilateral negotiations have both advantages and disadvantages for the selling party. Because the buyer and seller are communicating directly with one another, the negotiations are easily kept confidential. The confidentiality of the negotiations helps both parties to explore the benefits of the potential transaction without disrupting the productivity of management and employees who are not engaged in negotiations. A big drawback to bilateral negotiations from the seller's point of view is the potential to undervalue the company. In order to alleviate this concern, sellers may ask for a go shop provision that allows them to explore alternative offers. Buyers will often object or try to dissuade the seller from seeking alternative offers from other interested parties as it puts the potential acquirer in a weaker position. The acquirer may be forced to pay a higher price or may lose the deal to a higher bidder. To avoid any potential competing offers, buyers will often seek to have the target company sign a no shop provision which precludes the target company from soliciting alternative offers.

PUBLIC AND CONTROLLED AUCTIONS

As is the case with any auction, multiple interested parties seeking to acquire an asset will often compete with one another in order to be the buyer who is willing to pay the highest price. The competition traditionally results in a higher sales price for the asset. This dynamic holds true for art, collectibles, automobiles and for companies. For this reason, sellers will often initiate the sale of a business, division or asset through the auction process. There are two types of auctions used by corporate sellers: public auctions and controlled auctions. If a seller initiates the auction process using a full public auction, the seller is seeking maximum exposure in an effort to obtain the highest sales price from any interested party. Through the full public auction process, the seller believes that the benefit of the publicity generated by a public auction outweighs the cost of the loss of confidentiality. Effectively, the company has announced to the world that it is for sale. Oftentimes the seller will issue a press release stating that it has retained investment bankers to explore strategic alternatives. This is the industry equivalent of putting a for sale sign on the lawn of the corporate headquarters. A seller who wishes to receive the benefits of the auction process, yet who wants to maintain a level of confidentiality, may engage in a limited or controlled auction process. In a controlled auction, the seller identifies a number of potential buyers who would be interested in acquiring the business or asset. Once identified, these potential acquirers are invited to bid.

THE AUCTION PROCESS

When a seller determines that it is time to sell a business, asset or division through the auction process, it must first identify the investment bank most capable of helping it meet its objectives. Certainly maximizing the sale proceeds is a major consideration. However, sellers may have other considerations such as time to close and identifying the right buyer for the asset. Corporate sellers will effectively interview investment bankers through a process known in the industry as a "bake-off" or "beauty contest." During this process, the investment bankers represent the strengths and reasons why the firm would be the most suitable to represent the seller in the auction process. If more than one candidate is identified as being a suitable choice, the decision may ultimately come down to a question of fees. Once the investment bank is selected the seller will sign the engagement letter. The engagement letter will authorize the investment banker to represent the seller and to advise management as to the best path forward. The fees to be paid to the investment bank and the scope of authority of the bank to act on the seller's behalf are all detailed in the engagement letter. Once the execution of the engagement letter has been completed the auction process includes the following:

1. Identify prospective buyers
2. Develop business profile
3. Draft confidentiality agreements
4. Compile confidential information memorandum/CIM
5. Provide bidding procedure letter
6. Create data room
7. Accept indications of interest
8. Deliver management presentations
9. Bid evaluation
10. Receive letters of intent
11. Distribute final bid letter
12. Receive final bids
13. Select buyer
14. Execute definitive purchase agreements
15. Obtain fairness opinion
16. Closing of acquisition

IDENTIFYING PROSPECTIVE BUYERS

Once the engagement letter has been signed the investment bank will begin the auction process by identifying prospective buyers. The investment bank will compile a list containing both strategic and (potentially) financial buyers who have the financial resources to acquire the company. The investment bank will initially seek to identify strategic buyers who may be interested in acquiring the company as strategic buyers are traditionally willing to pay more than financial buyers.

DEVELOPING THE BUSINESS PROFILE

The investment bank and seller will work together to develop a business profile designed to be distributed to potential acquirers. The business profile is often referred to as a 'teaser" in the industry as it provides an overview of the business for sale, but does not disclose the name of the company or any confidential details. The teaser is a brief summary designed to pique the interest of the recipient. The teaser will provide general information, such as the industry and nature of the business, an overview of the revenue, a basic profit and loss detail and reason for sale.

DRAFTING CONFIDENTIALITY AGREEMENTS

The seller's legal counsel will draft a confidentiality agreement to be provided to a recipient of the teaser who wishes to receive additional information regarding the company. Both the seller and potential buyer will sign the confidentiality agreement prior to disclosing any additional information to the recipient. The confidentiality agreement is designed to protect the seller by restraining the recipient from using or acting on the information in a way that could potentially harm the seller. Some of the actions a seller will seek to restrain are:

- Disclosure or use of confidential information
- Soliciting employees for hire, sometimes referred to as poaching
- Contacting or soliciting customers or suppliers
- Colluding with other buyers, sometimes known as an anti-clubbing provision

- The purchase of the seller's common stock, sometimes known as a stand-still agreement

In addition to the above items, the confidentiality agreement will traditionally include procedures by which the buyer may share the information with third parties such as bankers and attorneys. It's important to note that the term laid out in the confidentiality agreement should be sufficient enough to ensure that the seller is protected for a reasonable amount of time after the disclosures are made.

COMPILING THE CONFIDENTIAL INFORMATION MEMORANDUM (CIM)

The seller and the investment bankers will work together to develop a comprehensive profile of the business known as the confidential information memorandum or CIM. The CIM provides substantial detail relating to the business, its operations, its history, certified financial reports, assets, liabilities, management team, recent developments and projected financial performance. The CIM will only be provided to potential buyers who have signed the confidentiality agreement and will be used by the purchaser to determine If it wishes to move forward with due diligence or with making a bid.

CREATING THE BIDDING PROCEDURE LETTER

Once interested buyers have expressed an interest in moving forward with making a potential bid for the company, the seller and its bankers will create the bidding procedure letter. The bidding procedure letter will include a deadline for interested parties to submit a bid to acquire the company. It will also require the buyer to disclose how the buyer will finance and pay for the purchase. For example, will the purchaser be using cash on hand, debt financing or issuing stock to pay for the purchase. Additionally, the purchaser will be required to disclose the currency it intends to use to pay for the purchase such as cash, stock or a cash-and-stock offer.

CREATING THE DATA ROOM

Once the seller has distributed the bidding procedure letter to interested parties, it will create a secure electronic data room where potential purchasers, investment bankers, accountants and attorneys can review and share documents relating to the potential transaction. The seller advises its bankers as to what information it will share in the data room and who should have access to the data. The sell-side bankers will then direct authorized users to where they can find the requested information. As one can imagine, the security of the online data room is a significant concern. The seller will traditionally outsource the hosting and security of the data room to a third party who specializes in creating secure online environments.

ACCEPTING INDICATIONS OF INTEREST

Once buyers have had an opportunity to review the confidential information memorandum as well as the data in the data room, the sell side investment banker will contact the receiving parties to gauge interest and ask them to submit a non-binding indication of Interest.

DELIVERING MANAGEMENT PRESENTATIONS

In addition to providing the confidential information memorandum and the documents in the data room, management will make presentations to interested parties to further clarify the information provided and to answer questions. The seller's management team will also use these presentations as an opportunity to create excitement among the buyers and present a strong case for the acquisition of the company.

BID EVALUATION

After the management presentations have concluded, buyers will submit an initial round of bids. The company and the sell-side banker will review the first round of bids and evaluate the strengths and weaknesses of each. Bids that are deemed to be too low or that are submitted by buyers who lack the financial resources to complete the transaction will be rejected. The remaining bids will be evaluated based on price, the currency to be received (cash, stock or both) and the financial strength of the counterparty / buyer.

RECEIVING LETTERS OF INTENT

Having evaluated the initial round of bids the seller will instruct its banker to request remaining bidders to submit a non-binding letter of intent to complete the transaction. The letter of intent contains additional information regarding the transaction, including:

- The structure of the transaction
- A valuation and price range
- Agreed upon reasons for a price adjustment, such as a material adverse change clause
- Any earn-out provisions for the seller(s)
- Any go shop or no shop provisions
- Any exclusivity periods
- Any break up fees to be paid if deal fails to close
- Any key management contract provisions
- Certification of financial statements
- Time frame to complete due diligence

Because the letter of intent is non-binding, the deal can still fail for any number of reasons.

DISTRIBUTING A FINAL BID LETTER

Once the letters of intent have been reviewed by the seller and the sell-side banker, a final bid letter will be drafted and distributed to the prospective buyers who have made it past the first round of bidding. The final bid letter will offer the buyers an opportunity to adjust their bid and to submit their final and best offer. The investment bank representing the seller may also include an offer of financing to purchasers along with the final bid letter. The offering of pre-arranged financing to buyers may help facilitate the closing of the transaction and is an opportunity for the investment bank to earn additional fees in the form of interest. This type of prearranged financing is often referred to as stapled financing among industry participants. While the sell-side banker may offer stapled financing to buyers, buyers are free to seek alternative financing options and some may be able to use cash on hand. A draft of a definitive purchase agreement is often included with the final bid letter.

RECEIVING FINAL BIDS

The final bid letter will detail the procedures under which the remaining bidders may submit a final bid. Interested buyers will submit a final bid that includes a firm price the buyer is willing to pay to acquire the company or asset for sale. Also included in the final bids are finance commitments from lenders and bankers who have agreed to provide financing to the purchaser. Including finance commitments provides the seller with a greater level of certainty that the purchaser will be able to close on the transaction. The buyer will also detail the currency it intends to use to make the purchase. While the seller may prefer an all-cash transaction, a buyer may wish to use its common stock as currency to pay for all or part of the acquisition. The final bid requires the buyer to certify that the bid is final and binding upon the buyer and will often include a certification of the approval of the board of directors to make the acquisition. Finally, the buyer will include a draft of a definitive purchase agreement with the final bid. On your exam you may see the final bidding procedure referred to as final bid placement..

SELECTING THE FINAL BUYER

Once the final bids have been submitted, the company and bankers will review the bids and select a winning bidder. There are many factors to consider When selecting the ultimate buyer. As noted earlier, a seller may prefer an all-cash offer to one that includes the stock of the buyer. Counterparty risk and regulatory risk are other factors to consider during the review process. Financially weak buyers may have a hard time closing, and as a result, may present substantial counterparty risk for the seller. Larger, more complicated transactions may present antitrust concerns that threaten the ability of the transaction to close. Other considerations include employment contracts, non-compete clauses and representations by the buyer regarding its intent to retain or eliminate employees..

EXECUTING DEFINITIVE PURCHASE AGREEMENT

After selecting the winning bidder, the buyer and seller will negotiate and agree to the final terms of the acquisition. Once all of the conditions are in place a final definitive purchase agreement will be signed by both the buyer and the seller. The definitive purchase agreement contains the final price, escrow provisions, financing commitments along with all the terms and conditions mutually agreed to by both parties.

OBTAINING A FAIRNESS OPINION

In preparing a fairness opinion, an investment bank performs a comprehensive appraisal of the value of the business and compares it to the price offered to acquire the business. In order to ensure that the price represents an appropriate valuation, the seller, buyer or both may retain an outside investment banker to evaluate the fairness of the offer. While not required, the seller wants to be certain they receive an appropriate value for the business and the buyer wants to ensure that they do not overpay. The valuation metrics that may be used to arrive at the range of detailed valuations will be included in the fairness opinion and these valuation methods are detailed later in this book. In the case of publicly traded companies, the board of directors have a fiduciary duty to its shareholders and obtaining a fairness opinion for an M&A transaction provides all interested parties with the assurance that the board is meeting its obligations. In the case of the seller, the fairness opinion does not state that the price is the highest value of the business and in the case of the buyer, it does not state that the price is an extreme bargain. The fairness opinion provides a range of valuations for the business and states that a transaction within this range is fair and reasonable from a financial perspective. Additionally, the fairness opinion does not provide advice to the board of directors. Ultimately it is up to the board of each company to proceed with the transaction. It is important to note that while obtaining a fairness opinion helps assure stockholders that the board is meeting its fiduciary duty, obtaining a fairness opinion does not relieve the board of directors of its fiduciary duty to act in the best interest of its stockholders. Obtaining a fairness opinion is also incredibly helpful for M&A transactions that require shareholder approval. If shareholder approval is required, the fairness opinion will be distributed to stockholders and can be used to help stockholders make an informed decision regarding the approval of the transaction. A fairness opinion that is distributed to stockholders must disclose any potential conflict of interest that exists between the investment bank preparing the opinion and the parties to the transaction. A current or previous material relationship and compensation to be received are two areas of concern. Any fees to be received by the author of the fairness opinion must be disclosed in the opinion. Part of the fee disclosure requirement includes contingent fees that may be received by the investment bank for providing financing and if the fees to be received are contingent upon the successful completion of the transaction. While the firm must disclose that it is going to receive a fee, it is not required to disclose the dollar amount to be received.

> **TAKE NOTE !**
>
> A fairness opinion would not be required for an initial public offering, subsequent primaries, registered secondary offerings, stock buybacks or hostile takeovers accomplished using a publicly announced tender offer.

CLOSING OF THE ACQUISITION

Having executed a definitive purchase agreement and reviewed the fairness opinions both parties sign off and complete the transaction. The closing of the transaction is the time when ownership is transferred to the buyer and the payment is received by the seller. For large or complicated transactions, the closing may be contingent upon receiving regulatory approval or meeting certain other conditions. If these conditions cannot be met, the transaction will not close and as a result the payment of a breakup fee may be required.

OTHER M & A TRANSACTIONS

In addition to the M&A transactions detailed above, you are likely to see numerous other types of transactions on your exam. Each of these transactions have their own unique structure and rationale for being completed. Other transactions you are likely to see include:

- Reverse mergers
- Consolidations
- Forward triangular mergers
- Reverse triangular mergers
- Split-offs
- Spin-offs

REVERSE MERGERS

In a reverse merger sometimes referred to as an alternative public offering or APO, a private company gains control of a publicly traded company and becomes a publicly traded company as a result. In a reverse merger, shareholders of the private entity exchange their shares for shares in the publicly traded company. Once completed, the public market will provide liquidity to its owners who wish to monetize his / her holdings and will allow the company to use its stock as currency to make an acquisition. In a reverse merger a large private company may acquire a smaller publicly traded company or the publicly traded company may simply be a shell corporation. The reverse merger may be seen as a cost-effective and efficient way in becoming a publicly traded company. Rather than filing a full registration statement to go public, the transaction is reported to the SEC as a nonscheduled material event on form 8K.

CONSOLIDATIONS

In a consolidation, sometimes referred to as a merger consolidation, two companies have agreed to form a new corporation intended to acquire each individual company to form a new combined entity. The shareholders of the original companies exchange their shares on a predetermined basis for shares of the new combined entity. For example, Company X and Company Y have agreed to merge and have formed Company Z. Shareholders in company X and Company Y will exchange their shares for shares in the newly-created Company Z, which will now be the surviving combined entity.

FORWARD TRIANGULAR MERGERS

As the name implies, a forward triangular merger involves three entities, the buyer or the acquiring company, a subsidiary of the buyer and the target company or seller. With this type of merger the target company is acquired into the subsidiary of the buyer. Once completed the target company becomes part of the subsidiary of the buyer.

REVERSE TRIANGULAR MERGER

In a reverse triangular merger the buyer acquires a target company and folds its own subsidiary into the target company so that the subsidiary ceases to exist and the target company becomes a subsidiary of the buyer. A reverse triangular merger would most likely be used when the target company has substantial revenue and contracts that would terminate upon being acquired. This type of transaction allows the target company to remain in existence and the contracts to survive the change in ownership.

SPLIT OFFS

A split off effectively breaks a company into two pieces, the original entity and the newly-formed split-off entity. During times of division between shareholder groups over the future or value of a company, a split-off transaction may be the best alternative for all parties. One group of shareholders will own the original entity and the other shareholders will receive the shares of the newly-created split off company. The assets and liabilities will be distributed among the two entities based on an agreed-upon method and the transaction will have no tax implications to shareholders.

SPIN OFFS

A spin-off transaction may be undertaken when a corporation is seeking to separate a subsidiary company or division into its own publicly traded company. A corporation may find it beneficial to engage in a spin-off when the subsidiary or division no longer fits into its corporate objectives. Another reason to engage in a spin-off would be when the board of directors feel the value of the two independent companies would exceed the current market value of the company with the division. Stockholders will retain their interest in the company and will receive newly issued shares of the now independent company created by the spin-off. The transaction will have no tax implications to shareholders and the market price of the parent company will be reduced by the value of assets that have now been spun off into a new independent company.

VALUATION

The key to completing any merger or acquisition is arriving at an appropriate value for the business. Sellers want to maximize the premium to be received upon closing, while buyers want to ensure that they do not overpay for a business. There are a multitude of ways to value any business and different bankers may arrive at very different valuations for the same business based on the valuation method used by each banker. Because there is substantial public information available for publicly traded companies, it is usually much easier to value a publicly traded company than it is to value a private company. Some of the valuation methods you will be required to master to pass your exam are:

- Precedent transaction analysis
- Comparable company analysis
- Pro forma analysis
- LBO analysis
- Discounted cash flow analysis

A much more detailed examination of all valuation methods is presented later in the book, but each are presented here for introductory purposes.

PRECEDENT TRANSACTION ANALYSIS

This type of analysis is similar to the comparable home sales analysis a Realtor may do when listing a home for sale. In order to determine the fair market value for the potential listing, the realtor looks at the sales price for similar homes. With this type of analysis, the bankers will review the valuations of M&A transactions within the same industry and for similar businesses. This form of analysis will often be used when the proposed transaction is contemplated for a company with a limited peer group and when there are few publicly traded companies.

COMPARABLE COMPANY ANALYSIS

This type of analysis is often used when there are a number of publicly traded companies within the peer group of the proposed transaction. The banker will compile a list of similar companies and look at the multiple of each to determine a multiple range for the industry or peer group. Bankers will often use the price-earnings multiple, price to book and enterprise value to EBITA as a basis for clear comparable company analysis.

PRO FORMA ANALYSIS

For transactions involving a strategic buyer, bankers will create pro forma financial statements in an effort to value both the target and the combined business. Pro forma financial statements are presented in three columns. The first two columns show the financial performance of the strategic buyer and that of the target company as they now exist. The third column shows the hypothetical financial performance of the combined entity. The process of creating pro forma financial statements detailing the hypothetical performance of the combined company is a process known as recasting. Investment bankers will take into consideration all potential cost-savings of the combined entity when creating pro forma financial statements. Pro forma assets, liabilities, income and expenses will all be projected and if the financial benefits are positive, synergies exist between the companies that will provide a benefit to the buyer.

LBO ANALYSIS

Because a leveraged buyout includes the issuance of a substantial amount of debt, the capitalization of the target company will be dramatically changed. As a result, bankers must analyze how the change in capitalization impacts the profitability of the corporation. Further, the change in the capital structure can also alter the cost of capital for the target company. Bankers will analyze pro forma financials based on the change in the capital structure and determine a present value for the future cash flows to be generated by the business (known as discounted cash flow analysis). This combined analysis is then used to determine if the projected rate of return meets the required rate of return for the financial buyer.

DISCOUNTED CASH FLOW ANALYSIS

Discounted cash flow analysis or DCF is often seen as a more accurate way to value a business than its earnings as reported under generally accepted accounting principles. This is because a company's earnings are often impacted by non-cash charges such as depreciation, asset impairments, granting stock options and inventory write-downs. To perform this type of analysis, analysts will project the amount of cash flow the company will generate each year in the future. Once the analyst has projected the cash flows to be generated each year during a set period, the analyst will discount each of these cash flows into a present value and add the values together to arrive at a lump sum present value. If the price the financial buyer is paying for the company is less than the present value of its cash flow, the acquisition should be made. While DCF analysis tends to be a better way to value a business than its GAAP earnings, if the analyst's projections are wrong, the estimated value of the future cash flows will be inaccurate. Because the analyst is trying to model or predict what will happen in the future, it is quite possible that unforeseen changes can impact the level or present value of future cash flows. For example, if interest rates unexpectedly increase during the projected period for which the analysis was performed, the present value of the future cash flows will be less than projected. In this case, the discount rate used by the analyst will prove to have been inaccurate and their analysis would have overvalued the business. Unforeseen changes in a company's revenue, expenses or capital structure can also impact its cash flow and as a result its present value. Analysts should only perform discounted cash flow analysis for companies that have predictable cash flow and should not be used to value start up companies or companies with limited revenue.

THE STRUCTURE OF THE TRANSACTION

While the price to be paid for the acquisition is the most important consideration, the structure of the transaction is almost equally as important. Acquisitions can be structured as either stock sales or as asset sales. Each of these structures have substantial tax implications for both the buyer and the seller. In a stock sale, the buyer acquires the entire entity outright and the stockholders are the sellers. The buyer acquires all of the assets and liabilities and upon completion, the target company is absorbed into the buyer and ceases to exist. When a corporation is being sold outright, sellers tend to prefer stock sales as it eliminates all current and any potential contingent liabilities that may arise in the future. Additionally, for tax purposes, a stock sale does not create a tax liability for the corporation. The tax liability will be borne by the stockholders who sell the shares to the acquirer. The acquisition of a company may also be structured as an asset sale. Upon completion, the shares of the target corporation are still owned by the stockholders and the target corporation has effectively become a shell corporation. The ability to exclude the liabilities from the asset sale is extremely attractive for the buyer. A partial acquisition such as that of a division of a company may also be structured as an asset sale. In a partial asset sale, the buyer acquires specified assets of the corporation without taking on the liabilities or the assets it does not want. With this type of asset sale, the corporation will have a tax liability if the asset was sold at a price exceeding its book value carried on the corporation's balance sheet. If the corporation ultimately decides to distribute these proceeds to shareholders through a special dividend, the proceeds will be taxed twice. How to structure the transaction is often an intensely negotiated part of the acquisition process. Buyers often favor asset sales and sellers traditionally prefer stock sales. There is a section of the Internal Revenue Code that allows for an acquisition completed as a stock sale to be treated as an asset purchase for tax purposes. The section of tax code that allows for this treatment is Section 338 (H) (10) and is often referred to as a 338 (H) (10) election. Classifying a transaction in this manner allows the buyer to step up the value of the assets from the cost basis on the seller's balance sheet to the fair market value at the time they are purchased. If the buyer elects to sell the assets in the future, this benefits the buyer by reducing the potential for any negative tax implications. Additionally, the higher value of the assets provides the buyer with additional tax benefits and allows them to depreciate the assets from a higher cost basis. The seller will have to pay taxes on the difference between the book value and the fair market value of the assets being acquired. However, the buyer will often pay a premium to the seller to compensate the seller for the negative tax impact

CASH AND STOCK TRANSACTIONS

When the purchaser uses cash to acquire a company, both parties know with absolute certainty what the transaction will cost the buyer and the amount that will be received by the seller. Using cash in lieu of stock to pay for an acquisition also ensures that the acquirer's shares are not diluted by issuing stock to pay for the purchase. While the certainty provided by a cash transaction has its advantages, there are several other features that should be noted, including:

- The receipt of a cash payment creates a tax liability to selling shareholders
- Cash offers usually result in a lower total value than one includes stock
- It is difficult to make large acquisitions in cash

When the buyer of a company uses its own stock to pay for the acquisition, the shareholders of the target company tender their shares in exchange for shares in the acquirer. The use of stock in an acquisition has its advantages and disadvantages for both the buyer and the seller. One of the advantages from the buyer's perspective is the fact that it can conserve cash. Another advantage is the buyer may be able to use an inflated stock price to acquire a target company. This is particularly true in the case when the acquirer has seen its stock appreciate substantially over a period of time. From the seller's standpoint, a stock transaction is usually completed at a premium to a cash transaction and the receipt of the acquirer's shares does not create a tax liability for the seller. The seller will transfer his / her cost basis of the tendered shares to the shares of the acquirer. For example , Mr. Walsh purchased 2,000 shares of ABC at $22, 3 years ago. With ABC trading in the marketplace at $35, XYZ announces that it will be purchasing ABC in a stock transaction worth $60 per share. The terms of the offering are that owners of ABC will exchange each share of ABC for one share of XYZ. Upon completion Mr. Walsh receives a share of XYZ worth $60 for every share he owns in ABC. This exchange does not create a tax liability and should Mr. Walsh wish to sell his shares in XYZ at some point in the future, his cost basis would be $22 per share. The preceding was a simple example used to illustrate that the tendering of shares does not create a tax liability at the time of the exchange. However, in the real world, When the purchaser offers a fixed ratio of shares such as 1:1, 2:1 or 3:1, neither party knows the ultimate value of the transaction. Once the offer has been made the price of the acquirer's shares fluctuate in the market. If the price of the acquirer's shares fall, the sellers will receive a lower value. Alternatively, if the price of the acquirer's shares increase, sellers will receive a higher value. In order to manage this uncertainty, the parties may include certain terms in the purchase agreement. One such term or clause that may be added is a collar. When the parties to a stock transaction include a collar, the parties agree to a minimum value and maximum value of the transaction. By setting a floor for the acquirer's stock price, the sellers know what the worst case scenario is. By setting a cap for the acquirer's stock price, the buyer knows the maximum value of the transaction. With a collar both parties have effectively agreed to a range of values for the deal. As with many purchase agreements, the collar may include a material adverse change clause or a MAC clause. If the price of the acquirer's shares fall below the floor set by the collar, the seller has the right to terminate or renegotiate the transaction. A variation of the collar agreement is a floating collar. With a floating collar, the buyer and seller agree to a price range for the acquirer's stock. As long as the price of the stock remains within that range (collar), the purchaser will acquire the seller's company for a fixed number of shares. If the price of the acquirer's stock falls below the lower end of the range, the seller has the right to receive additional shares. If the price of the stock rises above the high end of the range, the buyer has the right to reduce the number of shares to be paid. For example, lets assume that QWER Manufacturing Co. has agreed to acquire RTY Industries in an all-stock transaction and that QWER has offered to exchange 3 shares of QWER for each share of RTY. At the time the transaction is agreed to, QWER is trading at $40 per share. The current price of the offer values RTY Industries at $120 per share. QWER and RTY further agreed to complete the transaction at the current exchange rate of 3:1 so long as the price of QWER remains between $38 and $42 per share. As a result, the deal values RTY between $114 and $126 per share. If the price of QWER drops below $38 per share the number of shares to be paid for each share of RTY will be increased. Alternatively, if the price QWER increase is above $42, the number of shares will be reduced. A third variation of a collar may be used to adjust the number of shares to be received by the target in a fixed price offering. If in the above example, QWER had offered to pay shareholders of RTY a fixed price of $120 in stock so long as the price of QWER remained between $38 and $42, The price of the deal is known, but the number of shares to be received is variable. In this case shareholders of TRY will receive between 3.16 (120/38) shares and 2.86 (120/42) shares of QWER.

INTERNATIONAL IMPLICATIONS

Large multinational corporations engaging in international M&A need to perform additional due diligence prior to closing any transaction. Currency implications, local regulations and US laws all must be taken into consideration. As the value of one currency fluctuates relative to another, the value of the transaction may rise or fall and as a result make the transaction more or less attractive. Additionally, these currency fluctuations may negatively impact the repatriation of foreign profits. The tax laws and regulations in the foreign country need to be taken into consideration as these can reduce profits and increase costs. The Bank Secrecy Act and the US Patriot Act are designed in part to protect our nation from terrorism and other criminal activities. The Department of The Treasury operates the Office of Foreign Assets Control (OFAC). OFAC maintains a list of designated countries, specified foreign nationals and blocked persons who are sponsors of terrorists or who are suspected or known to be terrorists. A key focus of OFAC is to guard against money laundering. Banks and broker dealers are prohibited from transacting business with any individual or entity appearing on the OFAC list. If a bank or broker dealer identifies an account belonging to anyone appearing on this list, a report must be made to the Department of Treasury within

CHAPTER 3 Mergers and Acquisitions

10 days of discovery. The report will be filed with The Financial Crimes Enforcement Network or FinCen. OFAC also oversees the list of countries the U.S has placed embargoes on. No U.S. corporation may transact business in these countries. In addition to guarding against transacting business with prohibited individuals or in prohibited countries, corporations contemplating an international acquisition also need to comply with the Foreign Corrupt Practices Act. This act prohibits any U.S. company from making improper payments directly or indirectly through a subsidiary to any party in a foreign country in an effort to gain business. This rule also applies to a US subsidiary of a foreign company, foreign private issuers who are reporting issuers and to foreign companies whose shares trade domestically through American depository receipts. The Foreign Corrupt Practices Act effectively acts as an anti-bribery statute. These anti-bribery provisions are enforced by both the SEC and the Department of Justice. Should an investment banker discover that a client or a target has made any payments in violation of the Foreign Corrupt Practices Act, a report of the violation should be made to both the SEC and the DOJ.

PROTECTIVE MEASURES AND TAKEOVER DEFENSES

It is not unusual for a publicly traded company to find themselves on the receiving end of an unwanted or hostile takeover attempt. Often in a hostile takeover the buyer will circumvent negotiations with management and take their proposal directly to shareholders. The unwanted suitor will make a tender offer to acquire the shares at a stated price and shareholders who are interested in selling may tender his / her shares to the potential buyer. Another approach that may be used in a hostile takeover; is for the potential buyer to acquire a substantial stake in the target company's common stock and then approach management regarding a potential sale. If the unwanted suitor finds that management is uncooperative or is not interested, the potential buyer may seek to use the voting power of its large stake to change management or the board of directors in an effort to win support for the acquisition. Publicly traded companies who are concerned about the adverse impact of a hostile takeover, may employ a number of takeover defense strategies in an effort to make a hostile takeover less attractive or less likely. A potential target may enact these protective measures if the company is on the receiving end of a hostile takeover or if the company feels that certain events have taken place that make the company vulnerable to a hostile takeover. For example, if the company has suffered a series of setbacks and their stock price has fallen dramatically in the market, a potential suitor may believe that the company in its weakened state is vulnerable. Often the potential buyer believes that the low price represents a good value and that its long-term prospects are much better then the stock price reflects. To guard against an unwanted takeover a company may:

- Require that the board of directors approve any hostile takeover by a super majority
- Stagger the election of the board of directors so that the entire board may not be replaced by an unwanted suitor during any single election.
- Enact a shareholder rights plan also known as a poison pill. Contingent upon certain events such as an activist investor acquiring 5 or 10% of the company, the poison pill will trigger a rights offering providing existing shareholders with the opportunity to purchase a large number of additional shares. The potential acquirer does not participate in the rights offering and this will dilute the ownership of the potential acquirer
- Offer golden parachutes to senior management. A golden parachute provision may be offered to senior management in the event of a takeover or change in management. Golden parachutes are large severance packages designed to make a takeover more costly and less attractive.

TAKE NOTE!

If the terms of the severance payments to be made as part of the golden parachute provision are greater than three times the annual salary of the recipient, the corporation may lose the tax deductibility of those payments. Additionally, the recipients may find themselves subject to a 20% excise tax applied to the portion of the severance payments that exceed three times his/her annual compensation .

CHAPTER 3

Pretest

MERGERS AND ACQUISITIONS

1. You are working as an investment banking representative at a firm that has been retained to identify target companies for a potential acquisition. When developing a strategy to approach shareholders, which would be the least useful?
   A. Recent 8K filings
   B. Recent 13 D filings
   C. Recent 13 F filings
   D. Recent 13 G filings

2. Smart Capital is a private equity firm that has acquired a manufacturer of industrial control systems. Smart Capital is looking to return capital to itself without selling the business. Which of the following would allow the firm to accomplish this objective?
   A. A minority recapitalization
   B. A majority recapitalization
   C. A dividend recapitalization
   D. An equity recapitalization

3. A family owned business leader is interested in participating in a liquidity event and wants to receive a substantial payment, but wants to retain control over the business. Which of the following would be the best transaction to meet this requirement?
   A. A majority recapitalization
   B. A minority recapitalization
   C. A debt recapitalization
   D. An equity recapitalization

4. LeverUp is an LBO firm seeking investment opportunities among various industries. Which of the following would be the best candidate for acquisition?
    A. ChipCo a rapidly growing manufacturer of microchips
    B. BuildCo a slow growing asset heavy manufacturing company
    C. BioCo a promising biotechnology company with 3 drugs in late state trials
    D. EcomCo an asset light high margin ecommerce company

5. The owners of SIA, a long established and profitable business, feel that the time is right to pass the business on to new owners. Having built the business over a period of many years, the current owners are seeking to sell the business to a buyer who knows the business and wants a certain level of anonymity. Which of the following would be the best strategy for the owners?
    A. A controlled auction
    B. A public auction
    C. Bilateral negotiations
    D. A confidential auction

6. As it relates to M and A, which of the following statements is correct ?
    A. In an acquisition, the target company ceases to exist and the target's shareholders will own a portion of the combined company in all cases
    B. In an acquisition, the target company ceases to exist and the target's shareholders will own a portion of the combined company, only if stock is used in whole or in part as currency
    C. In an acquisition, the target company ceases to exist and the target's shareholders will own a portion of the combined company, only if stock is used as the sole currency
    D. In an acquisition, the target company ceases to exist and the target's shareholders will own a portion of the combined company, only if stock is used to fund majority of the purchase

7. Selling a business through an auction is a long and complicated process. Of the choices listed below, which would be the last task performed?
    A. Creation of the confidential information memorandum / CIM
    B. Creation of the data room
    C. Draft confidentiality agreements
    D. Distribute the bidding procedure letter

8. A sell-side banker has been retained to identify potential buyers for their client. When contacting potential interested parties the banker would use which of the following to drum up interest?
   A. A preliminary offering document
   B. A preliminary confidential information memorandum
   C. A teaser
   D. A term sheet

9. A sell-side banker has assisted the seller in preparing a confidentiality agreement. The purpose of the agreement is to restrain all of the following, except:.
   A. The recipient from colluding with other buyers
   B. The recipient from contacting vendors
   C. The recipient from contacting the seller's bankers
   D. The recipient from purchasing the stock of the seller

10. Qualified interested parties who have signed the confidentiality agreement will be able to review detailed information regarding the seller:
    A. In an electronic environment
    B. Though an offering memorandum
    C. Through an offering circular
    D. Though due diligence meetings

CHAPTER 4

Tender Offers and Financial Restructuring

INTRODUCTION

In this section we are going to review the rules and regulations surrounding tender offers, financial restructuring transactions resulting from a bankruptcy filing as well as the reports that are required to be filed with the SEC. A complete understanding of these concepts will be required in order for you to successfully complete the Series 79 exam.

TENDER OFFERS

A tender offer is public solicitation made by a person or firm who is seeking to purchase all or part of the outstanding securities of an issuer at a specific price. If a third party is making a tender offer to acquire all or part of a company, the buyer will generally publish an announcement in the financial newspapers stating the price and the number of shares the buyer is willing to acquire. This type of tender offer would be seen as part of a hostile takeover attempt with the buyer circumventing management to go directly to shareholders. In the case of a third party making a partial tender, the buyer may be an activist investor seeking board representation to facilitate change at the target or to gain support for an acquisition. In the case of an issuer buyback, the issuer itself makes a tender offer for its securities. The SEC has issued strict guidelines that must be followed by all parties to the tender including investors who tender their securities.

If the issuer, another company or person makes a tender offer for securities the offeror must file schedule TO with the SEC as soon as practical, but no later than the commencement date of the tender. Should any entity other than the issuer itself purchase more than 5% of an issuer's outstanding securities as a result of the tender, that entity must file form 13D with the SEC in addition to schedule TO. SEC Rule 14D-9 requires schedule 14D-9 or TO to be filed by:

- The subject company, its officers, directors, employees and affiliates
- Any bidder, affiliate of the bidder or owner of the securities
- Any party that makes a recommendation or solicitation to shareholders relating to the tender

In addition to the requirements listed above, if the bidder, its affiliates or if the subject company, its officers, directors or affiliates make any recommendations or solicitations regarding the tender, schedule 14D-9 or TO is required to be filed within 10 business days. It is important to note that parties who provide advice in the normal course of business who are not participating in the tender offer, are not required to file schedule 14D-9 or TO so long as the advice rendered is provided on an unsolicited basis. Broker dealers, investment advisers, bankers and attorneys who are not engaged in the tender process would all be exempt from filing so long as the advice was unsolicited. If the subject company merely announces that it has received a tender offer and is in the process of its evaluation, a filing would not be required. As part of this announcement the target may identify the party making the offer and that the board will be making a recommendation shortly.

Schedule 14D-9 or schedule TO is used to provide investors with the details of the offer being made. Schedule TO must be filed for all tender offers including offers made by third parties, issuer buybacks and going private transactions. The information provided in these filings will generally be the basis for the information in the proxy statement. In addition to the terms of the offering, schedule 14D-9 or TO will include:

- A term sheet summarizing the offering
- Background information on the parties making the offer
- The purpose of the transaction
- Information on the subject (target) company
- Financial statements
- Information about parties retained or compensated as part of the offer
- Source of funds
- Information relating to past transactions and agreements
- Details of the negotiations

CHAPTER 4 Tender Offers and Financial Restructuring

The guidelines to be followed by parties making a tender offer include:

- The offer must detail the price or number of shares to be received by investors who participate in the offer. If the buyer is offering to use its own shares to pay for the tender, the tender is known as an exchange offer.
- The offer must be open for 20 business days from the day it is announced.
- If any of the terms of the tender are changed, the tender must remain open for at least 10 business days from the day the change in the terms was announced.
- A covered person making a tender offer for stock may not buy the stock or the convertible securities of the issuer in the open market during the term of the tender. However, the party may purchase nonconvertible bonds.
- In addition to prohibiting the party making the tender from purchasing common stock and convertible securities, SEC Rule 14e-5 also prohibits coveryered persons from making purchases. A covered person includes an individual or investment bank involved in the tender process.
- If the duration of the offer is extended, the announcement extending the offer must be released no later than the opening of the exchange on the business day following the original expiration date for exchange-listed securities. The announcement must include the amount of securities tendered to date.
- If a tender offer is extended for securities that are not listed on an exchange, the announcement must be made no later than 9:00 a.m. EST the business day following the original expiration and must also include the amount of securities tendered to date.
- SEC Rule 14 D - 10 requires the buyer to pay the best price and to provide equal treatment to all shareholders interested in tendering shares to the buyer. The buyer may not engage in preferential treatment for institutional shareholders over retail shareholders and all shareholders must receive the same price.

In addition to the above rules there are a few exceptions you may need to be familiar with for your exam. One is that an exemption to the best price rule is applied to compensation received as part of a pay package for officers and directors of the target company. The compensation package would have to be approved by the target's compensation committee if the compensation is to be paid by the target company to an officer or director. If the buying company is providing the compensation package to management, the compensation package would have to be approved by the buyer's compensation committee. There is also an exemption to SEC Rule 14e-5 which allows for open market purchases to be made by covered investment banks or dealer managers provided the following conditions are met:

- The transactions are executed on an agency basis
- Information barriers exist and transactions are not executed as part of the tender process
- Principal transactions executed by non market makers

The guidelines to be followed by parties receiving a tender offer include:

- Shareholders must be notified of the tender offer no later than 10 business days after the tender is announced.
- Management of the company subject to the tender offer must advise shareholders as to management's opinion on the offer (i.e., accept, decline, or neutral) no later than 10 business days from the date the tender was announced.
- A party making a tender offer must pay the price offered for the securities to the extent the offer was made.

Investors may only tender securities that they actually own. An investor may not sell short into a tender, which is known as short tendering. Investors are considered long the security if they:

- Have possession of the security
- Have entered into an unconditional contract to acquire the security but have not yet done so (this is test terminology for having purchased the stock and the transaction has not yet settled)
- Own a convertible bond, preferred stock right or warrant
- Are long call options and have issued exercise instructions.

Additionally, investors may only tender their securities to the extent of their net long position. SEC Rule 14E - 5 prohibits investors from engaging in the manipulative practice of short tendering. If an investor is short against the box or has written calls with a strike price lower than the tender price, then the investor's net long position will be reduced.

EXAMPLE

If an investor owns 1,000 XYZ and has written 5 XYZ June 40 calls when a tender offer is announced at $42 for XYZ, the investor could only tender 500 shares. If the same investor was long 10 XYZ put contracts, the investor's ability to tender shares would not be impacted regardless of the strike price.

SEC Rule 14e-3 Prohibits any person in possession of non-public information regarding a proposed tender from acting on the information and from disclosing the information to a third party. The knowledge of this non-public information constitutes material inside information. Additionally, an investment banker is prohibited from sharing information regarding a proposed tender with any representatives who are not engaged in the proposed transaction. Investment banking professionals may discuss the proposed tender with the officers and directors of the purchaser or the target company. The details of the proposed tender may also be discussed with key employees, accountants, attorneys or advisors of the purchaser or target company.

During a partial tender the exact amount of securities to be accepted from all tendering parities is not known. As a result, an investor who has a convertible security may tender an amount equal to the amount to be received upon conversion. If the investor is informed that his/her tender has been accepted, he/she must convert the securities and deliver the subject securities.

Another type of tender offer you may see on your exam is known as a Dutch auction. An issuer may use this type up tender to facilitate a large buy back. During a Dutch auction the issuer will announce a range of prices at which it is willing to repurchase its own securities. For example, TRY Inc. announces that it is willing to repurchase 10 million of its class A common shares between $45 and $50 per share. Investors who are interested in selling their shares will tender their shares at a stated price. Based on the prices received during the Dutch auction, the issuer will set a final price for the tender. All shares tendered at or below the final price will be purchased by the issuer up to the maximum number of shares stated in the tender. Investors who tendered shares at a price above the final price will have their shares returned to them. Investors who tender their shares as part of a Dutch auction are not required to stipulate a price for their shares. An investor who tenders their shares without a stated price is agreeing to tender their shares at the final auction price. If the number of shares tendered exceeds the number of shares stated in the tender offer, tendering shareholders will sell their shares on a pro-rata basis and the rest will be returned. The final type of tender you may need to be familiar with for your exam is known as a "mini tender". With a mini tender a purchaser announces their intention to purchase less than 5% of the issuer's common stock. So long as this stake purchased is less than 5%, the buyer will be exempt from filing schedule TO as well as form 13 D. Even though the purchaser is exempt from filing schedule TO and form 13 D, the tender is still required to remain open for a minimum period of 20 business days and is still subject to all antifraud provisions. The price at which a mini tender is announced is traditionally at a discount to the market price. Regulators often express concern that mini tenders will be used to take advantage of unsophisticated investors.

ISSUER BUYBACKS AND GOING PRIVATE TRANSACTIONS

Issuers may repurchase their own shares in order to fund stock purchase plans or stock option plans or to retain control of the company. These are just a few of the legitimate reasons a company may repurchase its own shares. Certain restrictions are placed upon issuers who repurchase their own shares in order to ensure that they are not trying to manipulate their share prices. SEC Rule 10b-18 sets guidelines for how an issuer or an affiliate may repurchase its own shares. SEC Rule 10b-18 states:

- For Nasdaq Global Market and listed securities (reported securities), the issuer may not buy on the opening print or within 30 minutes of the close of the market. This is known as the safe harbor.
- For actively traded issues with ADTV of greater than $1,000,000 and a public float of at least $150,000,000, the safe harbor will begin 10 minutes prior to the close.
- For Nasdaq Capital Market securities, purchases may not be made unless there is at least one independent bid.
- The issuer may only enter orders through one broker dealer or market maker on a given trading day.
- For reported or Capital Market issues, the issuer may purchase the greater of 25 percent of the ADTV for the preceding four calendar weeks or one round lot.
- For non-Nasdaq securities, the issuer is limited to the greater of one round lot or an amount that does not exceed 1/20 of 1 percent of the outstanding shares for the preceding five days, exclusive of securities owned by affiliates.
- For reported securities, the issuer may not enter a bid that is higher than the best independent bid or make a purchase at a price that is higher than the last independent sale, whichever is higher.

- For Capital Market securities, the purchase price or bid price may not be higher than the lowest independent offer.
- For non-Nasdaq OTC equities, the price may not be higher than the lowest independent offer obtained after a reasonable inquiry has been made.

Within these safe harbor guidelines, the repurchasing of securities by issuers or affiliates will not be deemed manipulative. If the repurchase of securities by an issuer would cause the number of shareholders to fall below 300 or cause the securities to be delisted from an exchange or from the Nasdaq, the issuer must file Form 13e-3 with the SEC. This is typically the result of a going private transaction. In addition to form 13 e-3, issuers who go private must file financial reports, a 14A proxy and the opinions of any financial advisors with the SEC. The issuer will forward a term sheet detailing the transaction and proxies to investors. Should the issuer engage in subsequent transactions that would materially affect the filing, the issuer must notify the SEC within 10 days after the transactions are executed. When management of a company decides to take the company private, it allows the current management to stay in control of the company rather than selling the company to another buyer or to private equity. Operating a private company will provide management with more control, reduced regulations and substantial cost savings.

THE TWO STEP MERGER

If the buyer is acquiring a target company using its stock as part of the consideration to be paid, traditional one step mergers require shareholder approval. As a result, one-step mergers can often take many months to complete. This extended time frame puts the buyer at a disadvantage and may allow for competing offers or takeover defenses to emerge. In an effort to avoid delays and shareholder approval, a buyer may seek to acquire a company through a two-step merger. This process will traditionally begin with the acquirer making a tender offer directly to shareholders to purchase the shares at a stated price or exchange rate. The buyer makes the tender offer contingent upon being able to purchase a substantial majority of shares through the tender. In order to satisfy shareholder rights and avoid a vote, in most cases the tender will be contingent upon receiving 90% or more of the outstanding shares. If the buyer is able to successfully purchase 90% or more of the outstanding shares, the buyer is able to complete the acquisition with the filing of a short-form merger agreement. The short-form merger agreement is effectively a contract between the buyer and the seller stating the terms and conditions of the sale.

The short form merger agreement does not require shareholder approval and upon execution any shareholder who did not tender their shares will be forced to do so. This process is sometimes referred to as "squeezing out" the remaining shareholders. Since a tender offer is required to remain open for 20 business days, the two step merger allows the transaction to be completed as quickly as possible. A two step merger conceivably could be completed within a month and without requiring proxies to be sent to shareholders.

FINANCIAL RESTRUCTURING

It is not unusual for over-leveraged companies to find themselves struggling to make timely interest and principal payments on their bonds or other credit facilities. Companies may find themselves having difficulty servicing their debt during economic downturns, structural changes in their industry, the loss of major customers or through mismanagement. During times of financial stress, a company may try to resolve its financial problems by reducing expenses, laying off employees, selling assets, restructuring its debt or in extreme cases by declaring bankruptcy. Reducing expenses and laying off employees may improve cash flow and may provide the company with enough breathing room to service its debt. The company may also seek to sell assets and use the proceeds to make interest payments or to pay down principal. Selling assets and paying down principal will reduce both the assets and liabilities on the corporation's balance sheet. Creditors of struggling corporations often find themselves with little choice but to work with the debtor to restructure the terms and conditions of the loan to improve the chances of being repaid. If all of the above actions are not enough to improve the corporation's liquidity and ability to meet its financial obligations, the company may resort to filing bankruptcy. There are two main categories of bankruptcy filings you need to be familiar with on your exam, Chapter 11 bankruptcy and Chapter 7 bankruptcy.

FILING CHAPTER 11 BANKRUPTCY

In times of extreme financial distress a corporation may seek protection from its creditors by filing Chapter 11 bankruptcy. The bankruptcy filing acts as a stay of all collection activities by creditors and is designed to provide a forum to resolve all claims. Bondholders and general creditors including vendors and holders of unsecured debt will be required to submit their claims and seek repayment through the bankruptcy court. In a Chapter 11 bankruptcy filing, management of the company seeks to reorganize the business and its financial obligations. Chapter 11 is known as a reorganization. It is undertaken with the hopes that the company can survive, emerge from bankruptcy and be run as a leaner, more profitable enterprise. During this process management of the now bankrupt company remains in control of the company. Management must develop a plan to repay creditors and is now acting in a fiduciary capacity on behalf of those creditors. Management's retention of control over the company is known in the industry as debtor-in-possession (DIP). That is to say that, the parties who borrowed the money on behalf of the now-bankrupt company are still in control or possession of the company or the asset. The filing of bankruptcy is made by petitioning the court in the debtor's jurisdiction. The management of the company may voluntarily file the petition for bankruptcy in an effort to end collection efforts and to restructure. Alternatively, a company could be forced into involuntary bankruptcy through a bankruptcy petition made by its creditors. The filing of bankruptcy creates an estate for the corporation. As such all assets and liabilities will become part of the estate. The corporation will be required to set up a new estate or debtor in possession bank account to receive money and to make payments to creditors and other parties. As part of the process the debtor-in-possession is required to file financial and operating reports monthly detailing its progress and condition. Once the petition for bankruptcy has been granted by the court, the debtor-in-possession has the exclusive right to file a reorganization plan with the court for 120 days. At the court's discretion, this time may be extended to allow management additional time to file a plan for large and complex bankruptcies. Once the reorganization plan has been submitted, the plan must be approved by both creditors and the court. If management's plan is not acceptable or if desired, creditors, at the expiration of the 120-day period may file their own reorganization plan. Prior to voting on the plan, the debtor-in-possession must submit a financial disclosures statement to the court. This financial disclosure statement is submitted to ensure that the creditors are provided with enough information regarding the debtor's financial position to make an informed decision. Not all classes of creditors will vote on the reorganization plan. Creditors who are to be repaid in full (unimpaired creditors) under the reorganization plan will not vote. Only creditors who are required to accept less than the full value of their claim (impaired creditors} will vote on the reorganization plan. Additionally, the bankruptcy filing may have many different classes of impaired creditors who will all need to vote as part of their class. A class of impaired creditors will be deemed to have approved the plan, if creditors holding 2/3 of the principal obligations have approved the plan and these impaired creditors represent at least 50% of the total number of impaired creditors in that class. For example, XYZ Inc has filed for bankruptcy and 12 impaired creditors hold $100 million dollars of claims against the estate. In order for this class to approve the reorganization plan, at least 6 of the creditors holding at least $66.67 million must approve the plan. Most corporate bankruptcies contain multiple classes of impaired creditors. Each of these impaired creditors vote within their respective class. In large complex bankruptcies it is not unusual to have classes who approve the reorganization and classes who do not approve the reorganization. In cases like this, the court can decide that the plan is fair and reasonable to all creditors and approve the plan. The process of approving the reorganization plan over the objection of dissenting classes is known as a "cramdown". In order for the court to approve the plan through a cramdown, at least one impaired class must have approved the plan.

ESTATE OPERATION AND PAYMENT PRIORITIES

Corporate estates are ongoing entities that continue to conduct business. During the reorganization process, the court is not required to approve day to day management decisions, the court is only required to approve major issues such as union contracts, certain asset sales and the like. In addition to the claims of creditors, the estate is required to pay a large number of administrative and operational expenses. Subsection 507 of the US Bankruptcy Code sets the priority of claims for unsecured creditors. Administrative estate expenses are given the highest payment priority. The following are all considered administrative expenses of the estate:

- Current wages and salaries
- Legal and accounting expenses
- Trustee expenses
- Cost of estate operation and maintenance
- Payments to post-bankruptcy vendors
- Payments for goods received 20 days prior to filing bankruptcy
- Taxes

After administrative expenses have been paid, the bankruptcy code prioritizes claims in the following order:

- Claims incurred post-filing during the course of business but prior to the appointment of a trustee for involuntary bankruptcy petitions
- Employee back wages up to $10,000 for each individual or outside corporation earned up to 180 days prior to filing bankruptcy
- Contributions to employee benefit plans
- Payments to owners preferred stockholders and common stockholders

In addition to the ongoing expenses of the estate, payments and proceeds must be allocated among the respective creditors and shareholders. As a general rule creditors are always given priority over owners. As such, payments will be made to bondholders and general creditors prior to any payments being made to stockholders. Once a company has filed for bankruptcy, secured creditors who have a claim against specific assets are always in the best position. For example, XYZ had borrowed $500,000,000 some years ago to build a new corporate campus by selling mortgage bonds to investors. The corporate campus was pledged as collateral for the bonds. The company has now filed for bankruptcy and the mortgage bondholders have a lien on the corporate campus. The bond trustee will now seek to obtain possession of the real estate and sell it in an effort to repay the bondholders. If the value of the real estate has fallen below the principal amount owed on the bonds, the bondholders will be unsecured on the difference. If in the above example the trustee was only able to obtain $450 million through the sale, the mortgage bondholders would have an unsecured claim for the remaining $50 million. Alternatively, if the value of the real estate exceeds the principal amount due, the bondholders are not entitled to receive the increased value. However, bondholders may be entitled to recover certain expenses and interest from the amount exceeding the principal amount owed. In order for a lien to be valid, the trustee must file the lien against the property with the court in the jurisdiction where the asset is located. The lien will prohibit the asset from being sold to another party prior to the lien being satisfied. The process of filing a lien acts as a declaration of the lender's claim against the asset and the process is known as perfecting the lien. There are times when multiple lenders have extended credit to the same borrower and each holds a secured claim. In these instances, the lenders will often enter into an intercreditor agreement (sometimes referred to as an intercreditor deed) which will act as a framework for the prioritization of their claims in the event of default. While secured creditors are required to file a lien against the specified asset to protect their claim, unsecured creditors are not required to file a claim. During the bankruptcy process the debtor will file a schedule of creditors listing the names of the creditors and the amounts owed to each. There may be instances when the debtor fails to list a creditor or the creditor disputes the debtor's classification of the liability or the amount owed. If the now bankrupt company fails to include or qualifies a liability as liquidated, disputed or contingent, the unsecured creditor must file a proof of claim with the court to protect its claim against the estate. Even though unsecured creditors are not required to file a proof of claim, most will file the claim to ensure that their claim is protected. In order to protect the interests of all unsecured creditors the trustee will appoint a creditors' committee. The creditors committee will be made up of the largest unsecured creditors and the committee is responsible for acting in a fiduciary capacity to protect the rights of all unsecured creditors. The priority of claims during the bankruptcy process is as follows:

1. Secured creditors (mortgage bonds, collateral trust certificates, Equipment trust certificates and other loans secured by equipment and assets)
2. Unsecured creditors (debentures, general creditors)
3. Subordinated creditors (subordinated debentures mezzanine lenders)
4. Preferred stockholders
5. Common stockholders
6. Warrant holders

While the priorities of above spell out who is entitled to receive payments or proceeds from the estate, in most instances all equity holders are wiped out.

It's important to remember that a chapter 11 filing is designed as a reorganization of the business and that the business continues to operate. Most of us are familiar with many national companies who have operated uninterrupted during the course of a chapter 11 bankruptcy. Many airlines, retail stores and restaurant chains have entered and emerged from bankruptcy with little impact to its customers. Because the business continues to operate, it may require financing during the time it is in bankruptcy. Companies may seek debtor-in-possession financing as a means to finance its continued operations and ultimate exit from bankruptcy. Lenders who provide debtor-in-possession financing are given a superpriority claim and are entitled to receive payments prior to any other unsecured creditor including those providing administrative services to the estate. Because of the complex nature of debtor-in-possession financing and the implications to the business and other creditors, debtor-in-possession financing must be approved by the court.

FILING CHAPTER 7 BANKRUPTCY

Unlike a chapter 11 bankruptcy proceeding, a chapter 7 bankruptcy is an outright liquidation of the company. A company would file Chapter 7 bankruptcy when it is clear that there is no potential for the company to reorganize and continue operating. A company may elect to file chapter 7 bankruptcy if its Chapter 11 reorganization plan is unsuccessful. The management and board of directors are removed and a trustee is appointed to oversee the liquidation of assets and the payments to creditors. The trustee files the plan with the court and may continue to operate the day-to-day business during the liquidation period. The Trustee's main objective is winding down operations, liquidating assets and recovering maximum value for creditors. The trustee may engage the services of accountants, appraisers, liquidators or other professionals to assist end the asset sales. All creditors (secured and unsecured) and equity holders must file a claim within 90 days of the first creditors' meeting in order to be entitled to recover funds.

DISTRESSED ASSET SALES

Once a corporation has entered bankruptcy, raising and recovering funds are often primary objectives of the debtor or the trustee. Corporations with large balance sheets and substantial assets may seek to sell off assets in an effort to meet its objective. Having entered bankruptcy, corporate assets are often subject to claims, liens or encumbrances that make asset sales difficult to accomplish. Further, the sale of major assets may require shareholder approval. In an effort to speed up and simplify asset sales, the debtor or the trustee may file a petition with the court seeking approval to sell assets. Section 363 of the bankruptcy code allows for the court approved or sponsored sale of assets. Once sold, the assets are transferred to the buyer with a clear title free of any claims or liens. The financial distress of a bankrupt seller often places substantial pressure on the company to raise funds as quickly as possible. This added pressure may result in assets being sold substantially below their fair market value to an opportunistic buyer. As part of the court approved sale process, procedures have been put in place to ensure that assets are not sold at an unreasonable price. Under Section 363, asset sales begin when the debtor or trustee negotiates with an initial purchaser. The initial purchaser performs the due diligence on the assets and submits an initial bid. This initial bid sets a floor for the price of the assets and allows the debtor or trustee an opportunity to shop the assets in an effort to receive a higher sales price. The firm that submits the initial bid and performs the due diligence is known in the industry as a "stalking horse" and the price it has submitted is known as a stalking horse bid. If the seller is able to obtain a higher bid from another party, the stalking horse will be provided with an opportunity to increase it's bid. If the stalking horse matches the best bid, the stalking horse will acquire the assets. If the asset is ultimately sold to another party the stalking horse will be paid a breakup fee and will be reimbursed for its due diligence expenses. In addition to the benefit of allowing assets to be transferred free of liens, asset sales under Section 363 include:

- Protection from fraudulent transfer claims
- Certain contracts may be assigned without consent
- Exempt from shareholder approval insert and state laws
- Expedited antitrust waiting periods the large purchasers

While there are substantial benefits to Section 363 asset sales, there are also a few drawbacks. Potential bidders may be concerned that the transparent nature of the bidding process will make it more likely that they will be out bid. Additionally, if the court finds that the sale was conducted in a manner inconsistent with the approved method, the court may block the sale.

A secured creditor may bid on an asset by submitting a credit bid. In lieu of cash, a secured creditor with an undisputed claim and perfected lien may offer to extinguish all or part of the debtor's liability in exchange for clear title to the asset. For example, a creditor who has loaned $250,000 to a now bankrupt company for the purchase of a large piece of manufacturing equipment holds a note secured by that piece of equipment. Let's assume that after 4 years the remaining principal on the note is $220,000. The creditor seeking to recover as much of the principal as possible submits a credit bid in the amount of $180,000 in exchange for clear title to the manufacturing equipment. If the credit bid is accepted the lender will receive a clear title to the equipment and is now able to sell the equipment in an effort to recover the principal of the loan.

CHAPTER 4

Pretest

TENDER OFFERS, AND FINANCIAL RESTRUCTURING

1. A large conglomerate has made a tender offer to acquire all of the outstanding stock of a target company and is taking the offer directly to the target company's shareholders. Which of the following would not require the filing of schedule 14D-9 or TO?
    A. An affiliate of the buyer makes a recommendation regarding the offer.
    B. An affiliate of the target company makes a recommendation regarding the offer.
    C. A party makes a solicitation to shareholders regarding the offer.
    D. A broker dealer responds to a large number of shareholder inquiries seeking advice regarding the offer.

2. Under SEC Rule 14e-5, which of the following would be allowed to purchase securities in the open market during the term of a tender offer?
    A. A large investment adviser with dictionary authority over $1.5 billion who has reported a large position in the subject security on form 13F.
    B. An officer of the target company's investment bank
    C. An officer of the acquirer's investment bank
    D. An attorney who prepared schedule TO for the acquiring company

3. SEC Rule 14D-10 states that buyers must pay the best price to all shareholders. During an acquisition, which of the following would be exempt from this rule, if properly approved ?
   A. A large employee pension plan administered for the benefit of the target company's employees owns a substantial portion of the outstanding stock
   B. A large endowment for a university feels the offer undervalues the stock and demands a premium to support the acquisition.
   C. The President and CEO are both offered a 15% premium price on their holdings as an incentive pay package
   D. A hedge fund has filed a 13D and is looking to replace the board of directors and who opposes the acquisition, is offered a 10% premium from the buyer to purchase its stake.

4. XYZ has just announced a tender offer to acquire QWER at a price of $40 per share. Which of the following securities holders would not be allowed to tender shares?
   A. A party who has entered into a contract to acquire shares of QWER but who has not yet acquired the shares.
   B. A party who is long 20 deep in the money call options with an expiration date exceeding the expiration of the tender offer.
   C. A party who is long a QWER issued security providing the right to acquire shares at a set price but who has not yet done so.
   D. An investor who owns 500 shares of QWER being held in an out of state safety deposit box

5. XCV has decided to take itself private by executing substantial orders to repurchase the majority of its own stock. XCV will be required to file form 13e-3 with the SEC, if the number of shareholders falls below:
   A. 500
   B. 400
   C. 300
   D. 200

6. A clothing retailer has deceived to seek protection from its creditors under a chapter 11 filing. The estate is now being operated under court supervision. Which of the following would not be considered to be an administrative expense of the estate ?
   A. Legal and accounting expenses
   B. Payments to post bankruptcy vendors
   C. Employee wages owed prior to the filing
   D. Taxes

CHAPTER 4 Pretest 113

7. A group of senior bondholders provided a mortgage on the office building of a now bankrupt computer company. The balance on the loan is $3.2 million. In an attempt to remain in business, the debtor in possession enters into a sale and leaseback arrangement for the building. The proceeds of the sale are $3.6 million. Which of the following is correct ?
   A. The bondholders are entitled to the entire proceeds of the sale.
   B. The bondholders are only entitled to the principal amount due
   C. The bondholders are entitled to the principal amount due plus certain expenses
   D. The bondholders are entitled to the principal, interest and certain expenses

8. In order to purchase a billion dollar office building in Chicago, a software application company obtained the capital from 4 different lenders through the sale of bonds. Each group of bondholders have a claim on the office building. The company has been forced into bankruptcy. The claims of the secured creditors will be prioritized through:
   A. A court ordered agreement
   B. A court ordered liquidation
   C. An intercreditor deed
   D. A perfected lien

9. ERT Manufacturing has been operating under chapter 11 bankruptcy for the last several years. It has become clear that the business will not be able to continue on as a going concern and has elected to move into a chapter 7 liquidation. Which of the following is correct?
   A. Unsecured creditors will be required to file a proof of claim within 90 days
   B. Both secured and unsecured creditors will be required to file a proof of claim within 90 days
   C. Unsecured creditors will be required to file a proof of claim within 60 days
   D. Both secured and unsecured creditors will be required to file a proof of claim within 60 days

10. A corporation operating under bankruptcy protection has begun selling off assets to raise much needed capital. Which of the following is not correct as it relates to asset sales under section 363 of the bankruptcy code?
    A. All contract assignments must receive consent to transfer
    B. The seller or trustee will engage in negotiations with a stalking horse bidder
    C. Asset sales are exempt from shareholder approval
    D. The court may block sales if the assets are sold outside of an approved method

CHAPTER 5

Issuing Corporate Securities

INTRODUCTION

The Securities Act of 1933 was the first major piece of securities industry regulation that was brought about largely as a result of the stock market crash of 1929. Other major laws were also enacted to help prevent another meltdown of the nation's financial system, such as the Securities Exchange Act of 1934, but we will start our review with the Securities Act of 1933 because it regulates the issuance of corporate securities.

The Securities Act of 1933 was the first major piece of securities industry legislation, and it regulates the primary market. The primary market consists exclusively of transactions between issuers of securities and investors. In a primary market transaction, the issuer of the securities receives the proceeds from the sale of the securities. The Securities Act of 1933 requires nonexempt issuers (typically corporate issuers) to file a registration statement with the Securities and Exchange Commission (SEC). The registration statement, formerly known as an S-1, is the issuer's full-disclosure document for the government. The registration statement must contain detailed information relating to the issuer's operations and financial condition and must include:

- A balance sheet dated within 90 days of the filing of the registration statement.
- Profit and loss statements for the last 3 years.
- The company's capitalization.
- The use of proceeds.
- Shareholders owning more than 10 percent of the company's securities.
- Biographical information on the officers and directors.

The registration statement will be under review by the SEC for a minimum of 20 days. During this time, known as the cooling-off period, no sales of securities may take place. If the SEC requires additional information regarding the offering, the SEC may issue a deficiency letter or a stop order that will extend the cooling-off period beyond the original 20 days. If the SEC has issued a stop order, the 20-day cooling-off period will begin again once the resubmission of the registration statement has been completed. A registered representative may only begin to discuss the potential offering with customers after the filing date.

THE PROSPECTUS

While the SEC is reviewing the securities' registration statement, registered representatives are very limited as to what they may do with regard to the new issue. During the cooling-off period, the only thing that a registered representative may do is obtain indications of interest from clients by providing them with a preliminary prospectus, also known as a red herring. The term "red herring" originated from the fact that a preliminary prospectus must have a statement printed in red ink on the front cover stating: "these securities have not yet become registered with the SEC and therefore may not be sold." An indication of interest is an investor's or broker dealer's statement that it might be interested in purchasing the securities being offered. The preliminary prospectus contains most of the same information that will be contained in the final prospectus, except for the offering price, the effective date, and the proceeds to the issuer. The preliminary prospectus will usually contain a price range for the security to be offered. If the securities are ultimately sold at a price outside of the range contained in the preliminary prospectus and the adjusted offering price is disclosed in the final prospectus, the issuer will not be required to file an amendment unless the maximum aggregate price deviates from the range by more than 20%. If the issuer fails to file the final prospectus within 15 days of the effective date, It must file a post effective amendment to disclose the change All information contained in a preliminary prospectus is subject to change or revision. The preliminary prospectus must be given in hard copy to expected purchasers at least 48 hours before the sale is confirmed if the company has not been a reporting company under the Securities Exchange Act of 1934. This is done to ensure that the final prospectus is not the first piece of information forwarded to the purchaser.

THE FINAL PROSPECTUS

All purchasers of new issues must be given a final prospectus before any sales may be allowed. The final prospectus serves as the issuer's full-disclosure document for the purchaser of the securities. If the issuer has filed a prospectus with the SEC and the final prospectus can be viewed on the SEC's website, a prospectus will be deemed to have been provided to the investor through the access equals delivery rule. The access equals delivery rule only applies to the final prospectus during the offering and during any aftermarket delivery requirements. A preliminary prospectus must be physically sent to potential purchasers. Once the issuer's registration statement becomes effective, the final prospectus must include:

- Type and description of the securities.
- Price of the security.
- Use of the proceeds.
- Underwriter's discount.
- Date of the offering.
- Type and description of underwriting.
- Business history of issuer.
- Biographical data for company officers and directors.
- Information regarding large stockholders.
- Company financial data.
- Risks to purchasers.
- Legal matters concerning the company.
- SEC disclaimer.

FREE WRITING PROSPECTUS

A free writing prospectus is any form of written communication published or broadcast by an issuer which contains information about the securities offered for sale that does not meet the definition of a statutory prospectus. Common examples of a free writing prospectus include:

- Marketing materials
- Graphs
- Term sheets

- Emails
- Press releases

The free writing prospectus should include a legend recommending that the individual read the statutory prospectus to obtain more information relating the securities being offered. A hyperlink will be used in many cases to direct the reader to the statutory prospectus. An issuer who meets the definition of a well-known seasoned issuer may use an FWP at any time before or after the filing of a registration statement. A seasoned issuer may only use an FWP after the filing of the registration statement with the SEC. An unseasoned or non-reporting issuer may use a free writing prospectus only after a registration statement is filed with the SEC and must either send a statutory prospectus with FWP or must include a hyperlink to a statutory prospectus. Issuers who use free writing prospectuses will file them with the SEC over the SEC's website.

PROVIDING THE PROSPECTUS TO AFTERMARKET PURCHASERS

Certain investors who purchase securities in the secondary market just after a distribution must also be provided with the final prospectus. The term for which a prospectus must be provided depends largely on the type of offering and where the issue will be traded in the aftermarket. If the security has an aftermarket delivery requirement, a prospectus must be provided by all firms that execute a purchase order for the security during the term. The after market prospectus delivery requirements may be met electronically and are as follows:

- For IPOs: 90 days after being issued for securities quoted on the OTC MKT or in the Pink OTC, 25 days for listed or Nasdaq securities.
- Additional offerings: 40 days for securities quoted on the OTC MKT or in the Pink OTC. No aftermarket requirement for listed or Nasdaq securities.

SEC DISCLAIMER

The SEC reviews the issuer's registration statement and the prospectus but does not guarantee the accuracy or adequacy of the information. The SEC disclaimer must appear on the cover of all prospectuses and states: "These securities have not been approved or disapproved by the SEC nor have any representations been made about the accuracy or the adequacy of the information."

MISREPRESENTATIONS

Financial relief for misrepresentations made under the Securities Act of 1933 is available for purchasers of any security that is sold under a prospectus that is found to contain false or misleading statements. Section 11 of the Securities Act of 1933 allows purchasers of the security to seek financial relief from any or all of the following:

- The issuer.
- The underwriters.
- Officers and directors.
- All parties who signed the registration statement.
- Accountants and attorneys who helped prepare the registration statement.

Section 11 of the Securities Act provides the parties listed above (excluding the issuer itself) with an affirmative defense against claims made as a result of false information. The parties must be able demonstrate that they had no knowledge of the fraud or misrepresentations and must refer the matter to the SEC. A due diligence meeting will be held during the cooling-off period to ensure that the information contained in the prospectus is accurate. Included in The Securities Act of 1933 is SEC Rule 176. SEC Rule 176 allows an underwriter to assert a due diligence defense to claims provided it can demonstrate it engaged in a substantial and extensive review of all facts submitted by the issuer. If the underwriter's investigation does not meet the definition of a reasonable investigation, the underwriter may be sued under liability standards of the Securities Act of 1933. The level of due diligence required is partially determined by:

- The type of securities being offered
- The type of issuer
- The existence of a relationship between the issuer and underwriter
- The role of the underwriter
- The type of underwriting agreement

In addition to the firm being held liable for sales that violate the Securities Act of 1933, the registered persons who offer securities whose prospectus or registration statement makes false representations or who fail to perform his / her own due diligence in regards to any false representations or statements may be civilly liable for losses suffered by investors to whom he/ she made such sales. The civil liability will be limited to the amount invested, plus a reasonable rate of interest, minus any dividend or interest income received from the investment.

TOMBSTONE ADS

SEC Rule 134 allows certain types of advertisements to be run relating to a new issue. Tombstone ads are the only form of advertising that is allowed during the cooling-off period. A tombstone ad is an announcement and description of the securities to be offered. A tombstone ad lists the names of the underwriters, where a prospectus may be obtained, and a statement that the tombstone ad does not constitute an offer to sell the securities and that the offer may only be made by a prospectus. Tombstone ads are traditionally run to announce the new issue, but they are not required and do not need to be filed with the SEC. Tombstone ads may also include:

- The amount of the security to be offered
- The date of sale
- A general description of the issuer's business
- The price of the security

FREE RIDING AND WITHHOLDING/FINRA RULE 5130

A broker dealer underwriting a new issue must make a complete and bona fide offering of all securities being issued to the public and may not withhold any of the securities for:

- The underwriters.
- Another broker dealer.
- A firm employee or a person who is financially dependent on the employee.
- Roommates who share expenses with the rep
- Boyfriends and girlfriends whose rent is paid by the rep
- An employee of another FINRA member.
- Accountants, attorneys, and finders associated with the underwriting.
- Portfolio managers purchasing shares for his / her own account

TAKE NOTE!

An exception to FINRA Rule 5130 applies to employees of limited broker dealers who engage solely in the purchase and sale of investment company products or direct participation programs (DPPs). Employees of limited broker dealers may purchase new issues. This exemption applies only to the employees of the limited broker dealer, not to the firm itself.

These rules are in effect for initial public offering, but they are especially prevalent when dealing with a hot issue. A hot issue is one that trades at an immediate premium to its offering price in the secondary market. A broker dealer may not free ride by withholding securities for its own account or for the accounts of those listed above. FINRA Rule 5130 covers initial offerings of common stock only. Exempt from the rule are offerings of additional issues, bonds, and preferred shares. These offerings may be purchased by registered persons. FINRA Rule 5130 requires that a broker dealer (not the Rep) obtain an eligibility statement from all account owners who purchase a new issue of stock within 12 months prior to the purchase. This eligibility statement attests to the fact that the person is not restricted from purchasing new issues. If a member of the syndicate or selling group receives an order for a new issue from a financial intermediary such as a bank or an investment adviser, the member selling the securities to the customer of the financial intermediary may rely on the financial intermediary's representation that their client is not restricted from purchasing new issues. Some people may purchase hot issues so long as the amount is not substantial and they have a history of purchasing new issues. These conditionally approved people are:

- Employees of financial institutions not able to direct the securities business of the institution.
- Non-supported family members.
- Accounts where the restricted persons' interest is limited to 10 percent or less or where a maximum of 10 percent of the allocation of new issue is for the benefit of such persons. This is known as the carve out procedure.

There are several conditions to be aware of regarding the classification of restricted persons on the exam. If the information is included in the question, the exam is most likely testing your knowledge of the exemptions. In the absence of the conditions, it is best to classify the person as restricted. These conditions include the following:

- The restriction applies to purchases made through the employee's member firm. Purchases made by a family member at another firm where the registered rep (immediately family member) has no association or control over allocation would be exempt from this rule.
- Purchases by family members where the associated person has no ability to control or direct allocations would be exempt
- Family members who do not receive more than 25% of their income from the rep would also be exempt from from the definition of a restricted person
- Other family members such as aunts, uncles, cousins and ex spouses are all exempt from the definition of a restricted person.

It is interesting to note that if an offering of securities is underscubscribed and all public orders have been filled, a broker dealer who is acting as an underwriter may purchase the securities for its own account. This exemption does not extend to registered persons of the broker dealer. It only applies to the broker dealer's proprietary account.

UNDERWRITING CORPORATE SECURITIES

Once a business has decided that it needs to raise capital to meet its organizational objectives, it must determine how to raise the needed capital. Most corporations at this point will hire an investment banker, also known as an underwriter, to advise them. Investment-banking is the broad umbrella term used to describe a variety of investment banking services provided by FINRA members. Included in the definition of investment banking services are acting as an underwriter, syndicate or selling group member, financial adviser to an issuer regarding an M&A transaction, placement agent in a private transaction, providing capital or lines of credit. The underwriter works for the issuer, and it is the underwriter's job to advise the client about what type of securities to offer. The issuer and the underwriter together determine whether stocks or bonds should be issued and what the terms will be. The underwriter is responsible for trying to obtain the financing at the best possible terms for the issuer. The underwriter will:

- Market the issue to investors.
- Assist in the determination of the terms of the offering.

- Purchase the securities directly from the issuer to resell to investors.

The issuer is responsible for:

- Filing a registration statement with the SEC.
- Registering the securities in the states in which it will be sold, also known as blue-skying the issue.
- Negotiating the underwriter's compensation and obligations to the issuer.

TYPES OF UNDERWRITING COMMITMENTS

The agreement between the issuer and the underwriter spells out the underwriter's responsibilities to the issuer. The agreement may take a variety of forms and may include:

- Firm commitment
- Best efforts
- Mini-maxi
- All or none
- Standby

FIRM COMMITMENT

In a firm commitment underwriting, the underwriter guarantees to purchase all of the securities being offered for sale by the issuer regardless of whether it can sell them to investors. A firm commitment underwriting agreement is the most desirable for the issuer because it guarantees the issuer all of the money right away. The more in demand the offering is, the more likely it is that it will be done on a firm commitment basis. If the issue is in extremely high demand and is oversubscribed, the underwriter may exercise its greenshoe provision to cover overallotments. This will allow the underwriter to purchase an additional 15 percent of the issue from the issuer. In a firm commitment, the underwriter puts its own money at risk if it can't sell the securities to investors.

MARKET-OUT CLAUSE

An underwriter offering securities for an issuer on a firm commitment basis is assuming a substantial amount of risk. As a result, the underwriter will insist on having a market-out clause in the underwriting agreement. A market-out clause would free the underwriter from its obligation to purchase all of the securities in the event of a development that impairs the quality of the securities or that adversely affects the issuer. If a syndicate was underwriting a new issue for a biotech company with a drug in clinical trials and the FDA rejected the drug for use, the underwriters could invoke the market-out clause. Poor market conditions are not a reason to invoke the market-out clause. However, a substantial dislocation of the financial markets as the result of an external shock may be used as a reason for invoking the market-out clause. Finally, an underwriter would not be allowed to invoke the market out clause as a result of poor demand or its inability to sell the securities.

BEST EFFORTS

In a best efforts underwriting, the underwriter will do its best to sell all of the securities that are being offered by the issuer but in no way is the underwriter obligated to purchase the securities for its own account. The lower the demand for an issue, the greater likelihood that it will be done on a best efforts basis. Any shares or bonds in a best efforts underwriting that have not been sold will be returned to the issuer.

MINI-MAXI

A mini-maxi is a type of best efforts underwriting that does not become effective until a minimum amount of the securities have been sold. Once the minimum has been met, the underwriter may then sell the securities up to the maximum amount specified under the terms of the offering. All funds collected from investors will be held in escrow until the underwriting is completed. If the minimum amount of securities specified by the offering cannot be reached, the offering will be canceled and the investors' funds that were collected will be returned to them.

ALL OR NONE (AON)

With an all-or-none underwriting, the issuer has determined that it must receive the proceeds from the sale of all of the securities. Investors' funds are held in escrow until all of the securities are sold. If all of the securities are sold, the proceeds will be released to the issuer. If all of the securities are not sold, the issue is cancelled and the investors' funds will be returned to them. All contingent offerings must have a qualified financial institute QFI to act as an escrow agent for the offering. A general securities broker dealer, bank, or trust company may all act as an escrow agent.

STANDBY

A standby underwriting agreement will be used in conjunction with a pre-emptive rights offering. All standby underwritings are done on a firm commitment basis. The standby underwriter agrees to purchase any shares that current shareholders do not purchase. The standby underwriter will then resell the securities to the public.

TYPES OF OFFERINGS

Securities that are being sold under a prospectus may include securities that are part of different types of offerings. The different types of offerings include initial public offerings, subsequent primary offerings, and registered secondary offerings.

INITIAL PUBLIC OFFERING (IPO)/NEW ISSUE

An initial public offering is the first time that a company has sold its stock to the public. The issuing company receives the proceeds from the sale minus the underwriter's compensation.

SUBSEQUENT PRIMARY/ADDITIONAL ISSUES

In a subsequent primary offering, the corporation is already publicly owned and the company is selling additional shares to raise new financing. The shares being sold under a subsequent primary distribution may be offered at a stated price or the shares may be sold at the market once the issue is effective. If the issue is an at-the-market offering, the shares may be sold at different prices in the marketplace.

PRIMARY OFFERING VS. SECONDARY OFFERING

In a primary offering, the issuing company receives the proceeds from the sale minus the underwriter's compensation. In a secondary offering, a group of selling shareholders receives the proceeds from the sale minus the underwriter's compensation. A combined offering has elements of both the primary offering and the secondary offering or split. Part of the proceeds go to the company and part of the proceeds go to a group of selling shareholders.

FIXED PRICE AND AT THE MARKET OFFERINGS

Initial public offerings are conducted at a fixed or set price. In the case of common stock investors are provided with an expected range of prices and based on the demand for the issue, the securities will be priced on the day the SEC declares the registration effective. All investors who purchase securities through the offering will pay the same fixed price. Most issues are sold on a fixed price basis including bonds, preferred stock and most subsequent or follow-on offerings. Additional issues such as subsequent primaries or registered secondaries for issuers whose stock has an established market may be sold at the prevailing market price on the day the registration is deemed effective. Investors who purchase securities through an at the market offering will pay the prevailing market price at the time or times when sales are conducted.

AWARDING THE ISSUE

There are two ways in which the corporation may select an underwriter. A corporation may elect to have multiple underwriters submit bids and then choose the underwriter with the best bid. This is known as a competitive bid underwriting. Or, a company may elect to select one firm to sell the issue and negotiate the terms of the offering with it. This is known as a negotiated underwriting. Most corporate offerings are awarded on a negotiated basis, whereas municipal bond offerings are usually awarded through competitive bidding.

THE UNDERWRITING SYNDICATE

Because most corporate offerings involve a large number of shares and a very large dollar amount, the securities will be offered through several underwriters known as the underwriting syndicate. The syndicate is a group of investment banks that have agreed to share the financial responsibility of marketing the issue. Only FINRA member firms may participate in the underwriting of securities. FINRA member firms may only share discounts and concessions with other FINRA member firms. Banks and other financial institutions who are non FINRA members are also prohibited from receiving discounts or concessions. An exception to this rule is for foreign broker dealers in good standing with a foreign regulator who are not eligible for FINRA membership. If a member firm participating in the underwriting as a syndicate or selling group member is suspended during the offering, the suspended member may not receive discounts or allocations of securities However, the suspended member would be allowed to purchase shares at the public offering price. The managing underwriter, also known as the lead underwriter or book running manager, leads the syndicate. If the syndicate plans to stabilize the issue in the aftermarket to allow for an orderly distribution of the shares, only one bid may be placed, and the stabilizing bid must be entered at or below the offering price.

SELLING GROUP

The syndicate may form a selling group in an effort to help market the issue. Members of the selling group have no underwriting responsibility and may only sell the shares to investors for a fee known as the selling concession. Selling group members may also be thought of or referred to as placement agents. Selling group members must sign an agreement attesting to the fact that they will abide by FINRA rules regarding the granting of selling concessions.

Occasionally the employees of the issuer may assist in selling the securities of the issuer. This is allowed with the permission of the managing underwriter so long as the employees are not paid based on the sales and are not disqualified from or registered as agents of any broker dealer. However, if the issuer hires a group to act as sales agents for the issuer, FINRA member firms may not participate in the offering. A FINRA member firm who is not participating in the underwriting as a syndicate or selling group member may still be allowed to fill a customer's order and will be paid a fee known as the dealer's reallowance.

TAKE **NOTE!**

No member firm participating in the underwriting of securities may sell the securities at a discount to the public offering price to investors who receive research from the member

UNDERWRITER'S COMPENSATION

The group of broker dealers that make up the underwriting syndicate will be compensated based upon their role as a syndicate member. The only syndicate member that may earn the entire spread is the lead or managing underwriter.

MANAGEMENT FEE

The lead or managing underwriter will receive a fee known as a management fee for every share that is sold. In most cases, the managing underwriter is the firm that negotiated the terms of the offering with the issuer and formed the syndicate.

UNDERWRITER'S FEE

The underwriter's fee is the cost of bringing the issue to market and is a fee assessed for each share that is sold by the syndicate. If there is any money remaining after all expenses are paid, the syndicate members will split it based upon their commitment level in the underwriting.

SELLING CONCESSION

The selling concession will be paid to any syndicate member or selling group member who sells the shares to the investors. The selling concession is the only fee that the selling group members may earn.

 TAKE **NOTE!**

With the approval of the syndicate manager, a member of the syndicate or selling group may sell the shares to a FINRA member firm who is not participating in the offering. The FINRA member will receive part of the selling concession known as the reallowance.

UNDERWRITING SPREAD

The total amount of the management fee, the underwriting fee, and the selling concession make up the total underwriting spread. This is the difference between the gross proceeds of the offering and the net proceeds to the issuer.

PUBLIC OFFERING PRICE: $12

SELLING CONCESSION $1.50
UNDERWRITING FEE $.75
MANAGEMENT FEE $.25
PROCEEDS TO ISSUER: $9.50 PER SHARE

In this example the underwriting spread is $2.50 per share.

FACTORS THAT DETERMINE THE SIZE OF THE UNDERWRITING SPREAD

Many factors determine the amount of the underwriter's compensation for offering the securities on behalf of the issuer. Some of these factors are:

- The type of securities to be offered.
- The size of the issue.
- The quality of the securities to be issued.
- The perceived demand for the securities.
- The type of underwriting agreement.
- The quality of the issuer's business.

REVIEW OF UNDERWRITING AGREEMENTS BY FINRA

With certain exceptions, underwriting agreements must be submitted to FINRA's Corporate Finance Department for review no later than three days after the filing of any registration with the SEC or with any state regulator. If the offering is not required to be filed at either the federal or state level, as is the case with private placements, the agreement must be filed with FINRA at least 15 business days prior to the anticipated offering date. In most cases, the agreement is submitted by the managing underwriter. FINRA will review the maximum total compensation to the underwriters to ensure that the underwriter's compensation is fair and reasonable in light of the size and complexity of the offering. Documents relating to common stock, convertible bonds, preferred stock, non-investment grade bonds, Regulation A, Rule 147, DPPs, rights, warrants, and closed-end funds must be filed. The submission must include:

- The maximum offering price.
- The maximum underwriter's discount.
- The maximum estimated reimbursement for the underwriter's expenses.

UNDERWRITER'S COMPENSATION

The largest percentage of the underwriter's compensation will come in the form of the underwriter's discount. Other items received by the syndicate will also be considered compensation and are reported to the corporate finance department, such as:

- Reimbursement of costs not usually borne by the issuer.
- Options, rights, warrant or convertible securities.
- Common or preferred shares of the issuer.
- Finder's fees reimbursed by the issuer.
- Wholesaler fees
- Attorney fees
- Advisory and consulting fees
- The amount of any non-accountable expense allowance.
- Overallotment provisions (green shoe).
- Qualified independent underwriter fees
- Sales incentives
- Compensation received in connection with the exercise or conversion of any securities within 12 months after the effective date of the offering
- Breakup fees if the member participates in a revised offering
- Right of first refusal on future offerings

In addition to those items listed above awarding the underwriters securities, all other items will be deemed compensation to the underwriter if the fees are paid in cash or in securities of the issuer. If the underwriter receives shares from the issuer as part of the compensation, those securities must be held for 6 months from the effective date of the offering. Alternatively, if the underwriter receives options, rights or warrants, those securities may be exercised at any time, but the shares received may not be sold until 6 months after the effective date of the offering. For example If TRY Industries goes public and the offering is deemed to be effective on June 1, an underwriter who received shares in TRY as part of the compensation may not sell those shares until December 2. Alternatively, if the underwriter was granted options to purchase TRY stock, those options may be exercised at any time but the sale of stock received would still be restricted until December 2.

UNREASONABLE COMPENSATION

FINRA's Corporate Finance Department will review all of the compensation received by the underwriter and determine if the total amount of compensation is reasonable. All compensation received 180 days prior to the filing of the registration statement up to and including the date when sales begin will be considered to be underwriter's compensation. One of the main focuses of the CFD is to ensure that underwriters do not take advantage of issuers by demanding fees that are excessive. The Corporate Finance Department considers all of the following to be excessive and unreasonable:

- A non-accountable expense allowance greater than 3 percent of the underwriting spread.
- A greenshoe provision in excess of 15 percent of the offering.
- Freely transferable shares amounting to greater than 1 percent of the offering, which are not subject to a 6-month lock up.
- Warrants, rights, or options exercisable below the public offering price or with a duration greater than 5 years, or that total more than 10 percent of the number of shares offered.
- Receipt of restricted securities, rights, warrants or options that have more than one demand registration right or have demand registration rights for greater than 5 years or piggyback registration rights greater than 7 years
- Right of first refusal to additional offerings greater than 3 years or which requires payment greater than 1% of the offering or 5% of the underwriter's discount
- A termination or trail fee greater than 2 years requiring payment to be made to the underwriter if the issuer cancels the offering and switches underwriters.

If the CFD notifies the lead underwriter that the compensation is excessive the lead underwriter must inform the syndicate and adjust the compensation. In addition to those items listed above as being excessive, FINRA's CFD would not allow any underwriter to:
- Receive any payments, commissions or expense reimbursements prior to the public offering of securities (excluded is the advance payment for out pocket expenses for which the underwriter provides detailed accounting)
- Receive any payments to cover overhead of the underwriter such as salaries of investment bankers, compliance officers or support staff
- Receive any payments as compensation for an offering that was not completed

Once the CFD is satisfied that the compensation is reasonable the offering may proceed.

Specifically excluded from the definition of underwriter's compensation are the reimbursement of registration fees (blue sky fees) paid by the underwriter on behalf of the issuer. Also excluded from the definition of underwriter compensation are:

- Printing costs
- Accounting fees
- Fees received as compensation for providing a loan as part of an M&A transaction
- Fees received for acting as a placement agent
- The purchase of non equivalent or non convertible securities at a price reasonably related to the market price for the securities
- FINRA filing fees

 TAKE **NOTE!**

When determining the total amount of compensation received by the underwriter, FINRA's Corporate Finance Department will look back 180 days (6 months) and assume that any compensation received from the issuer was received as compensation for the offering.

The following are all exempt from the filing of the underwriting agreement with the Corporate Finance Department:

- U.S. government securities
- Municipal securities
- Redeemable investment company shares
- Variable contracts
- Private placements

OFFERING OF SECURITIES BY FINRA MEMBERS AND OTHER CONFLICTS

When a FINRA member firm wishes to raise money by offering securities for sale to investors special rules apply to the offering. When a FINRA member firm goes public it may not underwrite its own securities. The member wishing to go public must engage the services of a qualified independent lead underwriter. A qualified independent lead underwriter is a FINRA member who has been the book running lead underwriter in at least 3 offerings in the last 3 years. The member's participation in those offerings must have been for at least 50 percent of the shares being sold. The proceeds of member offerings must be placed in escrow and may not be released for use by the member until the member has completed a net capital computation and submitted it to FINRA. The computation must show that the member's AI:NC does not exceed 10:1 or that its net capital is greater than 120 percent of its required net capital. When calculating the net capital the member may use the funds being held in escrow as part of the calculation. If the net capital computation shows AI:NC of greater than 10:1 or if its net capital is less than 120 percent of its required net capital the offering will be canceled and the funds returned to investors. If the member calculates net capital using the alternative method the offering will be canceled if the member's net capital is less than 7 percent of aggregate debit items. When a FINRA member is offering securities for sale the member who is issuing the securities must file the underwriting agreement with FINRA's Corporate Finance Department. If the member is raising money for itself (or for an entity it controls defined as having at least a 50% ownership stake) through a member private offering (MPO) the member must file the private placement memorandum or term sheet with FINRA's CFD within 15 calendar days of the first sale. If no offering documents are to be used FINRA must be notified of that fact.

FINRA member firms who participate in the distribution of securities must disclose and manage conflicts of interest in accordance with FINRA regulations and The Securities Act of 1933. In addition to the potential conflicts contained in offering of securities of a member firm, The following potential conflicts are particularly noteworthy:

- The offering of securities by an affiliate of a member firm (an affiliate is any entity that is controlled by, controls or is under common control of the member)
- The offering of securities where 5% or more of the net proceeds excluding underwriter compensation is being used to repay a loan made by the member firm
- The offering of securities of an issuer controlled by or who controls of the member firm

For the purpose of the exam, the term control includes any entity that owns at least a 10% stake in the common stock, preferred stock or subordinated debt of an issuer. A partnership would be deemed to be controlled by any entity that has the right to 10% or more of the profits or losses of the partnership. If a member wishes to participate in an offering of securities where a conflict exists, the member must meet one of two conditions in order to be allowed to participate. One condition that may be met to allow the member to participate in the offering is the appointment of a qualified independent underwriter. The qualified independent underwriter must meet requirements very similar to those detailed above for a qualified independent lead underwriter in the offering of securities by a member firm. The one small difference is that the QIU must have been a manager or co-manager of the prior offerings and that their participation must be of similar size to the proposed offering. The independent underwriter will prepare the offering documents and the required disclosures. Of particular importance is the prominent disclosure of the conflicts of interest and the responsibilities of the firm acting as the qualified independent underwriter. These disclosures must clearly inform the investor as to how the potential conflicts may impact the offering and must be included in the prospectus or offering memorandum.

 TAKE NOTE!

A member firm who has a conflict of interest who is participating in an offering of securities may not place the securities in the account of a discretionary customer. The member must obtain the written authorization of the customer to purchase the securities prior to allocating any securities to the customer's account.

SYNDICATE OPERATIONS

The agreement among the underwriters must clearly state how the syndicate will handle the repurchase of shares trading at a premium. If a client "flips" the hot issue in the secondary market and the shares are repurchased by the book running lead underwriter, those shares must be used to cover any syndicate short position. If shares are returned to the syndicate as a result of a client failing to pay, those securities may also be used to cover a syndicate short position. If no short position exists the shares may be used to cover unfilled qualified customer orders at the offering price. Any account to receive these shares must receive the shares through a random allocation process. In the extremely unlikely event that no unfilled orders exist, the syndicate may sell the shares in the market and anonymously donate the profits to an unaffiliated charity. If a purchaser sells the stock (flips) within 30 days of the offering the syndicate may not seek to reclaim any sales credit earned by the agent or member unless the stock was sold back to the syndicate's penalty bid. If the securities are sold back to the penalty bid the syndicate may reclaim the selling concession paid to the member. Issuers who are going public are allowed to direct stock to the officers, directors, and employees of the company. The number of shares directed to the employees of the issuer are part of and are not in addition to the number of shares being underwritten. Syndicate managers are ultimately responsible for establishing the process by which orders will be filled. The order allocation process will be clearly spelled out in the in syndicate agreement. In many underwritings the syndicate will set aside a block or pool of shares specifically for institutional investors. Syndicate members and its representatives will compete with each other to receive shares from the pool to fill customer orders. This is a process known in the industry as a "jump ball". The institutions who receive shares will designate which underwriter is to receive the sales credit for the shares. The remaining profit on the shares will be allocated among the underwriters based on its participation. In order to ensure managers do not receive all or most of the the sales credits for sales, syndicates usually place a maximum amount that may be received by the managers through the jump ball process. A variation of the jump ball process calls for all of the sales credits and profits for sales from the institutional block to be allocated among the syndicate members based on its participation. This is known as a fixed pool. The amount of shares that remain available after the shares that have been set aside for institutional investors may be sold by syndicate members to retail clients. These shares represent each member's allocation. A member's allocation is known in the industry as its "free retention". Representatives at the syndicate member will compete with each other to receive allocations for his / her retail clients.

TAKE NOTE!

Syndicate members may not allocate shares of hot issue to the accounts of individuals who are in a position to direct business to the firm. This includes portfolio managers who may direct execution business to the member as well as officers and directors of companies who have been an investment banking client in the last 12 months or when the company is an anticipated investment banking client. Doing so is a violation known as spinning.

SYNDICATE SHORT POSITIONS

In an effort to cover a short position created in the syndicate account as a result of overallotments, the syndicate manager may enter a covering bid. The syndicate manager must record information relating to the syndicate's short position within 30 days of the issue's effective date. If the security is trading at a premium to the offering price, covering transactions will result in losses for the syndicate. If offered, in cases like this, a syndicate may elect to exercise its greenshoe option to cover the short position. This will allow the syndicate to purchase up to an additional 15 percent of the offering from the issuer. The syndicate will purchase the securities from the issuer at the original price to cover overallotments. However, should the security be trading at a discount to the public offering price, covering the short position in the secondary market will result in a profit for the syndicate. The syndicate agreement will detail how any losses that result from covering the syndicate short position will be distributed.

EXEMPT SECURITIES

Certain securities are exempt from the registration provisions of the Securities Act of 1933 because of the issuer or the nature of the security. Although the securities may be exempt from the registration and prospectus requirements of the act, none are exempt from the antifraud provisions of the act. Examples of exempt securities are:

- Debt securities with maturities of less than 270 days and sold in denominations of $50,000 or more.
- Employee benefit plans.
- Option contracts, both puts and calls on stocks and indexes.
- Examples of exempt issuers are:
- U.S. government
- State and municipal governments
- Foreign national governments
- Canadian federal and municipal governments
- Insurance companies
- Banks and trusts
- Credit unions and savings and loans
- Religious and charitable organizations

TAKE NOTE!

Insurance and bank holding companies are not exempt issuers.

EXEMPT TRANSACTIONS

Sometimes a security that would otherwise have to register is exempt from the registration requirements of the Securities Act of 1933 because of the type of transaction that is involved. Issuers who are seeking to raise money through an exempt transaction may test the waters by soliciting interest from potential investors and by holding "demo days" prior to selecting the type of transaction. The following are all exempt transactions:

- Private placements/Regulation D offerings
- Rule 144
- Regulation S offerings
- Regulation A offerings
- Rule 145
- Rule 147 intrastate offerings

PRIVATE PLACEMENTS/REGULATION D OFFERINGS

A private placement is a sale of securities that is made to a group of accredited investors where the securities are not offered to the general public. Accredited investors include institutional investors and individuals who:

- Earn at least $200,000 per year if single,

  or

- Earn at least $300,000 jointly with a spouse,

  or

- Have a net worth of at least $1,000,000 without the primary residence.

The SEC has recently added a new category that will allow an individual to qualify as an accredited investor. Individuals who meet certain educational or certification requirements can now meet the definition of accredited investor. Included in this category are individuals who have an active Series 7, 65 or 82 license. Reasonable efforts must be made to ensure purchasers meet the definition of an accredited investor. Brokerage accounts, bank accounts, credit reports and tax documents may be used for verification purposes. An existing partnership which consists of both accredited and non-accredited investors will be seen as one purchaser under regulation D and allowed to purchase the shares. Partnerships formed specifically to purchase shares of the offering would have all of the partners' financial status reviewed independently to determine the eligibility of each partner.

Sales to nonaccredited investors for private placements are limited to 35 in any 12-month period. No commission may be paid to representatives who sell a private placement to a nonaccredited investor. If the issuer is not going to allow offers to be made to non accredited investors no disclosure documents are required to be provided. For private placements being offered to both accredited and non-accredited investors, all investors must be provided with an offering memorandum. All investors in private placements must hold the securities fully paid for at least six months and sign a letter stating that they are purchasing the securities for investment purposes. Stock purchased through a private placement is known as lettered stock, legend stock, or restricted stock, because there is a legend on the stock certificate that limits the ability of the owner to transfer or sell the securities. There is no limit as to how many accredited investors may purchase the securities. The limits on the amount of money that may be raised under the various regulation D offerings are as follows:

- Regulation 504 D allows issuers to raise up to $10 million.
- Regulation 506 D allows issuers to raise an unlimited amount of capital.

PURCHASER'S REPRESENTATIVE

A purchaser's representative is an individual designated in writing by the prospective purchaser to represent the purchaser when evaluating the suitability of a private placement. A purchaser's representative may not:

- Receive a blanket appointment to represent the investor for all private placements.
- Own more than 10 percent of the issuer's stock.
- Be an officer, director, employee, or affiliate of the issuer, unless he or she is a close relative of the prospective purchaser.

For private placements exceeding $5 million, the offering will be limited to institutional, accredited, and nonaccredited investors who together with their purchaser's representative have the financial and business knowledge to evaluate the offering. The issuer in a private placement may not advertise the issue or hold a seminar open to the general public. However, a seminar held exclusively for qualified potential purchasers would be allowed. The JOBS Act now allows investors to view private placement documents online so long as the website requires an investor to submit a questionnaire documenting assets, income, and investment experience. This questionnaire must be reviewed and if qualified for participation the issuer or broker dealer may assign the investor a username and password granting them access to view the details of the offerings. The JOBS Act also allows offerings conducted under regulation 506 D to advertise and generally solicit investors to participate in the offering.

RULE 144

Regulates how control or restricted securities may be sold. Rule 144 designates:

- The holding period for the security.
- The amount of the security that may be sold.
- Filing procedures.
- Method of sale.

Control securities are owned by officers, directors, and owners of 10 percent or more of the company's outstanding stock. Control stock may be obtained by insiders through open-market purchases or through the exercise of company stock options. There is no holding period for control securities. However, insiders are not allowed to earn a short swing profit through the purchase and sale of control stock in the open market. If the securities were held less than six months, the insider must return any profit to the company.

Restricted securities may be purchased by both insiders and investors through a private placement or be obtained through an offering other than a public sale. Securities obtained through a private placement or other nonpublic means need to be sold under Rule 144 in order to allow the transfer of ownership. For reporting companies, restricted stock must be held fully paid for, for six months. After six months the securities may be sold freely by noninsiders so long as the seller has not been affiliated with the issuer in the last three months. It's important to note that rule 144 imposes a 12 month holding period for the restricted stock of non reporting issuers who fail to meet the requirements of adequate publicly available information. Rule 144 sets the following volume limits for both restricted and control stock during any 90-day period. The seller must file Form 144 at the time the order is entered and is limited to the greater of:

- The average weekly trading volume for the preceding four weeks,

  or

- 1 percent of the issuer's total outstanding stock.

Securities may be sold under Rule 144 four times per year. Restricted securities sold under Rule 144 become part of the public float and the seller, not the issuer, receives the proceeds of the sale. For orders for 5,000 shares or less and that do not exceed $50,000, Form 144 does not need to be filed. If the owner of restricted stock dies, his or her estate may sell the shares freely without regard to the holding period or volume limitations of Rule 144 so long as the decedent was not an affiliate of the issuer.

If the purchaser of restricted stock gifts the shares, to another person or to a trust, the holding period transfers to the recipient of the shares. Additionally, shares that have been pledged as collateral for a loan and subsequently surrendered will have the holding period transferred to the recipient.

TAKE NOTE!

There is a six-month holding period for control stock acquired through a private placement, and control stock is always subject to the volume limitations.

BROKER TRANSACTIONS UNDER RULE 144

A firm handling a customer's sale under Rule 144, except for in very limited circumstances, must execute the orders on an agency basis for the customer. The broker dealer may execute the order with a market maker or may inquire with customers who have expressed an unsolicited interest in the securities in the last 10 days or with a broker dealer who has expressed interest in the securities in the last 60 days. Firms that are classified as bona fide block positioners are allowed to purchase the stock on a principal basis.

RULE 144A

Rule 144A permits the resale of restricted stock to qualified institutional buyers (QIBs). A QIB is defined as a company that owns investments worth at least $100 million and includes:

- Corporations
- Partnerships

- Insurance companies
- Investment companies
- Banks
- Trust funds
- Pension plans
- Registered investment advisers
- Small business development companies

The broker dealer must verify that the customer meets the definition of a QIB, When determining the eligibility for a buyer to participate in a 144a transaction, the broker dealer may use any of the following:

- The purchaser's most recent, publicly available financial statements
- The purchaser's most recent publicly available information appearing in documents filed in an SRO
- The purchaser's most recent publicly available information appearing in a recognized securities manual or filed with a foreign regulator
- A certification by the purchaser's chief financial officer or other executive

The broker dealer may not rely on the information on the customer's account card.

> **TAKE NOTE!**
>
> A broker dealer will be considered a QIB if it owns $10 million worth of securities or if it engages in riskless principal transactions for other QIBs.

To qualify for the exemption provided under Rule 144A, the QIB must be purchasing the securities for its own account or for the account of other QIBs. Not all securities will be eligible for an exemption under Rule 144A. Ineligible securities include:

- Securities of registered investment companies.
- Securities of the same class as those listed on an exchange or Nasdaq.
- Certain warrants and convertible securities.

All purchasers of securities under Rule 144A must be informed that the seller is relying on the exemption provided under Rule 144A, and the issuer of the securities must be willing to provide financial information to owners and prospective purchasers. The PORTAL Market has been developed to help ensure compliance with Rule 144A and to help facilitate Rule 144A transactions. Transactions that qualify under Rule 144A may be executed without regard to any holding period otherwise imposed so long as the buyer is a QIB. However, the QIB is still subject to the holding period of the original purchaser.

PRIVATE INVESTMENT IN A PUBLIC EQUITY (PIPE)

Public companies that wish to obtain additional financing without selling securities to the general public may sell securities to a group of accredited investors through a private placement. The accredited investors in most cases will be institutional investors who wish to invest a large amount of capital. Common stock, convertible or nonconvertible debt, rights, and warrants may all be sold to investors through a PIPE transaction. Obtaining capital through a PIPE transaction benefits the public company in a number of ways:

- Reduced transaction cost.
- Term disclosure only upon completion of the transaction.
- Increased institutional ownership.
- Quick closing.

Securities sold through a PIPE transaction are subject to Rule 144. If the issuer files a registration statement after the closing of the offering, sales may begin immediately upon the effective date.

REGISTRATION RIGHTS AND LOCK UP AGREEMENTS

Hedge funds, venture capital firms and large institutions who invest directly in companies will include a stipulation regarding the ability to register and sell its shares as part of the consideration received in exchange for the investment. These large sophisticated investors will seek registration rights as part of their exit strategy. In the case of a private placement in a private company, the investor may be granted demand or piggyback registration rights in the event the company goes public through an initial public offering. An investor who has been granted demand registration rights, may as the name implies, demand that the issuer file a registration statement for its shares. Large investors with demand registration rights can effectively force (demand) that the company go public so that they may sell shares. Investors with piggyback registration rights cannot force the company to go public or to file a registration statement. Piggyback registration rights allow the investor to participate in an offering of securities as part of an IPO. In this case, the investor may be piggybacking a registration that was demanded by another investor who had been granted demand registration rights or one that was filed at the election of the company. From an investor's point of view demand registration rights are superior to piggyback registration rights because demand rights put the investor, not the issuer in control of the timing of an offering.

While investors seek to obtain the opportunity to register and sell shares, issuers often seek certain assurances that the investors will hold the securities for a minimum amount of time. Large investors and officers and directors who own pre IPO shares are often asked to sign lock up agreements that set restrictions on the sale of shares for a period of time. Because these investors often have a very low cost basis for the shares, being able to sell the shares in the secondary market post IPO often represents a huge opportunity to lock in substantial gains. Investors who are considering purchasing the shares either through the IPO or in the secondary market are often concerned with the huge amount of stock that could hit the market when these investors seek to lock in gains and sell large blocks of shares. The lock up agreement provides both protection and viability for investors regarding the potential negative impact these sales can have on the price of the stock.

 TAKE NOTE!

Restricted shares that are subsequently registered through demand or piggyback registration rights are exempt from Rule 144.

REGULATION S OFFERINGS

Domestic issuers who make a distribution of securities exclusively to offshore investors do not have to file a registration statement for the securities under the Securities Act of 1933. In order to qualify for the exemption offered under Regulation S, the issuer may make no offerings of the securities within the United States and may not announce or distribute literature relating to the securities within the United States. Securities distributed under Regulation S are subject to a distribution compliance period, during which the securities may not be resold to domestic investors. The distribution compliance period is 6 months for equities if the issuer is a reporting company and files 10-Qs,

10-Ks and 8-Ks, and one year for non reporting companies. The distribution compliance period is 40 days for debt. Sales of the securities may take place in off-shore markets anytime after the initial sale. Issuers must report the sale of securities under Regulation S by filing form 8K.

REGULATION A OFFERINGS

Regulation A allows US and Canadian issuers to raise up to $75 million in any 12 month period. A Regulation A offering provides issuers with an exemption from the standard registration process. This exemption from full registration allows smaller companies access to the capital markets without having to go through the expense of filing a full registration statement with the SEC. The issuer will instead file an abbreviated notice of sale or offering circular known as an S1-A with the SEC. Issuers are required to file 2 years of audited financial statements with the SEC and purchasers of the issue will be given a copy of the offering circular rather than a final prospectus. Purchasers of the issue must have the preliminary or final offering circular mailed to them 48 hours before mailing the confirmation. The same 20-day cooling-off period also applies to Regulation A offerings. Regulation A has two tiers, with Regulation A now sometimes being referred to as Regulation A plus. Tier 1 allows issuers to raise up to $20 million. Of this $20 million, no more than $6 million may be offered by selling shareholders. Tier 2 allows issuers to raise up to $75 million, of which no more than $22.5 million may be offered by selling shareholders. When determining the total amount of money raised through a regulation A offering, the look-back period includes money raised in the past 12 months.

CROWDFUNDING

Crowdfunding has become a popular way for issuers to raise capital from small investors. Issuers may offer securities to investors for purchase through a broker dealer or through a registered crowdfunding portal. The portal must be registered with the SEC and must also be a FINRA member firm. Issuers who raise capital through crowdfunding may not engage directly in crowdfunding as a way to sell shares to investors. Issuers who sell shares through crowdfunding must register the securities with the SEC by filing form C. Because most of the securities are speculative in nature, broker dealers and crowdfunding portals must offer educational material to investors who are considering purchasing securities offered through crowdfunding. The material must detail the risks involved in making investments in companies through the crowdfunding process as well as the fact that the securities have a limited amount of liquidity. Investors who purchase shares through crowdfunding may not sell the shares for 12 months. Shares however may be transferred earlier to a relative or to a trust controlled by the investor or as a result of death or divorce. Early transfer will also be allowed if the purchaser is an accredited investor or if the securities are part of an SEC registered offering. Investors who purchase shares are limited to the amount of securities they may purchase through the crowdfunding process in any 12 month period. Investors who have an annual income or a net worth of less than $124,000 are limited to purchasing the greater of $2,500 worth of securities or 5% of their annual income or net worth. If the investor uses the 5% calculation to determine their purchase limit the amount the person may purchase will be the lesser of the two amounts. Investors who have an annual income or a net worth greater than $124,000 may invest the lesser of 10% of their annual income or net worth up to a maximum of $124,000. Investment limits have been removed for accredited investors and issuers may raise up to $5 million through the crowdfunding process.

 TAKE **NOTE!**

If any covered person, such as an officer or director of an issuer, has been the subject of a disqualifying event, such as being convicted for securities fraud or having been barred by a regulator, the exemption from registration offered through Regulation A, Regulation D, and Regulation crowdfunding may not be used by the issuer.

RULE 145

Rule 145 requires that shareholders approve any merger or reorganization of the company's ownership. Any securities issued as a result of a merger or acquisition will be registered with the SEC using Form S-4. Stockholders must be given full disclosure of the proposed transaction or reclassification and must be sent a prospectus as well as proxies to vote on the proposal. Rule 145 covers:

- Mergers involving a stock swap or offer of another company's securities in exchange for a company's current stock.

- Reclassification involving the exchange of one class of the company's securities for another.
- Asset transfers involving the dissolution of the company or the distribution or sale of a major portion of the company's assets. In the case of a spin-off, the shareholder will retain the securities of the issuer and will receive shares of the newly independent company that was the subject of the spin off.

Rule 145 does not cover:

- Stock splits
- Reverse splits
- Changes in par value

It is interesting to note that any shareholder who owns restricted shares at the time the securities are exchanged under Rule 145, will receive newly issued shares subject to the remainder of the restricted period.

RULE 147 INTRASTATE OFFERING

Rule 147 allows an issuer to raise an unlimited amount of capital within one state. Because the offering is being made only in one state, it is exempt from registration with the SEC and is subject to the jurisdiction of the state securities administrator. In order to qualify for an exemption from SEC registration, the issue must be organized and have its principal place of business in the state and meet at least one of the following business criteria:

- 80% of the issuer's income must be received in that state.
- 80% of the offering's proceeds must be used in that state.
- 80% of the issuer's assets must be located in that state.
- A majority of the issuer's employees are based in-state.

All purchasers must be located within the state and must agree not to resell the securities to an out-of-state resident for 6 months.

If the issuer is using an underwriter, the broker dealer must have an office in that state.

The SEC has also adopted Rule 147A, which is largely identical to Rule 147. However, Rule 147A allows companies that are incorporated out of state to utilize the Rule 147 exemption so long as the company's principal place of business is in that state. Rule 147 A also allows issuers to use the internet and to advertise securities being offered through Rule 147. Offers may be made to residents while out of state. However, all sales are still limited to investors residing in the state where the offering is being conducted. Interestingly, an existing domestic partnership made up of partners from both in-state and out-of-state would be allowed to purchase these shares being issued under Rule 147.

RESEARCH REPORTS

Broker dealers that issue research reports must carefully supervise their associated people who issue the research reports. The review and approval of research is exclusively conducted by the research department and supervisory analysts. The member's investment banking department is strictly prohibited from exercising any control over the member's research department. Neither the investment banking nor any other non research department may have any review, approval, or veto power over the issuance of research reports. The investment banking department may only be contacted by the research department to ensure the accuracy of information. All written communications, including emails and instant messaging, between the two departments must be conducted through the legal or compliance department or the department must be copied on the communication. If the contact is oral, the communication must be done through an official of the legal or compliance department or in the presence of a member from the legal or compliance department. All other communication between investment banking and research is strictly prohibited. FINRA has recognized that certain small firms may not be able to absorb the costs associated with ensuring the barriers between research and investment banking. In order to alleviate the undue hardship, in limited circumstances, FINRA will allow personnel to act in a dual capacity. If during the last three years, on average, the member firm has participated in 10 or fewer underwritings as a manager or co-manager and has received $5 million or less in compensation, an investment banker may also function as a research analyst. This exception relieves the member from the obligation for the legal and compliance department to serve as the intermediary between investment banking and research. Further, this exemption also relieves the member firm from the prohibition regarding investment banking having a supervisory role in research. While this exception alleviates many provisions of the firewall or gatekeeper provisions, it does not eliminate the prohibition regarding communication between research and the issuer. Compensation for analysts may not be based on:

- Deal-related bonuses

- Percentage of investment deals
- Specific investment banking deals

If the analyst's compensation is in any way tied to the investment banking department it must be clearly disclosed in the research reports issued by that analyst. All analyst compensation should be reviewed by the firm's compensation committee and supervisory analysts. In order to ensure that analysts who issue research reports do not profit by trading the security just before or after they issue the report, the following rules have been enacted:

- Analysts may not trade against their recommendations.
- An analyst who is working on a research report may not trade the security that is the subject of the report until such time as the intended recipients of the report have had an opportunity to act on the report.
- Analysts may not receive pre-IPO shares from a company in a sector the analyst covers.

The personal trading rules apply to accounts owned by the analyst or under the control of the analyst or any member of the analyst's household. Exceptions would be made for hardship or emergency sales by analysts. Each exemption would have to be approved by the firm's legal or compliance department. It's important to note that a hardship exemption would not allow the analyst to trade against their own recommendation to cover expenses they knew were coming up, such as college tuition. Analysts may invest in mutual funds without restriction so long as the analyst does not own 1 percent or more of the fund and the fund does not invest more than 20 percent of its assets in a sector covered by the analyst. A broker dealer may prohibit analysts from owning securities issued by the companies or in the sector covered by the analyst. Should a broker dealer hire an analyst or assign a company to an analyst who already owns the stock in the company or sector they are now going to cover, the broker dealer must handle the sale of the securities in line with its policy of not allowing an analyst to own such securities. Research analysts who are primarily engaged in the preparation of research reports and those who report directly or indirectly to such persons must register with FINRA and are subject to both firm element and regulatory CE requirements. Individuals who only occasionally produce or prepare research do not meet the definition of a research analyst. In addition to the trading rules for analysts, the firm itself is precluded from establishing or adjusting it's inventory position in a security based on the prior knowledge of a research report. This is another variation of the prohibited practice known as trading ahead. Excluded from this rule are inventory adjustments solely based on the receipt of unsolicited customer orders, orders received from other broker-dealers, and adjustments made based on internal research reports that will not be made available to the public. Firms must maintain adequate supervisory systems to ensure all research related rules are followed but are not required to attest annually or otherwise relating to the adequacy of its research supervisory system.

REQUIRED DISCLOSURES FOR RESEARCH REPORTS

The issuance of research reports requires the member to make certain disclosures about the firm's ownership and relationship with the subject company. The firm must disclose:

- If the firm makes a market in the security.
- If the firm owns 1 percent or more of the subject security.
- If the analyst or a member of the analyst's household owns the security, has an interest in the issuer, or is an officer, director, or adviser to the issuer.
- If the member has received investment banking fees from the subject company within the last 12 months.
- If the member is seeking investment banking business from the subject company within the next three months.
- Any material conflict of interest known by the firm.

The disclosures required by the firm must appear on the first page of the research report in type of equal size. If the report contains research reports on six or more companies, the report may direct the reader to a location as to where the information may be found in print or electronic form. The firm must also disclose certain information relating to the firm's research and the market conditions. The research must disclose:

- A clear explanation of its rating system and an explanation of what each rating means.
- The percentage of subject securities that are rated buy, sell, or hold.
- Rationale to support the recommendation.
- The percentage of subject companies in each category with whom the firm has an investment banking relationship.
- Risk factors that may keep the security from reaching the firm's price target.
- The market price of the security at the time the recommendation was made.

- A three-year price chart for the subject security and information relating the firm's target prices and any changes to the target price for securities covered for at least one year.

If an analyst makes a public appearance on a television or radio program, the analyst is required to make similar disclosures if predictions are made. The disclosures that are required during the interview are:

- If the firm owns 1 percent or more of the subject security.
- If the analyst or a member of the analyst's household owns the security, has an interest in the issuer, or is an officer, director, or adviser to the issuer.
- If the issuer of the subject security is an investment banking client.
- Any material conflict of interest known by the firm.

A public appearance by an analyst is defined as any appearance where there are 15 or more attendees in person in a seminar, on a conference call, or through a webinar. A public appearance would also be defined as any event or call attended by one or more members of the media. Firms must maintain guidelines for disclosing all of the potential conflicts of interest by an analyst as part of the written supervisory procedures. Firms issuing research reports may not submit research reports to subject companies, and subject companies may not be informed of a ratings change until the end of the trading day one day prior to the public announcement. The only exception is for factual clarification. If the analyst requires a clarification from the subject company, only the part dealing with the facts in question may be sent to the subject company, with the approval of the legal or compliance department. In addition to preparing its own research, broker dealers may also use third-party and independent third-party research prepared by others. Third-party research is prepared by an affiliated party, and the broker dealer has control over the content of the report. The broker dealer is required to approve the research prior to its distribution. Independent third-party research is prepared by an unaffiliated party, and the broker dealer has no control over the content of the report. As a result, the broker dealer is not required to approve the content of the report. Regulation AC requires an analyst to certify each and every report issued by the analyst. This certification states that the opinion expressed in the research report is based on the analyst's own personal beliefs. Additionally, within 30 days of the end of every quarter, the analyst must recertify that each research report issued during the quarter reflects the analyst's personal beliefs. If the analyst fails to recertify all reports at the end of the quarter, each research report for the next 120 days issued by the analyst must be marked as uncertified. If a broker dealer terminates research coverage for a security it must publish a final research report containing the same scope of coverage as customarily published, unless doing so would be impractical. If for any reason a final report is not going to be published the broker dealer must state the reason for the termination of coverage. It is important to note that the termination or research coverage has no impact on the firm's ability to make a market in the security.

While it should go without saying, it is important to note for the test, that FINRA has an anti-retaliation rule that prohibits any person from retaliating or threatening an analyst who issues a negative report on an issuer. This includes making threats against an analyst who makes negative comments during a public appearance. The broker dealer must include safeguards against potential retaliation by investment bankers and other professionals in its written supervisory procedures.

RULE 137 NONPARTICIPANTS

Firms that are not participating in a distribution of securities may issue recommendations, information, or opinions relating to the securities that are in registration, if the issuer is a reporting company, as required by the Securities and Exchange Act of 1934. So long as the broker dealer did not receive compensation for issuing the report from the issuer, a selling shareholder, or a participant in the distribution, it will not constitute an offer of the securities.

RULE 138 NONEQUIVALENT SECURITIES

If a registration statement has been filed for a nonconvertible bond or a nonconvertible preferred stock, a broker dealer, who is a participant in a distribution of the securities, may in the normal course of business issue recommendations, information, or opinions relating to the issuer's common stock or convertible securities. If the registration statement covers common stock or a convertible security of the issuer, a broker dealer may only issue recommendations, information, or opinions relating to the issuer's nonconvertible debt or preferred stock.

RULE 139 ISSUING RESEARCH REPORTS

A broker dealer who is participating in a distribution of an additional issue may continue to issue research reports relating to the issuer if the issuer is a large reporting company under the Securities and Exchange Act of 1934 and:

The company is followed by analysts.

The information, opinion, or recommendation appears in a regularly published report.

Information, opinions, or recommendations that are at least as favorable as the current report must have been contained in the previous report.

The company that is subject to the offering is not highlighted or featured more prominently than other companies in the report.

If the broker dealer is not currently covering the company, the report is not considered to be issued with sufficient regularity. Any projections relating to the company's earnings may not extend past the current fiscal year. Broker dealers may issue reports for smaller issuers if the report contains information relating to a substantial number of issuers in the same industry as the issuer, or a list of securities currently recommended by the broker dealer, so long as the information relating to the registrant is not displayed more prominently than other information in the same report.

If the conditions for continuing to publish research reports are not met, managers, co-managers, and syndicate members participating in the underwriting of IPOs may not issue research reports relating to the IPO until 10 days have passed from the offering's effective date. The quiet period for managers and co-managers is reduced for secondary and follow-on offerings to 3 days from the effective date. Syndicate and selling group members have no quiet period for follow-on offerings. It is important to note that these rules are not in effect for the underwriting of debt securities. If the company is classified as an emerging growth company with annual revenue of less than $1.07 billion research reports may be distributed any time after the IPO. Additionally, the standard prohibition against a research analyst attending a pitch meeting to win the underwriting business is waived in the case of an emerging growth company so long as their involvement is limited to winning the underwriting or investment banking deal. One additional exception to the quiet period occurs in the event of a material development at the company. Should a material change take place (requiring the filing of an 8K) such as the approval of a new drug, research reports may be published and analyst appearances may take place with the approval of the firm's legal or compliance department.

RULE 415 SHELF REGISTRATION

Rule 415 allows an issuer to register securities that may be sold for its own benefit, for the benefit of a subsidiary, or in connection with business plans in an amount that may be reasonably sold by the issuer within a two-year period. The two-year window starts from the registration date and allows the issuer and the underwriters flexibility in the timing of the offering. Issuers who qualify as well-known seasoned issuers (WKSI, as defined on page 85) and who qualify for automatic registration may sell securities for up to three years. Rule 415 also allows the issuer to register to sell securities on a continuous basis in connection with an employee benefit plan or upon the conversion of other securities.

TAKE **NOTE!**

An issuer who loses its status as a well-known seasoned issuer may continue to sell the securities under Rule 415 until it files its next 10K.

SECURITIES OFFERING REFORM RULES

The SEC has adopted the securities offering reform rules, which are designed to modify and streamline the filing and communication requirements of issuers under the Securities Act of 1933. The rules focus on the following areas:

- The communications related to registered securities offerings.
- Registration and other procedures in the offering and capital-formation processes.
- The delivery of information to investors, including the timeliness of that delivery.

The rules adopted have placed an increased importance on the value of electronic communications and filing and have helped eliminate cumbersome and outdated filing requirements.

SEC RULE 405

SEC Rule 405 defines certain classes of issuers who may be entitled to use a streamlined registration process depending on how the issuer is classified.

Well-known seasoned issuers and seasoned issuers may take advantage of automatically effective shelf registration of securities by filing Form S-3 or F-3 in the case of a foriegn issuer . The registration of the securities covered under the filing of Form S-3 or F-3 is effective immediately upon filing.

WELL-KNOWN SEASONED ISSUER (WKSI)

An issuer that within 60 days of its eligibility determination has at least $700 million worth of voting and nonvoting common equity held by nonaffiliates or that has issued within the last three years at least $1 billion in nonconvertible securities for cash (excluding common equity). A WKSI also includes a company that is a majority-owned subsidiary of a WKSI. If during the course of an offering the WKSI sees the value of its securities fall below the required levels to be considered a WKSI, the issuer may continue to sell the securities until it files its next 10-K.

SEASONED ISSUER (PRIMARY S-3 ELIGIBLE)

An issuer that has a public float of $75 million and has been a reporting issuer under The Securities Exchange Act of 1934 for 12 months meets the requirements of Form S-3 to register a primary offering of securities.

UNSEASONED REPORTING ISSUER (NOT PRIMARY S-3 ELIGIBLE)

An issuer that is required to report under the Exchange Act but that does not qualify with the requirements of Form S-3 or F-3 to file a primary offering of securities.

INELIGIBLE ISSUER

A reporting issuer that is not current with the filing of reports required under the Securities Exchange Act. Ineligible issuers also include:

- Companies who have filed for bankruptcy within the last three years.
- Blank check companies.
- Shell companies.
- Issuers of penny stock.
- Issuers that are limited partnerships that don't have a firm commitment underwriting agreement to sell securities.

- Issuers that have been subject to a stop order or have been convicted of a felony or misdemeanor under the Exchange Act directly or indirectly through a subsidiary within the last three years.

In addition to the standard registration form S-1 discussed at the beginning of this chapter and the streamlined registration forms listed above, you may see the following forms on your exam:

- Form S-4 - Is used to register securities being issued as a s result of a business transaction such as a merger, acquisition, consolidation, asset transfers or in cases of reclassification of securities
- Form S-8 - Is used to register shares of securities being issued as part of an employee benefit plan
- Form S-11 - Is used to register securities being issued as part of an offer for a real estate investment trust (REIT)

ADDITIONAL COMMUNICATION RULES

An issuer who is a reporting company may continue to release regular business communications with forward-looking statements prior to the effective date of an additional offering of securities. A forward-looking statement is one that contains information about what may possibly happen in the future, such as projected sales or new products. If the securities being offered are the subject of an IPO for a non-reporting issuer, only standard factual business communications may be released by the company. Standard factual information contains information relating to products or services and is not intended to be used by potential investors to make an investment decision. These two safe harbors allow the companies to continue to communicate without violating the gun jumping provisions of the communications rules. The gun jumping rules are designed to limit communications during the time an issue is in registration and to prevent companies from trying to create more favorable market conditions for the securities than otherwise would exist. If the company is a reporting company under the Securities Exchange Act of 1934, the issuer may use forward looking statements in both their prospectus and annual reports provided that the statements are clearly identified as forward looking. Key words such as expect, predict, potential, and anticipate are all used to inform the reader that the statements are not facts but projections based on management's beliefs. If the company uses a third party to review the projections it must disclose the nature of any relationship, the qualifications of the reviewer, and the extent of the review. The company is under no obligation to have the projections reviewed.

Road shows are designed to help the company communicate the details of the offering to broker dealers and representatives. Road shows have been traditionally held at large hotels in financial centers across the country. More and more these road shows are being conducted over the Internet via webinars and are known as electronic road shows. These road shows may be broadcast live and recorded for playback and may be available on demand. If the recorded roadshow is for an IPO of equity securities, the recorded road show must be filed with the SEC unless at least one version is made available to the public in addition to the financial community. Recorded road shows for additional issues do not have to be filed with the SEC.

Certain conference calls and meetings attended by research analysts can be a cause for concern when an analyst is speaking with customers or potential customers regarding an M-A transaction or investment banking deal. Specifically prohibited are three-way communication involving the analyst, customers and any representative of investment banking, or the issuer. Analysts who attend in-person meetings should ensure that they do not speak to customers or potential customers in the presence of investment-banking agents or individuals representing an issuer. It's important to note that a research analyst may attend a meeting with an issuer who is an investment banking client to discuss the prospects of a merger or acquisition involving the issuer. However, the transaction must have been reported to the media and no members of investment-banking may attend.

Another circumstance that is often cause for concern is a joint due diligence meeting between the company, a research analyst and investment banking professionals. These joint due diligence meetings are prohibited prior to the issuer's selection of an underwriter. FINRA does not want investment banking professionals pressuring research analysts to issue favorable research regarding the company in an effort to be awarded the underwriting deal. Once the underwriting agreement is signed or underwriters have been selected, the joint due diligence meetings may take place.

DPP ROLL-UP TRANSACTIONS

From time to time one or more limited partnerships may wish to combine their operations and assets to achieve better returns and economies of scale. By combing the partnerships investors may be able to achieve better returns and realize greater liquidity for their partnership interests. Member firms who solicit votes from investors may receive a fee for their services so long as the fee is payable in equal installments regardless of the outcome, and the fee to be received does not exceed 2 percent of the value of the securities to be received upon exchange of the interests. Investors must receive full disclosure of all the related risk factors and be provided with a statement from the general partner as to its opinion regarding the fairness of the transaction. If an investment bank or investment adviser has issued a negative opinion regarding the transaction it must be disclosed to the investors. Failure to disclose a negative option in connection with a roll-up transaction constitutes fraud.

NASDAQ LISTING STANDARDS

Prior to having its stock trade in either the Nasdaq Global Select Market, Global Market or Capital Market, an issuer must meet certain standards. Issuers must apply and be accepted to have its stock trade in either marketplace. Issuers that want to have their stock trade in the Global Market must have a bid price of at least $5, meet stringent financial requirements, and be an issue with national interest. Issuers that cannot meet the financial requirements to trade in the Global Market may elect to have their stock trade in the Capital Market. In addition to having to meet lower financial requirements, the price of the security is only required to be $4. Prior to being accepted to trade in either market, an issuer is required to meet FINRA corporate governance standards and meet the following requirements:

- Maintain an audit committee with mostly independent directors.
- Solicit proxies.
- Provide annual and quarterly reports.
- Maintain at least two independent directors.

An issuer that has been informed by Nasdaq that it is in violation of Nasdaq listing standards will be given 30 days to correct any problems or face suspension. Note that if an issuer is suspended from trading in either market for failing to meet the continued listing standards and wants to resume trading in that market, the issuer must reapply and meet the initial listing standards

LISTING REQUIREMENTS FOR THE NYSE

Only corporations that meet the strict listing requirements may have their stock traded on the NYSE. In order to become listed, a company must have all of the following:

- At least 400 shareholders owning at least 100 shares.
- At least 1,100,000 publicly held shares with a market value of at least $100 million or $40 million for IPOs or spin-off companies.
- A bid price of at least $4 per share.

Companies must also meet at least one of the following:

- Total pretax earnings of at least $12 million over the last three years, with at least $5 million in the most recent year.
- Total pretax earnings of $10 million over the last three years with at least $2 million in each of the last two years
- Average global market capitalization of $500 million with revenues of at least $100 million for the latest fiscal year.

If the issuer ever wants to have its stock delisted from the NYSE, the following conditions must be met:

- The board of directors must approve the action.
- The 35 largest shareholders must be notified.
- The board's audit committee must approve the action.

MARKET MAKING DURING SYNDICATION

The SEC has set strict guidelines regarding the activity of market participants and other interested parties during syndication. Regulation M sets guidelines for:

- Syndicate members
- Issuers
- Passive market makers
- Stabilization of the issue
- Short sales prior to the issue's effective period

REGULATION M, RULE 101

Rule 101 regulates the activities of distribution participants, including syndicate members, selling group members, and other interested broker dealers. The focus of Rule 101 is to keep distribution participants from manipulating the secondary market for an issue during the distribution of a registered secondary or subsequent primary offering of shares. Rule 101 sets a restricted period that prohibits the participants from bidding for or buying the subject security for the period just prior to the effective date. The length of the restricted period depends on the level of trading activity in the security and the value of the public float. The lower the trading volume and value of the public float, the greater the ability of an interested party to manipulate the price of the security. The restricted period will begin as listed below or when the broker dealer becomes a participant, whichever occurs later.

Average Daily Trading Volume	Value of Public Float	Restricted Period
Less than $100,000	Less than $25 million	Five days prior to effective date
$100,000 or greater	At least $25 million	One day prior to effective date
$1,000,000 or greater	At least $150 million	No restricted period

The following are exceptions to Rule 101:

- Government and municipal securities.
- Nonconvertible investment grade bonds and preferred stock.
- Investment company securities.
- Unsolicited customer orders may be executed on an agency or principal basis.
- Odd lot orders.
- Exercising of options, rights, or warrants.

PENALTY BIDS

A syndicate manager may enter a penalty bid that will require the syndicate member, who sells securities back to the syndicate, to return the selling concession it originally received for selling the shares. A penalty bid will have the identifier PBID next to the market maker's Nasdaq symbol.

REGULATION M, RULE 102

Rule 102 regulates the activities of issuers during the restricted period. Issuers and selling shareholders may not bid for or purchase a covered security or encourage others to do so during the restricted period. An issuer during the restricted period also may not:

- Bid for or purchase actively traded securities of the issuer or an affiliate.
- Execute inadvertent orders or small orders known as de minimis orders.
- Participate in basket transactions that include the covered security.
- The following are exempt from Rule 102:
- 144a transactions
- Conversion of convertible bonds or preferred shares
- Odd lot orders
- Unsolicited purchases
- Transactions in exempt securities

REGULATION M, RULE 103

Rule 103 regulates the activity of market makers participating in a distribution. Market makers that are participating in a distribution may only act as passive market makers during the restricted period. Passive market makers may not enter a bid or buy the security at a price that exceeds the highest bid entered by an independent party. If the highest independent bid entered by a nonparticipant drops below the bid of the passive market maker, the passive market maker may remain as the highest bid until it purchases an amount equal to its volume restriction. The volume restriction in this case would be the lesser of two times the passive market maker's displayed size or the balance of its daily purchase limit. If there are no independent market makers, passive market making will not be allowed. The syndicate manager must apply for passive market making status on behalf of all syndicate members by filing part of the Underwriting Activity Form no later than one business day prior to the first full trading day of the restricted period. All participants who act as a passive market maker during the offering will have the identifier PSSM next to the market maker's Nasdaq symbol. A passive market maker is still required to display customer limit orders even if the displayed order would cause the firm to increase its bid above the highest independent bid. Passive market making may only take place for firm commitment underwritings.

PASSIVE MARKET MAKERS' DAILY PURCHASE LIMIT

A passive market maker's daily purchase limit is the greater of 30 percent of its ADTV or 200 shares. The number of shares in a passive market maker's displayed bid cannot exceed the size of its daily purchase limit. If a passive market maker exceeds this limit, it must withdraw from the market for the rest of the day. Only a passive market maker's net purchases count toward its daily purchase limit. A sell order, reported within 30 seconds of a purchase, will reduce the passive market maker's net purchase.

> TAKE **NOTE!**
>
> A market maker that is approaching its daily purchase limit may execute any single order, even if executing the order would cause the market maker to exceed its daily purchase limit.

REGULATION M, RULE 104

Rule 104 allows for the stabilization of a new issue in the secondary market provided that the issue is not being distributed at the market offering. In order to provide for an orderly distribution, and to ensure that the shares do not fall dramatically in the secondary market as a result of the increased supply, a syndicate may enter a stabilizing bid. A stabilizing bid may be entered at or below the issue's offering price. At no time may a syndicate member enter a stabilizing bid at a price that exceeds the issue's offering price. However, a stabilizing bid may have a lower price limit if the stabilizing bid is entered when the principal market for the security is open, and:

- The security traded in the principal market on the day preceding the initiation of stabilization or on the day stabilization began.
- The security is offered at a price that is greater than or equal to the last independent trade in the principal marketplace.

If the above conditions are met, then the stabilizing bid may be no higher than the last independent trade in the principal market. If the above conditions are not met, then the stabilizing bid may not be higher than the highest independent bid in the principal market. If a syndicate member is going to enter an initial stabilizing bid when the principal market is closed, then the stabilizing bid will be limited to the lower of the following:

- The price at which a stabilizing bid may have been entered in the primary market based on the closing price in the primary market.

  or

- The last independent bid or transaction in the marketplace where the issue will be stabilized.

Syndicates must notify the market in which it intends to stabilize the issue. Stabilization is the only form of security price manipulation allowed by the SEC. There is no time limit as to how long an issue may be stabilized; however, all syndicate accounts must be settled 90 days from the day the issuer delivers the securities to the syndicate. The following conditions apply to stabilizing bids entered on behalf of a syndicate:

- Only one stabilizing bid may be entered.
- The stabilizing bid will be a one-sided quote with no offer.
- The identifier SYND will identify the bid as a stabilizing bid.
- The market maker entering the stabilizing bid must confirm the request to stabilize the issue by filing an Underwriting Activity Report (UAR) no later than the end of the first day it entered the stabilizing bid.
- The UAR must include the identity of the security, the estimated effective date and pricing date, a copy of the cover page of the preliminary or final prospectus, and the date when the SYND identifier should appear next to the market maker's ID.
- Only issues sold through a fixed price offering on a firm commitment basis may be stabilized. Best efforts and at the market offerings may not be stabilized.

REGULATION M, RULE 105

Rule 105 restricts the purchase of subject securities to cover short positions. Rule 105 states that securities purchased through an offering may not be used to cover short positions established during the restricted period. The restricted period for selling securities short begins five days prior to pricing the issue. If the issue is priced within five days of the filing of the registration, then the restricted period under Rule 105 begins with the filing date. Offerings not done on a firm commitment basis as well as shelf registrations are exempt.

CHAPTER 5

Pretest

ISSUING CORPORATE SECURITIES

1. A syndicate has published a tombstone ad prior to the issue becoming effective. Which of the following must appear in the tombstone?
    I. A statement that the registration has not yet become effective
    II. A statement that the ad is not an offer to sell the securities
    III. Contact information
    IV. No commitment statement
        I. III and IV
        b. II and III
        c. I and II
        d. I, II, III, and IV

2. During a new issue registration, false information is included in the prospectus to buyers. Which of the following may be held liable to investors?
    I. Officers of the issuer
    II. Accountants
    III. Syndicate members
    IV. People who signed the registration statement
        a. I and III
        b. I, II, III, and IV
        c. I, II, and III
        d. I, II, III, and IV

3. A syndicate may enter a stabilizing bid:
   A. whenever the price begins to decline.
   B. at or below the offering price.
   C. to ensure an increase from the offering price.
   D. to cover overallotments only.

4. KNFL Has entered into a definitive agreement with SIA, to acquire SIA in an all stock deal, valuing SIA at $62 per share. In order to complete the transaction, KNFL will have to issue 25 million shares of common stock. Which of the following is correct?
   A. KNFL will issue the shares as part of an immediately effective shelf registration.
   B. KNFL will issue the share pursuant to Regulation 506 D to exchange shares directly with the shareholders of SIA.
   C. KNFL will issue and register the shares by furling form S-4 with the SEC.
   D. KNFL will issue and register the share by filing form S-8 with the SEC.

5. A corporation in your state wants to sell 1,000,000 shares of stock at $5 per share to investors. Which of the following is NOT a business requirement under Rule 147?
   A. 80 percent of corporate assets must be located in the state.
   B. 80 percent of proceeds must be used in the state.
   C. 80 percent of the income must be derived from activity within the state.
   D. 80 percent of the purchasers must be in the state.

6. A new research analyst has just joined a well regarded investment firm. As part of the onboarding process, the analyst is required to familiarize himself with the rules and regulations regarding making public appearances. Which of the following would meet the definition of a public appearance?
   A. The analyst attends a video conference call with analysts from two different firms and the president of a covered company.
   B. The analyst attends a meeting in a hotel conference room with 10 investors to discuss the impact of recent economic events
   C. The analyst joins a conference call with 5 members of the investing public and a reporter from a small local newspaper.
   D. The analyst observes a presentation made by another member of his firm's research department attended by 12 high net worth clients.

7. Which of the following is NOT a type of offering?
   A. Rule 149 offering
   B. Subsequent primary offering
   C. Secondary offering
   D. Combined offering

8. Once a company decides to raise long-term capital to meet its needs, it will do which of the following?
   A. Approach the money market to determine how much capital can be raised.
   B. Hire an underwriter to advise the issuer about the type of securities to issue.
   C. Hire a dealer to issue stock for public purchase.
   D. Hire a broker to issue stock for public purchase.

9. A firm participating in the offering of a private placement may sell the private placement to how many nonaccredited investors in any 12 month period?.
   A. 12
   B. 6
   C. 35
   D. 15

10. A company doing a preemptive rights offering would most likely use what type of underwriting agreement?
    A. Best efforts
    B. Firm commitment
    C. All or none
    D. Standby

CHAPTER 6

Financial Analysis

> **INTRODUCTION**
>
> One of the critical functions that must be performed by investment bankers is financial analysis. Financial analysis is concerned with the financial performance of the company. Prospective investment bankers will see a substantial number of questions on the exam requiring a mastery of corporate financial statements and how to extract information from these reports. Valuation analysis is used to examine the price the market is paying for the financial performance of the company. Or, in the case of an acquisition, the price that must be paid to acquire that financial performance.

Financial analysts examine the company's financial statements and financial ratios to ascertain the company's overall financial performance. The analyst will use the following to determine a value for the company's stock:

- Balance sheet
- Income statement
- Footnotes to financial statements
- Cash flow statement
- Financial ratios
- Liquidity ratios
- Valuation ratios

GAAP ACCOUNTING AND REPORTING

Generally Accepted Accounting Principles (GAAP) set standards for the classification and reporting of financial transactions. These standards set guidelines for how companies treat assets and include transactions on financial reports. All publicly traded companies are required to follow GAAP when reporting results to investors. By applying GAAP standards, investors have confidence that accountants and auditors have created an accurate and impartial report that is free from speculation. Additionally, investors have confidence that the classification of transactions will be applied consistently across all required reports and over all reporting periods. This will allow investors to easily compare the financial performance of the company over time. There are a number of GAAP principles applied by accountants and auditors. Four of these are objectivity, consistency, materiality and prudence. The Financial Accounting Standards Board (FASB) is an independent, not-for-profit organization, that establishes financial accounting and reporting standards for public and private companies that follow Generally Accepted Accounting Principles. The standards set by the FASB are recognized by the SEC as the proper method for financial reporting. GAAP requires public companies to report on their financial condition, profit-making operations and cash flow. In order to comply with this requirement companies must prepare a balance sheet, income statement, stockholders equity statement and a statement of cash flows.

THE BALANCE SHEET

The balance sheet also known as the statement of financial condition will show an investor everything that the corporation owns (assets) and everything that the corporation owes (liabilities) at the time the balance sheet was prepared. A balance sheet is a snapshot of the company's financial health on the day it was created. The difference between the company's assets and its liabilities is the corporation's net worth. The corporation's net worth is the shareholders' equity. Remember that the shareholders own the corporation. As the relation of the assets and liabilities change, stockholders equity changes. If assets increase while its liabilities remain constant, stockholders equity will increase. Alternatively, if a corporation's liabilities increase, while assets remain constant, stockholders equity will decrease. The basic balance sheet equation is:

Assets – liabilities = net worth

The balance sheet equation may also be presented as follows:

Assets = liabilities + shareholder's equity

The two columns on the balance sheet contain the company's assets on the left and its liabilities and shareholder's equity on the right. The total dollar amount of both sides must be equal or must balance. The entries on a balance sheet look as follows:

Assets	Liabilities
Current assets	Current liabilities
Fixed assets	Long-term liabilities
Other assets	Equity/net worth
	Preferred stock par value
	Common stock par value
	Additional paid in surplus
	Treasury stock
	Retained earnings

The assets are listed in order of liquidity. Current assets include cash and assets that can be converted into cash within 12 months. Current assets include:

- Money market instruments
- Marketable securities
- Accounts receivable net of any delinquent accounts
- Inventory including work in progress
- Prepaid expenses

Fixed assets are assets that have a long useful life and are used by the company in the operation of its business. Fixed assets include:

- Plant and equipment
- Property and real estate

Other assets are intangible / non-physical assets that belong to the company. Other assets include:

- Goodwill
- Trademarks
- Patents
- Contract rights

Intangible assets generally have significant value to the corporation, but are difficult to place a hard value on by outside companies. Corporations who acquire other companies at a price that exceeds the value of their assets will add the premium to the goodwill carried on its balance sheet. Companies who grow through inorganic (acquisition) strategies tend to have a large amount of goodwill on the balance sheet.

The liabilities of the corporation are listed in the order in which they become due. Current liabilities are obligations that must be paid within 12 months. Current liabilities include:

- Wages payable, including salaries and commissions owed to employees
- Accounts payable to vendors and suppliers
- Current portion of long-term debt; that is, any portion of the company's long-term debt due within 12 months
- Taxes due within 12 months
- Short-term notes due within 12 months

Long-term liabilities are debts that will become due after 12 months. Long-term liabilities include:

- Bonds
- Mortgages
- Notes

TAKE NOTE!

The corporation's debt, which comes due in five years or more, is known as funded debt.

Stockholders' equity is the net worth of the company. Stockholders' equity is broken up into the following categories:

- Capital stock at par: the aggregate par for both common and preferred stock
- Additional paid in surplus: sometimes known as capital in excess of par is any sum paid over par by investors when the shares were issued by the company
- Retained earnings: profits that have been kept by the corporation, sometimes known as earned surplus
- Treasury stock is carried at its cost in the stockholders equity section of the balance sheet. The value of the treasury stock reduces stockholders equity.

EXAMPLE

SIA has just gone public by issuing 100 million shares at $25. The common stock has a par value of $1. The CFO of SIA must now properly credit the cash proceeds to the current assets of the company in the form of cash. Excluding underwriters fees $2.5 billion will be credited to the cash account. The balance sheet must have a corresponding entry on the liability account. In our example the CFO will credit $100 million to the par value of common stock and $2.4 billion to capital in excess of par. These liabilities will be credited to the stockholders equity account as part of the liabilities section of the balance sheet. Of course the underwriters will be paid a fee for marketing the shares. The underwriter fees would reduce the amount of the proceeds credited to the cash account, but would not impact the entries to the stockholders equity account on the balance sheet.

	Balance Sheet ABC MILLS, Inc. As of December 31	
Assets		
Current Assets	Cash and Equivalents	$6,000,000
	Accounts Receivable	$12,000,000
	Inventory	$20,000,000
	Prepaid Expenses	$500,000
	Total Current Assets	**$38,500,000**
Fixed Assets	Buildings, Furniture & Fixtures	$50,000,000
	(Including $5,000,000 Depreciation)	
	Land	$20,000,000
	Total Fixed Assets	**$70,000,000**
Other Assets (Goodwill, Intangibles)		$2,000,000
Total Assets		**$110,500,000**
Liabilities and Net Worth		
Current Liabilities	Accounts Payable	$3,000,000
	Accrued Wages Payable Current	$1,500,000
	Portion of Long-Term Debt	$1,500,000
	Total Current Liabilities	**$6,000,000**
Long-Term Liabilities	7% 30-Year Convertible Debentures	$40,000,000
Total Liabilities		**$46,000,000**
Net Worth	**Preferred Stock $100 Par 7%**	**$25,000,000**
	Convertible noncumulative	
	250,000 shares issued	
	Common Stock $1 par 2,000,000	$2,000,000
	Shares Issued	
	Capital Paid in Excess of Par	$22,000,000
	Retained Earnings	$15,500,000
Total Net Worth		**$64,500,000**
Total Liabilities and Net Worth		**$110,500,000**

CAPITALIZATION

The term capitalization refers to the sources and makeup of the company's financial picture. The following are used to determine the company's capitalization:

- Long-term debt
- Equity accounts, including par value of common and preferred and paid in and earned surplus

A company that borrows a large portion of its capital though the issuance of bonds is said to be highly leveraged. Highly leveraged companies are at a greater risk of bankruptcy than less leveraged companies. Raising money through the sale of common stock is considered to be a more conservative method for a corporation to raise money because it does not require the corporation to pay the money back. When a company borrows funds, it is trying to use that borrowed capital to increase its return on equity. Many companies issue commercial paper to fund short term cash needs (270 days or less). The value of the commercial paper is not included in the capital structure of the company.

CHANGES IN THE BALANCE SHEET

As a business conducts its operations, its daily transactions will affect the balance sheet. Every transaction requires an offsetting transaction to the appropriate account. This is known as double-entry bookkeeping. For example, if ABC Mills wrote a check to a large vendor for $1,000,000, the company's cash would be reduced by $1,000,000 and the company's accounts payable would be reduced by $1,000,000. Transactions that affect the balance sheet include:

- Purchasing equipment for cash
- Depreciation
- Issuing securities
- Declaring a dividend
- Paying a dividend
- Conversion of convertible securities
- Bond redemption
- Stock splits

Purchasing Equipment for Cash: If the company purchases a piece of industrial equipment for cash, its long-term assets will increase and its cash and current assets will be decreased by the amount of the purchase.

Depreciation: This allows companies to amortize the cost of capital goods over their estimated useful life. As fixed assets wear out, their value declines. Companies may reduce the value of their assets through depreciation and may use the amount of the depreciation to offset taxes owed. Depreciation is a noncash charge that lowers a company's earnings and tax liability. Depending on the type of asset involved, depreciation may be taken as either straight line depreciation or as accelerated depreciation. Straight line depreciation is taken in equal amounts over the estimated useful life of the asset. A piece of heavy equipment costing $10,000,000 with a useful life of 10 years would be depreciated at $1,000,000 per year for 10 years. The value of the asset would be reduced by $1,000,000 per year on the balance sheet and that same $1,000,000 would be carried over to the income statement and used to reduce the company's earnings. Accelerated depreciation depreciates most of the value of the asset in the first few years of useful life and by lesser amounts during the remaining years. Depreciation impacts both the income statement and balance sheet of a corporation. A company's taxable income is reduced by the amount of the depreciation taken in the current period and accumulated depreciation reduces the value of the asset on the company's balance sheet.

Issuing Securities: If the company were to issue additional shares of $1 par common stock, the net worth of the company would increase by the amount of the par value sold, plus any paid in surplus. As a result of the issuance of the securities, the corporation's cash position would also be increased by the net proceeds of the offering.

Declaring /Paying a Dividend: When a cash dividend is declared, the corporation's retained earnings are reduced by the amount of the dividend and the company's current liabilities are increased by the amount of the dividend payable. Once the dividend is paid, the company's cash and current assets are reduced by the amount of the dividend paid. The payment of the dividend also eliminates the current liability that resulted from the declaration of the dividend.

Conversion of Convertible Securities: If the holder of a convertible bond converts the bonds into common stock, the par value of the bonds will be eliminated as a long-term liability and the par value will be credited to the equity account on the balance sheet.

Bond Redemption: Bonds are redeemed at maturity. If the corporation uses cash to pay off the principal amount of the bonds, the long-term liabilities and the cash and current assets of the corporation will be reduced by an equal amount.

Stock Splits: A forward stock split will increase the number of shares outstanding and reduce the par value of the shares. A reverse stock split will reduce the number of outstanding shares and increase the par value. Shareholders' equity is not affected as a result of a stock split.

An analyst may look at the balance sheet to determine the following financial information:

- Net worth
- Working capital
- Current ratio
- Quick assets
- Acid test ratio/quick ratio
- Cash assets ratio
- Debt-to-equity ratio
- Common stock ratio
- Preferred stock ratio
- Bond ratio

The following table details financial valuation ratios and formulas used by analysts and their purpose.

Measure	Formula	Purpose
Book value per share	Assets – liabilities – par value of preferred/no. of outstanding common shares	To determine the book value of the company's common stock
Tangible book value per share	Assets – liabilities – intangible assets – par value of preferred/no. of outstanding common shares	To determine the tangible book value of the company's common stock
Working capital	Current assets – current liabilities	To determine the company's liquidity
Current ratio	Current assets/current liabilities	A relationship between current assets and liabilities
Quick assets	Current assets – inventory	To determine highly liquid assets
Acid test/quick ratio	Quick assets/current liabilities	To determine the company's liquidity
Cash assets ratio	Cash & equivalents/current liabilities	The most stringent liquidity measure
Debt-to-equity ratio	Total long-term debt/total shareholders' equity	To examine the company's capital structure
Common stock ratio	Common shareholders' equity/total capitalization	To examine the company's capital structure
Preferred stock ratio	Preferred stock/total capitalization	To examine the company's capital structure
Bond ratio	Total long-term debt/total capitalization	To examine the company's capital structure
Interest Coverage Ratio	EBITDA/interest expense	To evaluate the company's ability to service its debt

THE INCOME STATEMENT

The income statement also known as the profit and loss statement details a corporation's revenue and expenses for the period for which it was produced. Income statements are usually prepared on a quarterly and annual basis. An analyst will use the income statement to determine a corporation's profitability. The three levels of earnings listed on the income statement are:

1. Operating income
2. Net income after taxes
3. Earnings available to common

Operating Income: Is the business profit or loss from operations and is also known as earnings before interest and taxes (EBIT). This details the business performance of the company and excludes one time items and other income and expenses

EBITDA: Earnings before interest taxes depreciation and amortization adds back accounting deductions taken for the depreciation and amortization of assets. EBITDA is a useful tool to measure the overall profitability of a company and an effective way to compare the performance of two companies. However, EBITDA does not measure a company's ability to generate cash nor a measure of cash flow. EBIT is lower than EBITDA

EBITDAR: Certain industries that require substantial leases to operate such as retail and restaurants may use EBITDAR as a way to measure performance. Earnings before interest taxes depreciation amortization and rent / EBITDAR adds back the rent paid by the company to EBITDA.

Net Income After Taxes: Is the corporation's earnings after all interest, federal and state taxes have been paid. Dividends to preferred shareholders will be paid from net income after taxes.

Earnings Available to Common: Is what is left from the corporation's net income after interest, taxes and after the corporation has paid preferred dividends. If the corporation wants to pay a dividend to common shareholders, the preferred dividends must have already been paid.

Funds From Operations (FFO): FFO is calculated by adding back depreciation to net income and adjusting for the impact of asset sales. FFO subtracts any gains from the sale of assets and adds back any losses on the sale of assets. Real estate investment trusts often use FFO as a performance measure

Net Operating Loss (NOL): If at the end of the fiscal year a C corporation suffers a net operating loss, that loss can be carried forward to reduce taxable income in future years. Currently corporations can carry the loss forward using it to reduce 80% of taxable income. Any remaining amount can be carried forward and used to reduce taxable income in future years.

Income Statement ABC Mills, Inc. January 1–December 31		
Net sales		$100,000,000
Expenses	Cost of goods sold	($45,000,000)
	General operating expenses (including $5,000,000 depreciation)	($32,000,000)
	Total	($77,000,000)
Operating income		$23,000,000
	Interest expense	($2,800,000)
Pretax income		$20,200,000
	Taxes at 36%	($7,272,000)
Net income after taxes		$12,928,000
	Preferred dividends	($1,750,000)
Earnings available to common		$11,178,000

By combining the information contained in the balance sheet and the income statement, an analyst can determine:

- Earnings per share primary
- Earnings per share fully diluted
- Price earnings ratio
- Dividend payout ratio
- Debt service ratio

Earnings Per Share Primary: Will tell the analyst how much of the company's earnings are credited to each common share.

Earnings Per Share Fully Diluted: Will tell the analyst how much of the company's earnings are credited to each common share after all convertible securities and all rights and warrants have been exchanged for common stock. If a question on your exam provides both primary and fully diluted earnings per share, it is best to use fully diluted earnings to answer the question.

Price Earnings Ratio: Will tell the analyst the relationship between the earnings per share and the common stock price.

Dividend Payout Ratio: Will tell the analyst how much of the earnings per share were paid out to shareholders as dividends.

Debt Service Ratio: Will tell the analyst the ability of the company to meet their debt service obligations.

Measure	Formula	Purpose
Earnings per share primary	Earnings available to common/no. of common shares	To determine the amount of the company's earnings for each share outstanding
Earnings per share fully diluted	Earnings available to common/no. of common shares	To determine the amount of the company's earnings for each share outstanding after all conversions
Price earnings ratio	Stock price/EPS	To determine a relationship between the stock price and the earnings per share
Dividend payout ratio	Annual dividends per common share/EPS	To determine how much of the company's EPS are paid out in dividends
Debt service ratio	EBIT/annual interest and principal payments	To determine the company's ability to meet its debt service needs

 TAKE NOTE!

Most balance sheets and income statements will include footnotes which give additional details regarding the items contained in the reports. These footnotes will detail the impact potential events may have on the financial information contained in the statements as well as any assumptions or calculations used to arrive at the information.

STATEMENT OF CASH FLOWS

The statement of cash flows also known as the statement of sources and use of funds is one of the 3 financial statements required to be prepared by reporting companies and distributed as part of its annual report. The statement of cash flows is used to measure changes in the company's cash position over time. Business operations, investing and financing activities will all impact the company's cash position and will be detailed on the statement of cash flows. The statement of cash flows provides a snapshot of the changes in the company's cash position over a specific period of time. While the statement of cash flows is very useful in determining how well a company manages its cash position, it cannot be used to predict the company's near term liquidity. The company could be holding excess cash to manage seasonality issues in its business or may be planning on using cash to reduce accounts payable. Effectively, the day after the statement of cash flows is created any business activity, investing or financing activity taken the following day would render the numbers obsolete. The statement of cash flows reflects the impact of activities that are sources and uses of cash. A source of cash increases the company's cash position, while a use of cash reduces the cash position. The impact of some of these activities is summarized as follows:

Business Activity	Cash Flow Impact	Cash Balance Impact
Liabilities increase	Source of cash	Cash balance increases
Liabilities decrease	Use of cash	Cash balance decreases
Accounts receivable increase	Use of cash	Cash balance decreases
Accounts receivable decrease	Source of cash	Cash balance increases
Accounts payable increase	Source of cash	Cash balance increases
Accounts payable decrease	Use of cash	Cash balance decreases
Increase in inventory	Use of cash	Cash balance decreases
Decrease in inventory	Source of cash	Cash balance increases
Depreciation added back	Source of cash	Cash balance increases

Investing Activity	Cash Flow Impact	Cash Balance Impact
The sale of an asset	Source of cash	Cash balance increases
The purchase of an asset	Use of cash	Cash balance decreases
Acquisition	Use of cash	Cash balance decreases
Sale of a division	Source of cash	Cash balance increases

Financing Activity	Cash Flow Impact	Cash Balance Impact
Issuing stock	Source of cash	Cash balance increases
Repurchasing stock	Use of cash	Cash balance decreases
Payment of dividends	Use of cash	Cash balance decreases
Issuing debt	Source of cash	Cash balance increases
Retirement of debt	Use of cash	Cash balance decreases

Keeping our company example of ABC Mills consistent, we have created the following hypothetical statement of cash flows. You can see how the depreciation from the balance sheet and the net income and preferred dividends paid have all carried over to impact the statement of cash flows.

Statement of Cash Flows ABC Mills, Inc. January 1–December 31		
Operating Activities		
Net Income		$12,928,000
	Depreciation	$5,000,000
	Reduction in Inventory	$2,000,000
	Increase in receivables	($500,000)
	Decrease in payables	($850,000)
Cash Flow From Operations		**$18,578,000**
Investing Activities		
Sale of mill		$4,800,000
Purchase of Timberland		($9,200,000)
Cash Flow from Investing Activities		**($4,400,000)**
Financing Activities		
Issuance of Bonds		$50,000,000
Stock Repurchase		($15,000,000)
Dividends Paid		($1,750,000)
Cash Flow From Financing Activities		**$33,250,000**

In further examining the statement of cash flows, if we were to assume that the company's cash balance at the beginning of the period was $185,000,000, we can use the statement of cash flows to calculate the cash balance at the end of the period. The cash balance in this case would be calculated as follows:

> Cash balance at the beginning of the period
> + Cash flow from operating activities
> − Negative cash flow from investing activities
> + Cash flow from financing activities

In this case the ending cash balance would be $232,428,000 found as follows:

$$\$185,000,000$$
$$+\$18,578,000$$
$$-\$4,400,000$$
$$+\$33,250,000$$

Cash Balance ABC Mills, Inc. As of December 31			
Beginning Cash Balance			$185,000,000
Net Income			
	Depreciation	$5,000,000	
	Reduction in Inventory	$2,000,000	
	Increase in receivables	($500,000)	
Cash Flow From Operations	Decrease in payables	($850,000)	$18,578,000
Investing Activities			
Sale of mill		$4,800,000	
Purchase of Timberland		($9,200,000)	
Cash Flow from Investing Activities			($4,400,000)
Financing Activities			
Issuance of Bonds	$50,000,000		
Stock Repurchase	($15,000,000)		
Dividends Paid	($1,750,000)		
Cash Flow From Financing Activities			$33,250,000
Ending Cash Balance			$232,428,000

It is interesting to note that if a company owns marketable securities and receives interest or dividends from those securities, the receipt would be classified under operational activities. Additionally, even though the issuance of bonds would be classified under financing activities, a company paying interest to its bondholders would classify that payment under operational activities. The reason for this is because the payment of bond interest is made pre tax from gross revenue. The issuance of equity and the payment of dividends are classified as financing activities on the statement of cash flows. Dividends are always paid after taxes.

THE IMPACT OF CONVERTING BONDS

The conversion of bonds into common stock has a substantial impact on the earnings per share for several reasons. First, when bonds are converted into common stock, the company loses the tax deduction created by paying interest on the bonds. Second, the conversion increases the number of common shares participating in the earnings per share calculation.

To calculate the impact of convertible securities, other potential dilutive securities and and common stock equivalents may have on the company's earnings per share use the following formula:

<u>Earnings available to common shareholders</u>
(Weighted Average number of common shares + Weighted average of common stock equivalents and other dilutive securities)

Let's take a look at an example of how the conversion of bonds would impact the earnings per share. Assume that ABC has issued the following convertible bonds:

Security	Conversion Price	Par value	Additional Shares
6% Convertible Bonds	$50	$100,000,000	2,000,000

Prior to the conversion ABC shows the following:

Common Stock $1 Par	10,000,000 shares outstanding
Taxable income	$50,000,000
Tax Rate	26%
Earnings available to common	$37,000,000
Basic EPS	$3.70 per share

Once the bonds have been converted ABC will now show the following:

Common Stock $1 Par	12,000,000 shares outstanding
Taxable income	$56,000,000
Tax Rate	26%
Earnings available to common	$41,440,000
Diluted EPS	$3.45 per share

Notice that taxable income increased by $6,000,000 as a result of losing the tax deductibility of the interest payment on the bonds. Subsequent primaries also have a substantial impact on the earnings per share calculation and in fact, are often quite dilutive since the company is increasing the number of shares outstanding. Series 79 test takers have reported seeing questions requiring prospective investment bankers to calculate the impact of a subsequent primary on earnings per share. Several of these questions have provided an earnings growth rate which must be taken into consideration. Lets review what would happen if ABC issued stock prior to the bonds being converted:

Common Stock $1 Par	10,000,000 shares outstanding
EBIT	$50,000,000
Tax Rate	26%
Earnings available to common	$37,000,000
Basic EPS	$3.70 per share

ABC is seeking to expand its manufacturing capacity and will be building a new plant. ABC plans to issue 2 million shares of common stock at $40 per share. ABC estimates that the increased capacity will allow it to grow its EBIT by 15 percent. Assuming ABC is correct in its projections, what would the EPS be after the issuance of the shares?

	Old	New
Common Stock $1 Par	10,000,000 shares outstanding	12,000,000 shares outstanding
EBIT	$56,000,000	$64,400,000
Interest Expense	$6,000,000	$6,000,000
Earnings Before Tax	$50,000,000	$58,400,000
Tax Rate	26%	26%
Earnings available to common	$37,000,000	$43,216,000
Basic EPS	$3.70 per share	$3.60 per share

CHAPTER 6 Financial Analysis

It is important to note that the interest payments associated with the 6% bonds ($6,000,000) were added back to determine the EBIT. The EBIT was then multiplied by the anticipated growth rate as follows:

$$\$56,000,000 \times 1.15 = \$64,400,000$$

Even though EBIT grew by 15%, EPS declined by approximately 2.7% as a result of the follow on offering of new common shares. Only shares that are part of a subsequent primary offering will dilute EPS. If a follow on offering is being conducted as a registered secondary, those shares are already outstanding and are being calculated in EPS. Further, if the follow-on offering is a combined offering of new shares being sold by the company and shares being sold by existing stockholders, only the new shares will have a dilutive impact. Lastly, if a company issues new common shares for the exclusive purpose of paying down existing debt, both the interest payments and the tax deductibility of the payments will be eliminated.

REFUNDING DEBT

When a corporation refunds its debt, it issues new bonds to pay off existing bonds. The process is very similar to the way a homeowner may refinance their mortgage. Often companies will seek to refund debt after interest rates have declined and the refinancing activity will result in a lower interest rate. This interest savings will not translate to an increase in net income on a dollar for dollar basis. Bond interest is paid with pre-tax dollars and a reduction in the interest expense will reduce the corresponding interest expense deduction. Lets review an example of how refinancing debt impacts a company's income statement.

Let's assume that a company has $500 million of 8 percent bonds outstanding and refunds the principal amount through the issuance of 6 percent bonds. This same company had net income of $210 million and was in the 26 % tax bracket

Bonds	$500 million @ 8%	$500 million @ 6%
Interest expense	$40 million	$30 million
Net Income	$210 million	$217.4 million

Notice how the net income did not increase by the full $10 million in interest savings. To determine the impact on net income, you must multiple the interest cost savings by the complement of the corporate tax rate. In this case $10 million x (100% - 26%) or $10 million X .74 = $7.4 million .

STOCK SPLITS AND STOCK DIVIDENDS

If a company declares a stock split or a stock dividend it impacts the stockholders equity section of the balance sheet. As we noted earlier in this chapter, the split changes the number of shares issued as well as the par value of the stock. Based on a 2:1 forward stock split consider the following:

Before Stock Split	Value	After 2:1 Stock Split	Value
10,000,000 shares issued with $1 par value	$10,000,000	20,000,000 shares issued with $.50 par value	$10,000,000
Capital paid in Excess of Par IPO @ $20	$190,000,000	Capital paid in Excess of Par IPO @ $20	$190,000,000

Although the par value and the number of shares issued has changed, the ultimate values carried in the stockholders equity section of the balance sheet has not changed. The payment of a stock dividend will impact the balance sheet differently than a stock split. Consider the following information if the same company paid a 10 percent stock dividend when the stock is valued at $40.

Before Stock dividend	Value	After 10% Stock Split	Value
10,000,000 shares issued with $1 par value	$10,000,000	11,000,000 shares issued with $1 par value	$11,000,000
Capital paid in Excess of Par IPO @ $20	$190,000,000	Capital paid in Excess of Par IPO @ $20	$230,000,000

Notice how the par value of the stock increased by $1 million based on the 1 million new shares being issued with a par value of $1. The company now must reduce its retained earnings based on the market value of the shares issued as the result of the stock dividend. In this case the retained earnings will be reduced by $40 million (1 million shares x $40) and paid in capital will be increased by the same $40 million. If a company pays a substantial stock dividend of 25 percent or more, the par value of the stock will be reduced and retained earnings will remain unchanged.

RETAINED EARNINGS

Retained earnings, also known as earned surplus, is the amount of undistributed earnings that a company has generated during profitable years, less losses incurred during unprofitable periods. The key word is "retained" any dividends paid to shareholders will reduce the amount of retained earnings. While most people think of dividends as being paid from the profits earned during the period when the dividends are paid, many companies will continue to pay dividends during unprofitable periods. During these unprofitable periods companies are paying dividends from the undistributed earnings retained from previous profits. On your exam you may see several questions relating to retained earnings and how it is impacted given various business events. You may also be required to calculate a company's projected retained earnings as follows:

SIA Co. produced $50 million in net income in the previous year and is projecting a growth rate for net income of 12%. At the end of the previous year SIA's retained earnings showed a balance of $134 million. In the following year, SIA has committed to paying $12 million in dividends. What is the projected retained earnings balance for SIA Co. at the end of next year?

Step 1- Calculate the net income for the following year as follows:

$50 million X 1.12 = $56 million

Step 2 - Subtract the dividends to be paid in the following year as follows:

$56 million - $12 million = $44 million

Step 3 - Add the current retained earnings to the previous retained earnings balance as follows:

$134 million + $44 million = $178 million

Net Income	$56 million
Dividends paid	$12 million
Retained Earnings Current Period	$44 million
Previous Retained Earnings Balance	$134 millon
Retained Earnings Balance	$168 million

PRO FORMA FINANCIAL STATEMENTS

There are times when companies experience one time or non recurring economic events that may dramatically affect its earnings or financial performance. The impact of these events under GAAP reporting may significantly distort the fundamental performance of the company. The impact may be so significant that the GAAP results may not accurately reflect the financial performance of the company. Pro forma financial statements provide a hypothetical projection of what the earnings would have been had these events not occurred. As such the pro forma reports will exclude the non recurring or unusual events so that investors can have a better understanding of the company's performance. While the SEC still requires all companies to report under GAAP, the SEC also allows companies to include additional pro forma reports and information to investors. Pro forma statements can be very useful, especially when they are presented during management's discussion on earnings calls. However, they can also be selectively edited to mislead investors. Accountants can remove selected items from GAAP reports and the resulting pro forma statements may make the company look stronger than it actually is. To help investors understand which items have been edited or adjusted, each entry that is reported using a pro forma non GAAP method should be clearly identified.

INVENTORY VALUATION AND ACCOUNTING

Companies who manufacture and sell products must properly value the inventory on its balance sheet. Manufacturing companies who produce finished goods will have inventory that consists of both work in progress and finished goods available for sale. Work in progress consists of the raw materials used to manufacture products and all goods in each stage of production, up to but not including, the finished products. Companies maintaining inventory purchased at wholesale prices who do not manufacture products would not have work in progress as part of its inventory. GAAP requires that companies value inventory at the lower of its historical cost or the current market price. The historical cost of the inventory is the price paid at the time of purchase. The market price for the inventory is the cost the company would have to pay today to replace the inventory stored in its warehouses and carried on its balance sheet. For example, assume XYZ purchased 10,000 coffee pots at a price of $40 and the current market price to replace the inventory was now $38. XYZ would have to carry the value of the inventory on its balance sheet at the lower replacement cost of $38. Companies must have inventory management systems in place that allow them to track inventory through the sales channel. Once inventory is sold, the sales generate cash or accounts receivable for the company. As sales are generated, the inventory systems will assign those sales to the units carried in inventory. These systems will help the company determine when to replenish its inventory and to assign a value to the inventory that was sold. The valuation method assigned to the inventory sold can have a substantial impact on the company's profit margin and as a result on its EBIT and EBITDA. When companies assign a value to the units sold, it may use one of the following methods:

First in, first out (FIFO) - this method of inventory management assigns sales to the oldest units in inventory, the units that were purchased first are the first units sold.

Last in, first out (LIFO) - this method of inventory management assigns sales to the newest units in inventory, the units that were most recently purchased are the first units sold

Weighted average - This method of inventory management assigns an average cost to all units in inventory, each unit sold is valued at the same weighted average cost regardless of when the units were purchased and without regard to the actual price paid for any particular unit.

Specific Identification - This method of inventory management matches the actual cost of the particular unit to each unit sold.

As prices of raw materials and wholesale goods change in the economy, the prices companies pay for inventory rise and fall. During periods of rising prices, companies are required to pay more to replace inventory. While during periods of falling prices, companies are able to replenish inventory at a lower cost. As the cost of inventory changes, the company's profit margins will be impacted by the fluctuating cost of goods sold. Companies may be tempted to change the inventory management systems to take advantage of the cyclical nature of prices in an effort to increase earnings or to lower its tax burden. It is important to be on the lookout for any changes a company may have made to its inventory valuation process and its potential impact on financial performance. If during periods of rising prices a company changes its inventory valuation method from LIFO to FIFO, COGS would decline while margins, net income and taxes would increase. If during this time, the company changed from FIFO to LIFO COGS would increase, while margins, net income and taxes for the company would fall. Alternatively, during periods of falling prices, if a company changes its inventory valuation method from FIFO to LIFO, COGS would decline while margins, net income and taxes would increase. If during this time the company changed from LIFO to FIFO, COGS would increase while margins, net income and taxes would decline. Changes to inventory valuation methods should be seen as potential red flags for lower quality accounting methods designed to manipulate current earnings. It is interesting to note, that two companies who are effectively in the same business, selling the same products, may report dramatically different results due to differences in inventory accounting methods.

In the next several pages we will be reviewing some of the following key ratios:

Measure	Formula	Purpose
Inventory turnover ratio	COGS / average inventory	To determine how quickly the company sells goods in inventory
Asset turnover Ratio	Sales / Average assets	To determine how efficiently the company uses assets to generate sales
Receivable turnover ratio	Sales / average receivables	To determine how quickly the company collects payment on credit sales
Gross profit margin	Gross profit / sales	To determine how much each dollar of sales remains to cover operating expenses
Operating profit margin	Income from operations / sales	to determine how much profit is made on each dollar of sales after subtracting variable cost
EBITDA profit margin	EBIDTA / sales	Useful in comparing comparing profitability of 2 companies
Net profit margin	Net income / sales	to determine the amount of income available as a percentage of sales
Payables turnover ratio	Income from operations / sales	To determine short term liquidity based on how quickly a company pays its creditors
Days sales outstanding	Accounts receivable /(Total credit sales / number of days in period)	To determine the average number of days it takes the company to turn sales into cash
Return on Assets	Net income / Average assets	To determine how efficiently assets are being used to generate earnings
Return on Common Equity	Net Income Available to Common Equity / Average common equity	To determine the rate of return available to common equity holders
Return On Invested Capital	EBIT (100- Tax Rate)/ Invested capital	To determine how effectively the company is investing capital

QWER Corp.	2019	2020	2021	2022
Income Statement				
Net sales	331,000	342,000	350,000	365,000
Cost of Goods Sold	150,000	155,000	180,000	194,000
Gross Profit	**181,000**	**187,000**	**170,000**	**171,000**
Expenses				
Marketing, Advertising, & Promotion	43,000	44,000	45,000	48,000
General & Administrative	10,000	11,000	14,000	16,000
Depreciation & Amortization	17,000	17,000	17,000	17,000
Income From Operations	111,000	115,000	94,000	90,000
Interest	1,500	1,500	1,500	1,500
Total Expenses	**71,500**	**73,500**	**77,500**	**82,500**
Earnings Before Tax	**109,500**	**113,500**	**92,500**	**88,500**
Taxes	8,483	10,908	11,598	10,322
Net Income	**101,017**	**102,592**	**80,902**	**78,178**
Balance Sheet				
Assets				
Cash	83,000	105,000	106,000	111,000
Accounts Receivable	6,000	7,000	8,000	9,000
Inventory	10,000	11,000	12,000	15,000
Property & Equipment	40,000	39,000	38,000	37,000
Total Assets	**139,000**	**162,000**	**164,000**	**172,000**
Liabilities				
Accounts Payable	4,900	5,200	5,600	7,100
Debt	30,000	30,000	30,000	30,000
Total Liabilities	**34,900**	**35,200**	**35,600**	**37,100**
Shareholder's Equity				
Equity Capital	70,000	70,000	70,000	70,000
Retained Earnings	35,300	64,000	90,000	110,000
Shareholder's Equity	**105,300**	**134,000**	**160,000**	**180,000**
Total Liabilities & Shareholders' Equity	**140,200**	**169,200**	**195,600**	**217,100**
Turnover Ratios & Profit Margins				
Inventory Turnover Ratio	N/A	14.76	15.65	14.37
Asset Turnover Ratio	N/A	2.27	2.15	2.18
Receivable Turnover Ratio	N/A	52.6	46.6	42.9
Payable Turnover Ratio	N/A	30.7	33.33	30.55
Gross Profit Margin	54.6%	54.6%	48.5%	46.8%
Operating Profit Margin	33.5%	33.6%	26.8%	24.6%
EBITDA Profit Margin	38.6%	38.5%	31.7%	29.3%
Net Profit Margin	30.5%	29.9%	23.1%	21.4%

To arrive at the above ratios and margins we used the formulas detailed in the table listed above the income statement and balance sheet. Below we will show the calculations for the results for the year 2020. After reviewing the calculations for 2020, it would be a good exercise for your exam to apply those calculations for the subsequent years.

Inventory Turnover Ratio = COGS / Average Inventory

$155,000 / (10,000 + 11,000) /2

$155,000/ 10,500 = 14.76

Asset Turnover Ratio = Sales / Average Assets

$342,000 / (139,000 + 162,000) / 2

$342,000 / 150,500 = 2.27

Receivable Turnover Ratio = Sales / average receivables

$342,000 / (6,000 + 7,000) / 2

$342,000 /6.5 = 52.6

Payable Turnover Ratio = COGS / average payables

$155,000 / (4,900 +5,200) / 2

$155,000 / 5050 =30.7

Gross profit margin = Gross Profit / sales

$187,000 / $342,000 =54.7%

Operating Profit Margin = Income From Operations / Sales

$115,000 / $342,000 =33.6%

EBITDA Profit Margin =EBITDA / Sales

$132,000 /$342,000 = 38.5%

Net profit margin = Net Income / Sales

$102,252 / $342,000 = 29.9%

CHAPTER 6 Financial Analysis

It is important to remember that Gross profit margin > Operating profit margin > Net profit margin

Now lets take a look at how to calculate the days sales outstanding or DSO given the following example:

Days Sales Outstanding = Accounts receivable /(total credit sales / number of days in period)

For the month of December:	
Credit Sales	$1,500,000
Cash Sales	$2,000,000
Total Sales Revenue	$3,500,000
Accounts Receivable Balance	$800,000
Number of Days in December	31
Days Sales Outstanding	**16.5**

The lower the number of days sales are outstanding the better it is for the company's liquidity. The longer it takes for a company to collect on its credit sales, the longer it takes for the company to turn accounts receivable into cash.

KEY OBSERVATIONS

From the information contained in the income statement and balance sheet in our above example we have extracted key performance indicators in the form of performance ratios and profitability margins. This allows us to make the following key observations regarding the financial performance of the company.

1. Inventory prices and margins were relatively stable during the period from 2019-2020
2. Inventory prices in 2021 and 2022 were increasing faster than the company grew its sales / or faster than the company could pass the increased inventory costs on to customers.
3. Margins and profitability were declining in 2021 and 2022
4. The company does not extend a lot of credit to its customers
5. The company does not use a lot of credit to purchase inventory

Ultimately on your exam you will not be required to interpret the results as good or bad in absolute terms due to the fact that different industries have different performance characteristics and expectations. For example, the asset turnover ratio for a retail company would be substantially higher than that for a utility company. It is important to be able to understand these observations as relatively good or bad given the information in the question. A question could be posed to you as follows:

All else being equal, which of the following companies exhibits the highest efficiency?

Company	Asset Turnover Ratio
Company A	.65 %
Company B	.50 %
Company C	1.27 %
Company D	.95 %

Company C has the highest asset turnover ratio and would be the company that most efficiently uses its assets to generate sales.

COMPARATIVE FINANCIAL ANALYSIS

In comparative financial analysis, it is important to be able to detect trends in the changes that occur over time in the different financial statements. This trend analysis is often referred to as "horizontal analysis," because the comparison implies a side-by-side analysis of the financial items in the statements. Two popular techniques in horizontal analysis are "year-to-year change" analysis and "index number trend series" analysis. Year-to year analysis, as the name implies, measures one year relative to a previous year. Index number trend series analysis is used when looking at financial statements covering periods greater than two years. The first year in the period is set as the base year with a value of 100% and the performance of each subsequent period is measured in relation to the base year as follows:

$$\frac{\text{Index year}}{\text{Base Year}}$$

An analyst reviewing the performance of the hypothetical company below from 20X1 - 20X4 would set the first period of 20X1 as the base year with a value of 100% and measure the performance of each subsequent year in relation to the base year.

CHAPTER 6 Financial Analysis

Results 20X1-20X4				
Year	20X4	20X3	20X2	20X1
Net Sales	$4.6 million	$4.2 million	$3.2 million	$3.5 million
Net Income	$2.1 million	$1.8 million	$1.2 million	$1.4 million

Performance Trend				
Year	20X4	20X3	20X2	20X1
Net Sales	131.4%	120%	91.4%	100%
Net Income	150%	128.5%	85.7%	100%

An analyst must also be able to compare financial reports between two companies. One exercise you may be required to do on the exam is to compare two income statements and based on the information, be able to answer the question presented. The following is an example of what you may be required to do.

XYZ Inc.	In 000s	SIA Inc.	In 000s
Sales	250	Sales	250
COGS	(67.5)	COGS	(80)
SG&A	(87.5)	SG&A	(100)
EBIT	95	EBIT	70
EBIT Margin	38%	EBIT Margin	28%
Interest Expense	(20)	Interest Expense	(5)
Taxable Income	75	Taxable Income	65
Taxes Paid	(25)	Taxes Paid	(15)
Net Income	50	Net Income	50
NET Income Margin	20%	NET Income Margin	20%

In looking at the income statements above, we notice that both companies have the same sales and net income even though cost of goods sold and SG&A are lower for XYZ than for SIA. In reviewing the income statements, we see that XYZ is paying substantially more in interest and taxes than SIA. There may be several reasons for this. First, XYZ may be substantially more leveraged than SIA and / or their credit rating could be much lower than that of SIA. A lower credit rating would force the company to pay higher interest rates on its debt. Further examination also shows that the operating margin is higher for XYZ than SIA, yet the net income margins are identical. These two companies may be in different states or different counties with drastically different tax rates. While there are many things that a company can do to try to control the profitability of the company and its margins, a company has very little control over the tax rates set by the government and interest rates set in the marketplace.

When an investment banker is performing a comparative analysis between two companies in the same industry of different sizes, it can be challenging to determine which company is performing better. To address this issue, the investment banker must create common size financial statements. Common-size financial statements compare the mix of assets, liabilities, capital, revenue, and expenses within a given industry without respect to relative size. Common-size financial statements present the items in a financial statement as percentages of a common base. By doing this a comparison among firms in the same industry is made possible despite differences in size. Using common-size financial statements to compare firms in different industries has drawbacks because the optimum mix of assets, liabilities, etc. will vary from industry to industry.

ACCOUNTING CHALLENGES

There are numerous items that can impact financial statements. Everything from changes in accounting methods and aggressive accounting practices to management of business and accounting decisions. Financial statements should be accurate and reflective of the company's performance and allow an investment banker to appropriately assess the financial position of the company. There are two quality measures that allow a banker to properly value a company, the company's financial reporting quality and the quality of the company's earnings. Financial reporting quality relates to the quality of the information contained in the financial reports including footnotes. This is a subjective evaluation to determine if the financial statements accurately reflect the financial condition of the company. The quality of the earnings relates to sustainability of the earnings.

High Reporting Quality - Allows for the accurate assessment of the company's financial performance

Low Reporting Quality - hinders the accurate assessment of the company's financial performance

Earnings quality or the quality of the reported results - relates to the earnings and cash flow generated by the business activities of the company and the sustainability of the earnings and cash flow in the future. High quality earnings are those which can be sustained over a long period of time. Low earnings quality are those which are difficult to sustain.

High Earnings Quality - increases the value of the company

Low Earnings Quality - decreases the value of the company

 TAKE **NOTE!**

A decline in revenue accompanied by an increase in net income, would be a red flag for low quality unsustainable earnings. This could be the result of earnings management, a decrease in taxes or falling interest expense. Alternatively, If a company reduces operating expenses during a period when revenue is flat and net income still declines, the company is likely to be paying higher interest rates and or higher taxes.

Aggressive accounting includes everything from overly optimistic projections to activities which could be deemed to be fraudulent, such as channel stuffing. Channel stuffing is a fraudulent activity undertaken by a company to increase the perceived value of its sales. Suppliers who engage in this activity will send customers more units than the customers order. In the short term this makes the sales volume and the company's financial performance look much better than it actually is. Customers will ultimately return the overages and the sales will be adjusted back to appropriate levels. Certain activities that take place in the "grey areas" of accounting may be justified and deemed acceptable if the auditors agree with the assumptions and accounting treatment of the activity. For example, a company may reduce loss reserves for bad debts taken against sales if it feels that business conditions are improving. In certain cases this may very well be justified. In other cases, it may be seen as manipulative in an effort to boost the company's performance. Additional examples of aggressive accounting practices include:

- Expense deferrals
- expensing stock options
- Asset value inflation
- Understating liabilities
- Taking an impairment charge against goodwill
- Recognizing revenue prior to fulfillment of the order or all obligations
- Capitalizing research and development expenses

- Capitalizing software expenses
- Capitalizing leases
- Employing a high discount rate when calculating defined pension liabilities
- Real earnings management and accounting earnings management

Real earnings management manages business activities such as research and development to manipulate earnings. Accounting earnings management makes classification choices in the accounting process to manipulate earnings. If we were to list the quality of reporting and earnings from high to low, the list would be as follows:

1. Reports are GAAP compliant, using conservative practices with high quality sustainable earnings
2. Reports are GAAP compliant, using conservative practices with low earnings quality
3. Reports are GAAP compliant, but accounting practices may be biased with emphasis placed on positive results while negatives may be hidden. Or, short term results are increased at the expense of long term reporting. Or, the reports contain contain evidence of earnings management or manipulation
4. Non compliant accounting practices
5. Reports contain fictitious transactions such as channel stuffing, fake bank accounts or assets

DEFERRED TAX ISSUES

There may be times when a company's taxable income materially differs from its accounting income. When this occurs, the company will have to classify the difference as either a deferred tax asset or as a deferred tax liability on its balance sheet. The creation of a deferred tax asset could be the result of:

- Net Operating Losses
- Tax overpayment
- Tax abatement or relief
- When revenue is subject to taxation prior to when it is taxable in the income statement

- Revenue recognition for multi year contracts where the revenue is recognized and taxes are paid in full in the first year, but the services must be provided over a number of years.
- Reserves taken against sales for future warranty issues

The deferred tax asset is carried on the asset section of the balance sheet. The deferred tax asset may be used to reduce the company's future tax liability. These deferred tax assets can be carried forward indefinitely to reduce tax liability, but can no longer be carried back to receive a return of taxes paid in previous years. The value of the deferred tax asset can be impacted by changes in the tax rate. If the tax rate increases, the value of the deferred tax asset goes up as it provides more protection from future tax liabilities. However, the value of the deferred tax asset will fall if the tax rate declines. To understand how to calculate the value of the deferred tax asset review the following example:

SIA Corp. has entered into a service contract worth $15 million to provide services over the next 3 years. For tax purposes, the CFO elects to declare the entire $15 million in the first year and pay taxes at a corporate rate of 26 percent, totalling $3.9 million. For accounting purposes, the income should be recognized over the period during which services are to be provided. In this case at a rate of $5 million per year. As a result, the taxable income for SIA has exceeded its accounting income by two thirds or by $10 million. The annual tax liability for the income received each year based on the 26% corporation tax rate is $1.3 million. In cases like these, there are two ways to value the deferred tax asset . One is found by subtracting the annual tax liability from the total tax liability paid. In this case $3.9 - $1.3 million = $2.6 million. The second is found by multiplying the amount by which taxable income exceeds the accounting income and multiplying the overage by the corporate tax rate. In this case $15 million - $5 million = $10 million X 26% = $2.6 million.

A deferred tax liability is carried on the liabilities section of the balance sheet and represents taxes that the corporation owes and must pay in the future. Some issues that can lead to a deferred tax liability are:

- Accelerated depreciation
- Rolling profits out to future periods

Deferred tax balances can have a significant impact on the cash flow of the corporation. An increase in deferred tax liabilities and a decrease in deferred tax assets are seen as sources of cash and improve cash flow. While a decrease in deferred tax liabilities and an increase in deferred tax assets would be a use of cash and would result in a reduction in cash flow. Clarification for the sources of deferred tax balances are usually found in the footnote section of the financial statements.

Accounting for investments in the stock of another company presents its own challenges. The method by which the company must account for the investment and any related income is contingent upon the percentage ownership of the company in question. There are three methods by which a company can account for the investment in the stock of another company.

1. The cost method will be used when the company owns less than 20 percent of the company
2. The equity method will be used when the company owns between 20 and 50 percent of the company
3. The purchase method requires consolidated financial statements to be prepared when the company owns more than 50 percent of the company.

The Cost method - Companies will carry the value of the stock on its balance sheet at the cost it paid to acquire the shares. Should the stock decline substantially the company will adjust the value of the asset doward to reflect the decline.

The Equity method - Companies who own a substantial portion of another company and have a significant amount of influence over the company, will record its proportionate share of the company's income or loss on the income statement under the heading "other income." For example, if SIA Co. Owns 40% of EZI Inc. and EZI reported net income of $200,000, SIA would record $80,000 of other income.

The Purchase Method / Consolidated Financial Statements - the parent company / company owning more that 50% of the subsidiary will incorporate the results of the subsidiary into its own financial statements. In the case of an acquisition, the purchase method must be used for cash transactions. If the acquisition creates goodwill as a result of any premium paid to acquire the asset, the company may be required to take an impairment charge against its earnings. To adjust the consolidated financial statements for the percentage of the subsidiary the company does not own, the percentage will be carried on an entry in the stockholders equity section of the balance sheet and on the income statement under an entry known as "non-controlling interest." For example, if SIA Co. owns 80% of EZI Inc. and EZI reported net income of $200,000, SIA would record $200,000 of income and reduce the income on the income statement with a non controlling interest entry in the amount of $40,000 to reflect the 20% of the company SIA does not own.

DEPRECIATION AND AMORTIZATION

On your exam you will be required to understand the difference between depreciation and amortization. Fixed assets with a finite useful life have the value of the asset reduced over that useful life. Similarly, intangible assets with a finite useful life such as intellectual property, patents and trademarks may be amortized. However, intangible assets with an indefinite useful life such as goodwill cannot be amortized. Intangible assets with an indefinite useful life are subject to an annual test to determine if the value of the intangible asset has fallen relative to the value carried on the balance sheet. If the value of the asset is less than its carrying value, the intangible asset is subject to an impairment charge. The impairment charge allows the company to record the loss as a charge against earnings and to reduce the value of the asset to its fair value. If a corporation was carrying an intangible asset with an indefinite useful life on its balance sheet at a value of $50 million and the annual test (mark to market) determines its fair value is $52 million, no charges will be taken. However, if that same asset was valued at $48 million, the company would be required to take an impairment charge of $2 million. The $2 million impairment charge would reduce the company's earnings and the asset would now be valued at its fair market value of $48 million on the balance sheet. If the $50 million asset listed above was a fixed asset with a useful life of 5 years, the asset depreciation schedule using straight line depreciation would look as follows:

Year	Opening Carrying Value	Depreciation	Accumulated Depreciation	Ending Carrying Value
1	$50,000,000	$10,000,000	$10,000,000	$40,000,000
2	$40,000,000	$10,000,000	$20,000,000	$30,000,000
3	$30,000,000	$10,000,000	$30,000,000	$20,000,000
4	$20,000,000	$10,000,000	$40,000,000	$10,000,000
5	$10,000,000	$10,000,000	$50,000,000	0

One form of modified accelerated depreciation is the double declining balance method. This form of depreciation allows the company to take a larger depreciation deduction in dollar terms during the first years and lower dollar values over the remaining years of an asset's useful life. Effectively, companies can take a depreciation deduction that is twice the straight line rate based on the carrying value of the asset. If the company who purchased the $50 million fixed asset listed above used the double declining balance method, the depreciation schedule would look as follows:

Year	Opening Carrying Value	Depreciation	Accumulated Depreciation	Ending Carrying Value
1	$50,000,000	$20,000,000	$20,000,000	$30,000,000
2	$30,000,000	$12,000,000	$32,000,000	$18,000,000
3	$18,000,000	$7,200,000	$39,200,000	$11,800,000
4	$11,800,000	$4,720,000	$43,9200,000	$6,080,000
5	$6,080,000	$6,080,000	$50,000,000	0

As you can see above the depreciation rate is 40 percent of the carrying cost of the asset, or 2 times the 20 percent deduction taken under the straight line method of depreciation. The final balance is depreciated to zero at the end of the asset's useful life. While the depreciation schedule above shows the full deduction of depreciation in the first year, often companies are only allowed to take 50 percent of the first year's depreciation. This would lead to a lower depreciation expense in the first year and somewhat higher depreciation expenses over the remaining years.

FIXED AND VARIABLE COSTS

Fixed costs are costs that a company must absorb and continue to pay regardless of the level of sales generated. Rent, salaries, leases, overhead and payments for equipment are just some of the fixed costs a business may be responsible for. Companies who have a substantial amount of fixed costs are said to have a high degree of operating leverage. A company that uses its operating leverage efficiently is able to use its fixed cost assets to generate profits. The sales generated by utilizing these fixed cost assets must be sufficient to cover the costs and generate a profit. Companies with substantial operating leverage tend to be more cyclical and see their earnings rise and fall based on the economic cycle. Variable costs are costs that raise and fall with the level or production or sales. Raw materials and other inputs that are used to create the products sold are all variable or direct manufacturing costs.

RESTRUCTURING CHARGES

Restructuring charges are usually the result of one time non recurring events such as layoffs, plant closings, exiting an unprofitable line of business or asset or inventory write downs. The charges are reflected in the income statement as non recurring operating expenses and net income will be reduced as a result of the charges. Further, most restructuring events will cause retained earnings to decrease. The exact details of the restructuring will often be disclosed in the footnotes to the financial statements. In the case of an asset or inventory write down, the value of the asset or inventory is reduced on the balance sheet and the corresponding reduction in value is carried over to the income statement as a restructuring expense. In these cases retained earnings are debited and there is no impact to the company's cash balance. Companies will often restructure their business to make needed adjustments to its assets and liabilities in order to improve profitability in the long run. In many casis, restructuring is undertaken during business or economic declines. Interestingly, certain expansion activities can also be seen as restructuring and the associated charges can be booked on the income statement under non recurring operating expenses. For example, if a company is increasing its footprint and acquires new office space and in order to attract top talent pays signing bonuses, these expenses can also be classified under restructuring expenses.

 TAKE **NOTE!**

If a company is involved in a lawsuit, the litigation expenses causes short term liabilities to increase and retained earnings to decrease.

Here is an example of a question you may see on the series 79 exam regarding the impact of non recurring charges.

EXAMPLE: XYZ, Inc. is a manufacturing company and has decided to consolidate two of its manufacturing facilities. XYZ has sold off one of its manufacturing plants at a pre-tax loss of $50 million. During this period the company reported net income of $281 million which included the negative impact of the asset sale. The company is subject to a marginal tax rate of 26% and has an overall effective tax rate of 22%. If all else remains unchanged, what would XYZ's net income be in the following period?

Pre Tax Loss	$50,000,000
Marginal Tax Rate	26%
Loss Adjusted for Taxes	$37,000,000
Prior Year Net Income	$281,000,000
Net Income	$318,000,000

The first step to solving this problem is determining which tax rate to use. If the question includes both a marginal tax rate and an effective tax rate, you must use the marginal tax rate. In this case the marginal tax rate is 26%. To determine the after tax impact the loss has on net income, you must multiply the loss by the complement of the marginal tax rate. In this case

$$\$50 \text{ million} \times (100\% - 26\%)$$

$$\$54 \text{ million} \times .74 = \$37 \text{ million.}$$

Once the after tax impact of the loss has been determined add it back to the net income to determine the net income for the following period.

$$\$281 \text{ million} + \$37 \text{ million} = \$318 \text{ million}$$

MARKET CAPITALIZATION

A company's market capitalization refers to the total value of all outstanding common shares. Market capitalization is divided into the following categories:

- Mega capitalization, companies with a market value greater than $200 billion
- Large capitalization, companies with a market value between $10-$200 billion

CHAPTER 6 Financial Analysis

- Middle capitalization, companies with a market value between $2-10 billion
- Small capitalization, companies with a market value between $300 million and $2 billion
- Miro capitalization, companies with a market value between $50 - $300 million
- Nano capitalization companies with a market value less than $50 million

MARKET INDEXES

Many market indexes have been developed to measure the performance of the overall stock market as well as the performance of sub sectors within the market. Investors may use these indexes as a way to measure the performance of the overall market and to measure the performance of a portfolio against a benchmark index. Market indexes are divided into two main types: capitalization-weighted and price-weighted indexes. The two types are characterized as follows:

Capitalization-Weighted Index: A market benchmark whose value is derived from the price action of the companies whose shares are included in the index. More weight is given to the price performance of the shares of the companies with the greatest market capitalization. Market capitalization is the total value of all the outstanding shares. The NASDAQ Composite, NASDAQ 100, NYSE Composite, Russell 2000, S & P 500, S & P 100, and Wilshire 5000 are all the capitalization-weighted indexes. The Wilshire 5000 provides the broadest coverage of all the indexes.

Price-Weighted Index: A market benchmark whose value is derived from the price action of the companies whose shares are included in the index. More weight is given to the price performance of the shares of the companies with higher stock prices. A change in the price of a $100 stock would have a greater impact on the value of the index than a change in the share price of a $10 stock. The Dow Jones Industrial, Transportation, and Utility averages are all price-weighted indexes.

International Indexes. Like the indexes created here in the United States, foreign markets also have created indexes to track the performance of their markets. The Nikkei in Japan, the FTSE in England, and the DAX in Germany all track the markets in their respective countries. Morgan Stanley created the EAFE as a single market capitalization-weighted index to track the combined performance of the markets in Europe, Asia, and the Far East.

CHAPTER 6

Pretest

FINANCIAL ANALYSIS

1. XYZ is a publicly traded company and reporting issuer with the SEC. It is preparing its annual report. Which of the following is not one of the financial statements to be prepared by XYZ and included in its annual report?
    A. Statement of depreciation and amortization
    B. Statement of sources and use of funds
    C. Income statement
    D. Balance sheet

2. As an investment banking representative you are reviewing the financial statements of GHJ Enterprises. Upon reviewing the statement of cash flows, you would identify which of the following entries as a source of cash?
    A. A decrease in liabilities
    B. An increase in accounts payable
    C. An increase in inventory
    D. A decrease in accounts payable

3. GMJ is a profitable electronics manufacturer with a long history of paying dividends to its shareholders. GMJ's balance sheet shows retained earnings of $620 million. Last year GMJ generated net income of $78 million and paid dividends of $15 million. GMJ is expected to grow net income by 8 percent in the current year and has announced it plans to increase its dividend by 5%. GMJ's retained earnings at the end of the current year is estimated to be:
    A. $688,490,000
    B. $687,740,000
    C. $703,490,000
    D. $698,000,000

205

4. A large conglomerate has experienced a substantial shock to its business and is required to take an usually large writedown at one of its divisions. The impact of the writedown will cause the financial performance for the quarter to be much lower than anticipated. In order to more clearly demonstrate the company's performance during the quarter, the best choice would be for:
   A. Management to clearly provide the details of the writedown during its earnings call
   B. The company to provide pro forma financial statements adjusting for the loss
   C. The company to use footnotes only on its financial statements prepared under GAAP
   D. The company to identify the assets that were subject to the writedown along with their current valuation

5. A large electronics retailer purchases TVs and audio equipment directly from manufacturers at wholesale prices. The inventory turns over very quickly for this large retailer. Under GAAP, the company:
   A. Must value its inventory under the FIFO method
   B. Must value its inventory at the market value
   C. Must value its inventory at the lower of LIFO or FIFO
   D. Must value its inventory at the lower of its cost or market value

6. After a substantial increase in the price of its stock SIA elects to declare a 2:1 forward split. Which of the following statements is correct regarding the impact of the stock split?
   A. Par value will decrease and capital paid in excess of par value will increase
   B. Par value will increase and capital paid in excess of par value will increase
   C. Par value will decrease and capital paid in excess of par value will remain constant
   D. Par value will decrease and capital paid in excess of par value will decrease

7. A manufacturer of heavy construction equipment has been experiencing a period of increased costs for raw materials. The company notes that it has substantial finished inventory and work in progress. Which of the following is correct regarding the company's inventory?
   A. If the company changes its inventory valuation method from LIFO to FIFO it would reduce its tax liability.
   B. If the company changes its inventory valuation method from LIFO to FIFO it would reduce its margins.
   C. If the company changes its inventory valuation method from LIFO to FIFO it would increase its tax liability.
   D. If the company changes its inventory valuation method from LIFO to FIFO it would not impact its tax liability.

8. Which of the following would allow an investment banker to determine how efficiently a company generates earnings?
   A. Return on common equity
   B. Return on assets
   C. Return on invested capital
   D. Net profit margin

9. An investment banking representative is comparing the financial performance of QWER and TRY. The representative notices that the sales and net income for the two companies are virtually identical. However, the COGS and SGA for QWER are both higher than that of TRY. Which of the following is correct?
   A. The interest and tax expense for QWER is lower than that of TRY.
   B. The interest and tax expense for QWER is higher than that of TRY.
   C. The difference between the two companies is the result of inventory valuation methods, with QWER using FIFO valuation and TRY using LIFO valuation.
   D. The difference between the two companies is the result of inventory valuation methods, with QWER using LIFO valuation and TRY using FIFO valuation.

10. CGC, a business operating in a niche industry, has just closed out its fiscal year end. CGC's taxable income is substantially different from its accounting income. Which of the following would create a tax deferred liability for CGC?
    A. CGC takes a charge against sales for future warranty expenses.
    B. CGC pays taxes on income prior to it being recorded on its income statement.
    C. CGC rolls profits out to future reporting periods.
    D. CGC operates in an industry that just received a tax abatement.

CHAPTER 7

Valuation

> **INTRODUCTION**
>
> Valuation analysis is used to examine the price the market is paying for the financial performance of a company. Investment bankers and analysts can use the analysis to identify opportunities to purchase attractively priced companies, to generate price targets and to avoid or short overvalued stocks. In the case of an acquisition, valuation is the key to the price that must be paid to acquire the financial performance. Two investment bankers looking at the same prospective stock or M&A target may arrive at different valuations and different opinions for the same company. The estimated valuations may vary based on different projections and valuation methods used in the analysis.

PRICE TO EARNINGS VALUATION

In the previous chapter we reviewed the basic concept of the price earnings ratio. In this section we will examine the multiple methods of valuation based on the PE ratio. There are numerous PE ratios that may be calculated using different inputs derived from the financial performance of the company. The PE ratios you are likely to encounter on your exam are the:

- PE Ratio based on the trailing earnings per share
- PE Ratio based on the projected earnings per share
- PE Ratio based on normalized earnings per share

If an investment banker were to calculate all of the above PEs for the same company, it is quite likely that they would all be different. The variation from one to another would be based on the different earnings per share data used in the denominator of the equation. Remember that the PE Ratio is found as follows:

$$\frac{\text{Price}}{\text{Earnings per share}}$$

To calculate the current price earnings ratio, the earnings per share for the trailing 12 months (preceding year) is used. If SIA Co. earned $4.00 per share and the market price of the stock is currently $50. Using the formula above SIA would have a current PE of 12.5. Based on the current PE the market is willing to pay $12.50 for each dollar SIA earns. The price earnings ratio is also known as the price earnings multiple and can be used to calculate an estimated stock price based on a change in earnings per share. For example, if SIA grew earnings per share by 7 percent, we can project a price for the stock as follows:

Current EPS X growth rate

$4.00 X 1.07 = $4.28

New earnings per share X PE multiple

$4.28 X 12.50 =$53.50

The current PE ratio represents a relationship between the current stock price and the past earnings performance of the company. The stock market tends to price equities based on what a company can do in the future, not what it has done in the past. As a result, many analysts believe that using a PE ratio based on a company's projected earnings represents a better valuation method. By valuing a current stock price based on its future earnings, investment bankers shift the focus from that past to the future performance of the company. Using the formula above, analysts and investment bankers who develop EPS estimates can use the PE multiple traditionally assigned to the company to create a price target for the stock. The biggest issue with calculating the forward or leading PE ratio is being able to accurately estimate the company's earnings per share for the future 12 months. If the estimate is inaccurate, or unforeseen events negatively impact the company's earnings the project price target will be too high and will overvalue the stock. Alternatively, if the earnings projections are too low, the price target for the company will undervalue the stock. Analysts and investment bankers are also faced with challenges when dealing with how the business cycle and non recurring one time events impact earnings. As the economy rises and falls many companies see their earnings follow the same trajectory. Trough earnings tend to occur during the bottom of the economic cycle, while peak earnings occur during the most prosperous times. In order to avoid mispricing a company, analysts and investment bankers will often "smooth out" the earnings fluctuations to develop a set of normalized earnings. Normalized earnings exclude non recurring events such as lawsuits and restructuring charges. Most normalized earnings projections will be created using a company's projected earnings based on an economy in "mid cycle" (i.e. between peak and trough) over an extended period of time. These normalized earnings projections will then be used to calculate a normalized earnings per share. Once the normalized EPS has been created, it can then be multiplied by the earnings multiple to develop a price target. If we were to look at a company in a cyclical industry such as steel, we would notice wide fluctuations in its earnings as the economic cycle rises and falls. Let's look at a hypothetical 4 year earnings cycle for US Steel.

Year	One	Two	Three	Four
Economic Condition	Peak	Recession	Trough	Expansion
EPS	$4.10	$2.80	$2.65	$3.40

From the above we can see that US Steel's earnings are dramatically impacted by the economic cycle. An investment banker taking a long term approach to this company may want to calculate the company's normalized earnings as a measure of its long term earning potential. Normalized or the average EPS over the period would be calculated as follows

$$\frac{(\$4.10 + \$2.80 + \$2.65 + \$3.40)}{4}$$

$$\$12.95 / 4 = \$3.23$$

Based on the reported results, the normalized earnings per share would be $3.23. If the stock was trading in the market at $38 per share, US Steel would have a normalized PE of 11.76. Found as follows Price / Normalized EPS or in this case 38 / $3.23 = 11.76

In 1953 Nicholas Molodovsky published an article entitled "A Theory of Price Earnings Ratios". In this article detailing the counter cyclical nature of PE ratios, Molodovsky theorized that EPS were at the lowest levels and PE ratios at the highest levels during times when the business cycle was bottoming out. Conversely, Molodovsky believed that earnings were at the highest levels and PE ratios were at the lowest levels in times of peak prosperity. Counter intuitively, the theory known as the Molodovsky effect postulates that the best bargains are found when purchasing stocks when the earnings are at the lowest and PEs are at the highest levels.

Investment bankers use a company's price earnings ratio as both a valuation tool for the company itself and as a way to compare the company's valuation to the market as a whole and to companies within its peer group. A relative PE can help bankers understand if the company is cheap or expensive on a relative basis. To calculate a relative PE ratio, use the following formula:

$$\frac{\text{PE of Company}}{\text{Market / Index PE}}$$

If we wanted to evaluate XYZ Technologies, a manufacturer of microchips currently trading at a PE of 28, to the semiconductor index with a PE of 31, we would be able to determine XYZ's relative PE as follows:

$$28 / 31 = .9$$

By calculating the relative PE ratio if all else were equal, it could be argued that XYZ is cheap compared to its peer group in the semiconductor industry. Alternatively, if XYZ had a PE of 40, its relative PE ratio would be 1.29 (40 /31) and it could be said that XYZ is overpriced relative to its peer group. Keep in mind these examples are based on a limited amount of information. There are many factors that would need to be considered to ultimately determine if a stock is relatively cheap or expensive when compared to the market or to its peers. Certain companies may historically trade at premiums or at discounts to the market or to its peers due to factors such as growth rates or perceived risks. Growth companies whose earnings are accelerating rapidly usually command higher PE ratios as investors are willing to pay more for a company whose earnings are increasing. On your exam, you could be faced with a question that asks you to determine if a company is cheap or expensive relative to the market based on its historical premium or discount to the market multiple. Consider the following example: SIA Co., traditionally trades at a 140 percent premium to the market multiple. An investment banker looking at the stock sees that its current PE ratio is 23. If the current market PE is 15, it could be said the SIA Co. is overvalued. Based on the historical premium of 140 percent and the market multiple of 15, SIA should be trading at a PE of 21. (15 x 1.4 =21)

On your exam, you may be provided with certain information regarding a company and be required to calculate the PE ratio. If you are given the annual dividend, the payout ratio and the dividend yield for a stock, you can calculate the PE ratio. As we mentioned in the previous chapter the dividend payout ratio is a relationship between the EPS and the annual dividend paid to each share. This tells us how much of the earnings a company pays out to its shareholders in the form of dividends. The dividend payout ratio is calculated as follows :

$$\frac{\text{Annual dividend per share}}{\text{EPS}}$$

CHAPTER 7   Valuation

The dividend yield is calculated using the same formula as for current yield as follows:

$$\frac{\text{Annual dividend}}{\text{Current market price}}$$

The EPS can be calculated from the annual dividend given the dividend payout ratio using the following formula:

$$\frac{\text{Annual dividend}}{\text{Dividend payout ratio}}$$

Finally, the market price for a stock can be calculated from the annual dividend and the dividend yield as such:

$$\frac{\text{Annual dividend}}{\text{Dividend yield}}$$

Having reviewed the calculations let's take a look at an example.

SJI is a utility company operating in the northeastern part of the United States. SJI pays its shareholders an annual dividend of $2.10 per share. As a utility company, SJI pays out a substantial portion of its earnings to shareholders and has a payout ratio of 60 percent. Based on its current market price, SJI has an attractive dividend yield of 4%. Using the above information we can calculate a number of variables.

1. SJI's EPS are $3.50. Found as follows: 2.10 / .6 = $3.50 (Annual dividend / dividend payout ratio
2. The current price of SJI is $52.50. Found as follows: 2.10/.04 (annual dividend/ dividend yield)
3. SJI has a PE Ratio of 15. Found as follows: $52.50/ $3.50 (price / EPS)

EARNINGS YIELD

A company's PE ratio is useful when making a comparison between two companies with positive earnings per share. However, during periods when a company is sustaining losses, the PE ratio would be a negative number and of no value. In fact, a negative PE might imply that a company was trading at a discount to one with a positive PE. This is clearly not the case. Calculating the earnings yield attempts to resolve this issue and to give analysts the ability to make a comparison between companies during periods of negative earnings. The earnings yield is the reciprocal of the PE ratio as follows:

$$\frac{\text{Earnings Per Share}}{\text{Stock Price}}$$

If we were to compare two steel companies at different phases of the economic cycle, it is likely that during times of expansion that they would both be generating profits. It is equally likely that they would both be sustaining losses during times of economic downturns. Let's take a look at how the PE and earnings yield for two steel companies might change with the change in the economic cycle.

Economy	Expanding	Expanding	Recession	Recession
Company	ABC Steel	XYZ Steel	ABC Steel	XYZ Steel
EPS	3.10	4.05	(1.15)	(1.75)
Price	38	51	22	31
PE Ratio	12.25	12.59	(19.13)	(17.71)
Earnings Yield	8.15%	7.94%	(5.22%)	(5.64%)

The earnings yield tells an investor how much in EPS a company generates for each dollar invested in a share of the stock. The earnings per share used in the calculation are the trailing EPS for the company. If we look at the earnings yield for both companies during the time when the economy was expanding and each company was earning a profit, we see that ABC Steel was generating 8.15 cents in earnings for each dollar invested. XYZ was generating 7.94 cents for each dollar invested. Durings times when the companies were losing money, the earnings yield tells an investor how much money the company is losing for each dollar invested.

PEG RATIO

As a way to account for the impact of a company's growth rate on its future earnings, investment bankers and analysts developed the PEG ratio. Many market participants consider the PEG ratio to be a better indicator of the true value for a company. The PEG ratio is a relationship between the PE ratio and the forward looking growth rate for the company's EPS. The formula is as follows:

$$\frac{\text{PE Ratio}}{\text{EPS Growth Rate}}$$

Like the PE ratio, lower PEG ratios represent lower valuations and potentially better values. A company with a PEG ratio of 1 represents a company that is considered to be fairly valued. While PEG ratios greater than 1 would be seen as overvalued. Consider the following example: SIA Co, Is trading in the market at $50 per share and its EPS for the trailing 12 months is $4.20.

CHAPTER 7   Valuation

SIA is expected to grow earnings by 14 percent. SIA's PEG ratio would be found as follows:

PE Ratio = 50/$4.2 = 11.9
PEG Ratio = 11.9 / 14 = .85

With a PEG ratio of less than 1, SIA seems to be undervalued by the market. As with any forward looking projections, the accuracy of the PEG ratio can be negatively affected by unforeseen events. An economic shock or the loss of a major contract could cause a company's growth to slow or to even turn negative. In these instances, the PEG ratio will have overvalued the stock. Additionally, the valuation or price target placed on the stock is only as good as the analysts' estimated growth rate. Different analysts often come up with different projected growth rates for a company's earnings. As a result the valuatations and price targets can vary significantly from one to another. Many investors are willing to pay a premium for companies whose earnings are growing faster than their competitors. As a prospective investment banker, being able to calculate the PEG ratio is an important part of the job description. Considering the following information for SIA Co.

Trailing 12 months earnings (net income)	$620 million
Projected 12 months earnings (net income)	$710 million
Stock Price	$24
Outstanding shares	350 million

Based on the information provided, the first step in calculating the PEG ratio would be to calculate the EPS based on the trailing net income as follows

$$\frac{\text{Earnings}}{\text{Number of shares outstanding}}$$

$620 million / 350 million =$1.77 per share

SIA's current EPS is $1.77 per share. Our next step in calculating the PEG ratio is to determine the current PE ratio.

$$\frac{\text{Price}}{\text{EPS}}$$

24/ 1.77 = 13.55

With SIA's stock price trading at $24 per share the company has a PE ratio of 13.55. Now that we have calculated the PE ratio, we must determine the projected earnings growth rate for SIA. The growth rate is a relationship between the projected earnings and the trailing or most recent earnings.

$$\frac{\text{Projected Earnings}}{\text{Trailing Earnings}}$$

$$\$710 \text{ million}/ \$620 \text{ million} = 1.14$$

To determine the growth rate you need to subtract the 1

$$1.14 - 1 = .14 = 14\%$$

The projected earnings growth rate for SIA is 14%. We are now able to calculate the PEG ratio for SIA by dividing the PE ratio by the earnings growth rate.

$$13.55 / 14 = .968$$

Based on the PE ratio of 13.55 and a projected growth rate of 14 percent the PEG ratio for SIA is .968. As mentioned earlier, a PEG ratio of less than 1 represents a situation where the stock is attractive and as a result may be undervalued.

Using the concept of the PEG ratio you may be required to calculate a price target for a stock based on the EPS growth and the PEG ratio. Consider the following information for SIA Co.

Current EPS	$1.20
Projected EPS	$1.38
PEG Ratio	1.2

Given the information above the first step would be to calculate the growth rate for SIA's EPS. The growth rate is found as follows:

$$\frac{\text{(Projected EPS - Current EPS)}}{\text{Current EPS}}$$

$$\frac{(1.38 - 1.20)}{1.20}$$

$$18 / 120 = 15\%$$

Based on the projected earnings per share, the growth rate for SIA is 15%. Next we must calculate the PE ratio using the PEG ratio and the growth rate. To calculate the the PE ratio, use the following formula:

PEG Ratio X Growth Rate

$$1.2 \text{ X } 15\% = 18$$

CHAPTER 7   Valuation

We can see that SIA has a PE ratio of 18. We are now ready to calculate a price target for SIA based on its PE ratio and its EPS estimate for next year.

Price Target = PE Ratio X EPS estimate
18 X 1.38 = $24.84

Based on the information provided we would calculate a price target for SIA of $24.84. Should the EPS estimate be inaccurate, the growth rate could be off and the price target for SIA may be overly optimistic or too pessimistic. The PEG ratio can be used to compare the relative valuations of different companies. It is important to keep in mind that the lower the PEG ratio, the less expensive a company is based on its projected growth rate. Higher PEG ratios represent companies where investors may be paying too high a price for the projected future growth. These companies may be seen as overvalued and vulnerable to a price decline. The PEG ratio should be used to conduct comparative analysis of similar companies within the same sector. The PEG ratio is not a useful tool when comparing companies in different industries and different growth cycles. For example, if we tried to use the PEG ratio to compare a high tech company to a mature steel company, the PEG ratios would be vastly different based on the difference in growth rates and industries. The PEG ratio is most useful when comparing companies in growth industries during periods of rapid earnings acceleration. The PEG ratio is not of much value when looking at mature companies or companies with negative earnings.

ENTERPRISE VALUE

A company's enterprise value can be thought of as the sum of all costs a buyer must pay to acquire the assets and financial performance of a business. The total enterprise value or EV includes the core operations, joint ventures, capital leases, non core assets and any non controlling interests. As a prospective investment banker it is important to have a full understanding of different ways to calculate the EV for prospective M&A transactions. Enterprise value is often thought of as the sum of a company's equity value plus its debt. The formula for calculating enterprise value is :

EV = Equity Value + Debt + Preferred Stock + Non-controlling Interest - Cash and Equivalents

The enterprise value requires the buyer to satisfy or assume the liabilities based on the claims of all capital providers (stockholders, bondholders) as well as all creditors and vendors. When considering the enterprise value of a company there are several things to keep in mind:

1. The equity component of the calculation is based on the market capitalization of the common and preferred stock
2. The debt component includes both long and short term debt, capital leases and and non controlling interests
3. The amount of cash and equivalents carried on the balance sheet reduce the enterprise value as the acquirer will assume control of these assets and it reduces the overall cost to the buyer. As a result, the cash on the balance sheet reduces the enterprise value
4. If a company has cash on its balance sheet and no debt, or more cash than debt, its enterprise value will be less than its market capitalization
5. If a company has more debt than cash on the balance sheet, the enterprise value will be greater than its market capitalization.

Let's take a look at the following information and use it to calculate the enterprise value for SIA.

Outstanding Common Stock	10 million
Stock Price	$45
Cash	$8 million
Short Term Debt	$3 million
Long Term Debt	$4 million
Non Controlling Interest	$7 million

The first step is to calculate the market capitalization for SIA:

$45 X 10 million = $450 million

Next we add total short and long term debt of $7 million

$450 million + $7 million = $457 million

From this figure we subtract the cash of $8 million

$457 million - $8 million - $449 million

Finally we add the value of the non controlling interest of $7 million

$449 million + $7 million = $456 million

The total enterprise value of SIA is $456 million. While in theory the enterprise value is what an acquirer would have to pay for a company, it is not actually reflective of what an acquirer would be willing to pay. Further, it is not indicative of what sellers would be willing to accept for the company. In the real world investment bankers often need to calculate the enterprise value based on a company's fully diluted share count. This assumes that all in the money options, rights and warrants have been exercised and all in the money convertibles have been converted into common shares. In extreme cases a company with a low market capitalization and a high level of net cash could have a negative enterprise value. These could be significant warning signs for a company who is in trouble or close to filing for bankruptcy. It is interesting to note that a company could have a negative enterprise value, but it cannot have a negative equity value, as the stock price can never fall below zero. Let's take a look at another example of how to calculate the enterprise value of a company using different data points. We can calculate the enterprise value for SIA using the data points below.

Net Income	$620 million
PE Ratio	11
Debt Net of Cash	$120 million

Equity Value = PE X Net Income

11 X $620 million = $6,820,000,000

In this case the equity of SIA is $6,820,000,000. To determine the enterprise value for SIA we must add the net debt on the balance sheet to the equity value. In this case SIA's enterprise value would be as folllows:

$$\$6,820,000,000 + \$120,000,000 = \$6,940,000,000$$

Now that we have covered 2 ways to calculate the enterprise value of a company, let's examine how to use the information to derive the stock price. If you are provided with the enterprise value of a company, the number of shares outstanding and the amount of cash and debt on its balance sheet the market value or equity value per share can be calculated. Using the following formula:

$$\frac{(\text{Enterprise value} + \text{cash} - \text{debt})}{\text{Number of shares outstanding}}$$

Enterprise Value	$20 million
Cash	$5 million
Debt	$10 million
Stock Price	Unknown
Outstanding shares	3 million

From the above information would have:

$$\frac{(\$20 \text{ million} + \$5 \text{ million} - \$10 \text{ million})}{3 \text{ million}}$$

$$15 \text{ million} / 3 \text{ million} = \$5$$

Simply calculating the enterprise value or equity value for a company is only the first step in utilizing this information. Your role as an investment banker will be to use this information to further develop an understanding of the relationship between the enterprise value and the sales or earnings of a company. Like all ratios, the lower the ratio, the less expensive the company is.

Enterprise Value: Sales - The enterprise value to sales ratio is useful when evaluating a startup company or a company with little to no earnings or very low profit margins

$$\frac{\text{Enterprise Value}}{\text{Sales}}$$

The pros and cons of EV:Sales ratios are:

Pros	Cons
Least likely measure to be manipulated through accounting adjustments	Revenue recognition issues create accounting issues between companies
Can be used to value unprofitable companies, start-ups and companies with low profit margins	Sales do not necessarily generate cash flow
Useful when comparing companies with different accounting practices	Does not consider cost structures of companies. Margins remain unknown
Useful when comparing companies with similar margins	Seasonality issues

Another variation of enterprise value to sales is the EV: net sales ratio. The company's sales are adjusted for any returns, allowances, refunds, industry discounts and any excise taxes collected.

Enterprise value : EBITDA - The enterprise value to EBITDA ratio, also referred to as the enterprise multiple, is used to value the overall company relative to its cash flows. The enterprise multiple is capital structure neutral and is an effective tool for measuring the relative value when comparing companies.

$$\frac{\text{Enterprise Value}}{\text{EBITDA}}$$

CHAPTER 7 Valuation

The pros and cons of EV: EBITDA ratios are:

Pros	Cons
It evaluates the impact of the company's cost structure	Cannot be used if company's EBITDA is negative
Is a better measure of value based on cash flow because depreciation and amortization are removed	Can be distorted by accounting issues and changes, such as revenue recognition and inventory management ie FIFO / LIFO
Provides for a large universe of comparable companies	Ignores certain real costs of business such as interest charges, depreciation and taxes
Most useful when comparing companies with similar levels of capital requirements / capital intensity	Hard to use for companies with large lease obligations such as retail chains. EV: EBITDAR would be more useful

It is interesting to note that EV: net sales may be preferred over EV:EBITDA as it allows for a better comparison of two companies who may employ different accounting methods. EV: net sales provides a fuller understanding of the company's ability to deploy its capital to generate a sufficient level of revenue. There are times when enterprise multiples are preferred over equity multiples, however both are useful valuation metrics. The following table details some of the characteristics of each:

EV Multiples	Equity Multiples
Are capital structure neutral	Easier for investors to understand
Less prone to accounting issues	More prone to accounting issues
Evaluate all claims on business from capital providers and creditors	Can be less subjective than EV multiples
Can be used to evaluate off balance sheet items	Better way to value equity

The enterprise value of a company may be greatly impacted by making an acquisition. The impact will be contingent on the currency the company uses to make the acquisition and the capital structure of the target. For example, let's assume that SIA, Co has entered into an agreement to acquire TRY industries for a total cost of $100 million. SIA will be using its stock as currency and borrowing money through the issuance of bonds on a 60/40 basis. The issuance of the securities to fund the acquisition would increase its enterprise value. If SIA had an enterprise value of $400 million prior to acquisition with its stock trading at $50, we would calculate the increase in its enterprise value by first determining how many shares the company would have to issue to fund the acquisition. The numbero shares :

$$\frac{\text{Cost of Acquisition Paid in Stock}}{\text{Stock Price}}$$

In this case SIA would be issuing 12 million shares to pay for 60 percent of the acquisition of TRY, found as follows: $60 million / $50 = 12 million shares. The issuance of the stock would cause SIA's market capitalization to increase by the same $60 million. The issuance of $40 million in bonds would cause SIA's enterprise value to increase by an amount equal to the new debt. Upon completion of the acquisition, SIA's enterprise value would increase by:

1. The increase in the market capitalization as a result of issuing stock, plus;
2. The increase in its outstanding debt issue, plus;
3. The amount of debt carried by TRY at the time of acquisition, minus;
4. Any cash on TRY's balance sheet at the time of acquisition

FREE CASH FLOW

Free cash flow is the cash flow generated by the enterprise's operating activities less its capital expenditure. Capital expenditures, usually referred to as CAPEX, includes the payments the company is required to make to purchase and maintain its physical assets such as its plant and equipment. CAPEX will tend to increase during times when the company is expanding its operations or entering new markets. Additionally, most businesses have ongoing CAPEX requirements to simply maintain its current level of production. If a company fails to maintain its assets, the assets' productivity will decline and the company will see its output and revenue fall. Free cash flow is therefore thought to be the cash flow generated by the business less the cash required to maintain or expand its operations. In turn, the free cash generated is available to the providers of capital to the business. The company can use the free cash flow to service its debt and to make interest and principal payments to bondholders, to pay dividends to its shareholders or to repurchase its shares. Free cash flow can be calculated based on the company's EBITDA or the EBIT. Both of which have already factored in the operating expenses or OPEX of the company. Operating expenses include the day to day expenses of the company such as salaries, rent, utilities and costs of goods sold. The main difference between CAPEX and OPEX is CAPEX are expenses incurred for major long term investments, while OPEX are expenses incurred for the daily operations of the company. Operating expenses reduce the taxable income of a company while CAPEX does not. The long term assets acquired as part of CAPEX are traditionally depreciated over the life of the asset. Even though free cash flow is not a GAAP accounting measure, it is very useful as it tells us how much cash a company has left after paying its operating expenses and capital expenditures. The following formulas can be used to calculate the free cash flow for a company:

Formula	Change in working capital
EBITDA - Taxes - CAPEX - increase in working capital	Increased
EBITDA - Taxes - CAPEX + decrease in working capital	Decreased
EBIT - Taxes - net CAPEX (CAPEX - Depreciation) - increase in working capital	Increased
EBIT - Taxes - net CAPEX (CAPEX - Depreciation) + decrease in working capital	Decreased
EBIT X(1-Tax Rate) + Depreciation and Amortization – Capital Expenditures – Increase in working capital	Increased
EBIT X (1-Tax Rate) + Depreciation and Amortization – Capital Expenditures + decrease in working capital	Decreased

It seems almost counter intuitive that an increase in working capital would be subtracted from free cash flow, and a decrease would be added to free cash flow, but remember that free cash flow is calculated to determine the amount of cash that is available to capital providers. Free cash flow assumes that the working capital will be used to meet the short term operating expenses of the business or invested in short term assets such as inventory and will not be available for capital providers. Free cash flow as calculated above is also known as free cash flow to the firm or FCFF. The free cash flow to equity calculation can be used to determine the amount of free cash flow available to equity holders. Unlike FCFF, the free cash flow to equity (FCFE) calculation is based on the net income of the company rather than EBIT or EBITDA. Remember that interest payments are made pre tax, so when calculating FCFE net debt service will be included in the calculation by basing it on net income rather than on EBIT or EBITDA. The formula to calculate FCFE is:

Formula	Change in working capital
Net income + depreciation and amortization – CapEx – increase in working capital	Increased
Net Income + depreciation and amortization – CapEx + decrease in working capital	Decreased

SIA Co	In Millions
EBIT	420
Interest Expense	51
Tax Expense at 28%	117.6
Net Income	251.4
Depreciation	90
CAPEX	150
Change in Working Capital (decrease)	(31)

Using the above information for SIA Co. we can calculate both the FCFF and FCFE as follows:

FCFF	Calculalation	FCFE	Calculation
EBIT	420	Net Income	251.4
Taxes	-117.6	Depreciation	+90
Net CAPEX	- 60 (150-90)	CAPEX	-150
Decrease in working Capital	+31	Decrease in working Capital	+31
FCFF	273.4	FCFE	221.4

There are many uses for FCFF and FCFE and both can be used to create a multiple to value the corporation. FCFF is known as the unlevered cash flow as it is the cash flow generated before any interest expenses are factored into the equation. Therefore when calculating a multiple based on a company's unlevered free cash flow or its FCFF, we use the the enterprise value in the numerator as follows:

$$\frac{\underline{\text{Enterprise Value}}}{\text{FCFF}}$$

CHAPTER 7 Valuation

When calculating a multiple for the business using FCFE we are using the cash flow generated after the impact of interest expenses or the company's levered cash flow. Levered cash flow assumes that the company has obtained borrowed funds. In this case we will use the equity value in the numerator as follows:

$$\frac{\text{Equity Value}}{\text{FCFE}}$$

It is important to note that a company's unlevered cash flow should always be greater than its levered cash flow. Financial leverage is the extent to which fixed-income securities are used in a firm's capital structure. Companies that borrow capital believe that the return on the borrowed funds will exceed the borrowing cost. Financial leverage differs from operating leverage which is the percentage change in EBIT that results from a change in the sales of the company.

PRICE TO FREE CASH FLOW

Once the free cash flow has been calculated, investment bankers will often want to analyze the price that the market is paying for the free cash flow. Like the PE ratio, the price to free cash flow utilizes the market price for the stock in the numerator. However, free cash flow per share is used in the denominator rather than EPS. Since we are calculating the price of the stock relative to the free cash flow per share, the equation uses FCFE as the basis for the free cash flow. Therefore, the equation is:

$$\frac{\text{Price}}{\text{FCFE Per Share}}$$

To illustrate this concept let's take a look at an example:

SIA Co	In millions except per share data
FCFE	$300
Stock Price	$45
Number of Shares Outstanding	50
FCFE per share	$6

Using the above information we determined that the FCFE per share was $6. This was found by dividing the total FCFE by the number of outstanding shares. Now we are ready to determine the price to free cash flow. Using the stock price of $45, we get a price to free cash flow of ratio (multiple) of 7.5 ($45/6). We can further use this information to calculate the FCF yield for the stock by inverting the equation and dividing the FCF per share by the price of the stock. In this case the free cash flow yield is 13.33% ($6/45)

PRICE TO BOOK

Investment bankers often use the price to book ratio to evaluate companies who operate in asset intensive industries such as oil exploration or manufacturing companies. Many analysts also use the price to book ratio as a preferred valuation method in the banking and finance industry. The price to book ratio tends to be a more stable measure of value when compared to earnings multiples, especially during times when companies are generating losses. One could take a big picture view of the company by measuring its market capitalization to its total book value as follows;

$$\frac{\text{Total Market Capitalization}}{\text{Total Book Value}}$$

A more stringent approach could be taken by subtracting the company's intangible assets from its book value to measure its market capitalization relative to its tangible book value using the following formula:

$$\frac{\text{Total Market Capitalization}}{\text{Total Tangible Book Value}}$$

This use of the price to book or market capitalization to book ratio may be used when considering an acquisition. Investment bankers and analysts who are looking for undervalued opportunities in the stock market may calculate the price to book ratio using the market price of a stock relative to the book value per share. The formula in this case is:

$$\frac{\text{Market Price}}{\text{Book Value Per Share}}$$

Like the big picture view above this calculation may be made more stringent by using the tangible book value per share as such:

$$\frac{\text{Market Price}}{\text{Tangible Book Value Per Share}}$$

As with most valuation ratios, lower price to book ratios represent better values based.

PRICE TO SALES

The price to sales ratio was developed in response to the difficulties found in properly valuing startup and early stage companies. Young companies who may have just completed an initial public offering often have not been able to translate sales into earnings. In these cases, the price to earnings ratios are of no value. A company's top line sales numbers are a reasonable way to place a value on companies in their early stages. Additionally, these revenue or sales numbers are free from the impacts of accounting adjustments. The formula for the price to sales ratio is:

$$\frac{\text{Share Price}}{\text{Sales Per Share}}$$

To find the sales per share the total sales or revenue number should be taken from the income statement and divided by the number of shares outstanding.

WEIGHTED AVERAGE COST OF CAPITAL

A company's weighted average cost of capital or WACC, is the weighted average after tax cost of obtaining capital through all capital sources. For most companies these capital sources include the issuance of common and preferred stock and the issuance of bonds. The weighted average cost of capital is the average after tax cost that a company would expect to pay to finance its assets. The WACC is calculated using the cost of each source of capital. The cost of each equity and debt issue is then multiplied by its percentage contribution to the company's capital base and added together to arrive at the WACC. To simplify the concept the formula is:

WACC = Weighted Average Cost of Debt + Weighted average cost of Equity

There are several factors that can further impact a company's capital costs. These factors include the expenses incurred to issue and underwrite the securities. These costs are sometimes referred to as flotation expenses. Fees or discounts paid to underwriters and legal costs are just a few of the expenses that can reduce the proceeds to the issuer and increase its capital costs. The cost of issuing debt securities has several additional factors that must be considered. First, the nominal yield is effectively the pre tax cost for borrowing the funds without considering any flotation expenses. However, in addition to the underwriting and floatation expenses, any original discount passed on to investors will increase the pre tax cost to the company. The example below illustrates this point.

SIA, Co is seeking to expand its operations and will be issuing $10 million worth of 10 year bonds. The bonds will be issued at par with a 7 percent coupon. SIA's nominal pre tax cost of capital is $700,000 per year ($10 million X 7%). In order to issue the bonds, SIA engaged an underwriting syndicate and the fees paid to the underwriters and other legal and printing costs totaled $400,000. SIA's proceeds from the bond issuance were therefore reduced by an equal amount resulting in net proceeds of $9.6 million. SIA' s pre tax cost of issuing the bonds is found as follows:

$$\frac{\text{Annual Interest Expense}}{\text{Net Proceeds}}$$

In this case:

$$\frac{\$700,000}{\$9,600,000}$$

SIA's pre tax cost of issuing the bonds is 7.29%. If the bonds in the above example were issued at discount to investors to help market the issue, the discount would further reduce the proceeds to the company and increase its cost of capital. If we keep the flotation costs of $400,000 constant and if the bonds were issued at a price of $990 instead of par, the cost of issuing the 7 percent bonds would be 7.36% . The net proceeds to the issuer would be $9.5 million and the annual interest cost remains $700,000.

Let's look at the pre tax cost of issuing preferred stock. Preferred stock is an equity security with a fixed income component in the form of a stated dividend. Unless otherwise noted, assume that the par value for preferred stock is always $100. The dividend on preferred stock is stated as a percentage of par. If, instead of issuing 7 percent bonds to fund its expansion, SIA issued a 7 percent preferred stock; its pre tax cost of capital would look similar to the pre tax cost of capital for the bonds. Keeping the flotation costs at $400,000 and issuing $10 million worth of preferred stock the pre tax cost would be found as follows:

$$\frac{\text{Annual Dividend Expense}}{\text{Net Proceeds}}$$

CHAPTER 7   Valuation

In this case:

$$\frac{\$700{,}000}{\$9{,}600{,}000}$$

Once again the pre tax cost of capital is 7.29%. Any discounts passed along to investors at the time the preferred stock is issued would further increase the cost of capital. Without taking taxes into consideration the issuance of bonds and preferred stock look very similar. However, for tax purposes the payments made by the corporation to investors are treated very differently. The interest payments made to bondholders are made with pre tax dollars. This favorable tax treatment reduces the overall cost of raising capital through the issuance of bonds. In the case of preferred stock, the stated dividend paid to preferred stockholders is made with after tax dollars and as a result increases the cost of capital. Let's look at the after tax cost of capital for SIA. First, we will calculate the after tax cost of capital for the 7 percent bond issue. If SIA pays a corporate tax rate of 28 percent, the after tax cost of the bond issue would be found as follows:

Pre Tax Rate X (100%- Tax Rate)

7% X (100-28)

7% X .72 = 5.04%

Here we see that the after tax cost of issuing the bonds is substantially lower than the nominal cost / nominal yield. Because the dividend on the preferred stock is paid with after tax dollars we need to alter the formula. To find the after tax cost for the 7% preferred stock we would calculate it a follows:

Preferred Dividend Rate
(100% - Tax Rate)

$$\frac{7\%}{(100-28)}$$

7/.72 = 9.72%

Here we have an after tax cost for capital on the preferred stock of 9.72%. While the nominal pre tax cost of capital was similar for the two securities, once the impact of taxes are taken into account we see that the cost of the cost of capital obtained by issuing preferred stock was substantially higher than that of the bonds. In this case the after tax cost of issuing the preferred stock was 9.72% vs 5.04% for the bonds.

In the above examples SIA was issuing securities in an effort to fund an expansion of its operations. In order for the expansion to be successful, SIA would have to increase its EBIT by more than the cost of capital. To determine the required increase in earnings use the following formula:

$$\frac{\text{(Proceeds X After Tax Cost)}}{(100\% - \text{Tax Rate})}$$

Keeping our tax rate consistent at 28 percent we see that the required increase for the 7 percent bonds is calculated as follows:

$$\frac{(\$10,000,000 \times 5.04\%)}{(100\%-28\%)}$$

$$\frac{504,000}{.72} = \$700,000$$

Because the interest expense is covered with pre tax dollars the company only needs to increase its earning before interest and taxes by an amount equal to the annual interest costs. However, this is not the case with the issuance of preferred stock because the dividends are paid with after tax dollars. Using the same formula as above we calculate the following required increase in EBIT for the issuance of the preferred shares.

$$\frac{(\$10,000,000 \times 7\%)}{(100\%-28\%)}$$

$$\frac{700,000}{.72} = \$972,222$$

If SIA had earnings before interest and taxes of $5 million before the issuance of the bonds, it would have to increase EBIT to $5.7 million after the issuance to maintain the same level of earnings available to common stockholders. Similarly, SIA would have to increase its earnings before interest and taxes to $5.972 million to maintain the same level of earnings available to common stockholders after the issuance of the preferred stock. The following table details these requirements

	Bonds	Preferred Stock
EBIT	$5,700,000	$5,972,222
Interest Expense	$700,000	0
Earnings Before Taxes	$5,000,000	$5,972,222
Tax Rat 28%	$1,400,000	$1.672,222
Preferred dividends	0	$700,000
Earnings Available to Common Stockholders	$3,600,000	$3,600,000

CHAPTER 7 Valuation

Calculating the cost of common equity is more complicated than calculating the cost of debt or preferred stock. The cost of equity will be calculated using either the capital asset pricing model (CAPM) or based on the cash flows generated to common stockholders using the dividend growth model. There are several factors to consider when calculating the cost of equity using CAPM including:

1. The risk free return available in the market (rate of 90 day T bill)
2. The expected return of the stock market (S & P 500)
3. The required risk premium or excess return
4. The s nondiversifiable or systematic risk associated with the equity security (its beta)

A stock's beta is its projected rate of change relative to the market as a whole. If the market was up 10% for the year, a stock with a beta of 1.5 could reasonably be expected to be up 15%. This is the simplest way to estimate the expected return using beta. However, The calculation for CAPM is more complex. You must take the risk-free return into consideration.. The risk-free return is subtracted from the market return to determine the risk premium. The risk premium is the return investors demand in exchange for taking on the risk of purchasing securities. From there, multiply the beta times the risk premium and add back the risk-free rate to predict the precise expected return for the security. If using the same example of a stock with a beta of 1.5, a market return of 10%, and with the risk-free rate of 1% for the 90-day T-bill, your calculation would be as follows: Market return minus the risk-free rate (10-1) equals a risk premium of 9%. 9% multiplied by the beta of 1.5 equals 13.5%. Finally, add back the risk free rate of 1%, to determine the overall expected return, which in this example would be 14.5% found as follows (10-1) x 1.5 +1 = 14.5%. The expected return of the stock translates into the equity cost of capital. A stock with a beta greater than one has a higher level of volatility than the market as a whole and is considered to be more risky than the overall market. A stock with a beta of less than one is less volatile than prices in the overall market. If we keep all of the data from the above example constant, but change the beta of the stock from 1.5 to .8, the calculation would b as follows:

$$[(10-1) \times .8] +1 = 8.2\%$$

Changes in interest rates will impact the risk free rate and as a result the equity cost of capital (expected return) for both high and low beta stocks. However, these changes will not affect high beta and low beta stocks equally.

An increase in the risk free rate will result in a lower cost of equity for high beta stocks and in a higher cost of equity for low beta stocks. The impact of how a change in the risk free rate affects these stocks is detailed in the chart below.

Beta	Market Return	Risk Free Return	Cost of Equity
1.5	10	1	14.5%
1.5	10	2	14%
1.5	10	3	13.5%
.8	10	1	8.2%
.8	10	2	8.4%
.8	10	3	8.6%

In the above table the expected return for the market remained constant and the risk free rate increased as interest rates increased. It seems almost counter intuitive that the cost of equity for high beta stocks would fall while the cost for low beta stocks would increase, but when you realize that the risk premium has fallen as a result of the increase in the risk free rate, it makes more sense. The cost of common equity includes common stock and retained earnings. Both of these are found in the equity section of the balance sheet. Companies may create equity capital by issuing new common stock or by increasing retained earnings. On your exam you will be required to calculate the cost of common equity. However, you will not be given the formula so it is important to commit the calculation to memory as follows:

Cost of equity = [Beta X (market return - risk free rate)] + risk free rate

LEVERED AND UNLEVERED BETA

In our discussion above we introduced the broad concept of beta and how a stock's beta impacts both its expected return and the issuer's cost of equity capital. A company's levered beta takes into account the impact of the capital structure and its use of borrowed funds or leverage. Unless stated otherwise, the beta coefficient used in most cases is the levered beta. The greater the company's leverage, the greater its beta and the more of its earnings are committed to servicing debt. The unlevered beta removes the impact of the company's capital structure and its use of leverage and is based solely on the company's equity or assets. For this reason unlevered beta is sometimes referred to as asset beta. On your exam you will be required to calculate both the levered and unlevered beta. You will not be give the formulas and must commit them to memory as follows:

Unlevered Beta = Levered Beta / 1+ [(1-tax rate) X (debt/equity)]

Levered Beta = Unlevered Beta X 1+ [(1-tax rate) X (debt/equity)])

Let's look at how to calculate the unlevered beta given a levered beta.

Levered Beta	1.5
Debt/ Equity	40 %
Tax Rate	28%

$$\frac{1.5}{1+[(1-28\%) \times 40\%])} =$$

$$\frac{1.5}{1+(.72 \times .4)} =$$

$$\frac{1.5}{1.288}$$

In this case the unlevered beta would be 1.164. Now lets calculate the levered beta given an unlevered beta

Unlevered Beta	1.3
Debt/ Equity	30 %
Tax Rate	28%

Using the above formula and information provided we calculate the levered beta as follows:

Levered beta = unlevered beta X (1 + [(1- Tax Rae) X (Debt / Equity)])

$$1.3 \times (1+[(1-28\%) \times 30\%)]) =$$

$$1.3 \times (.72 \times .30) =$$

$$1.3 \times 1.216 = 1.58$$

COST OF EQUITY BASED ON ISSUANCE OF NEW COMMON SHARES

When a company seeks to raise capital through the issuance of new shares, the proceeds to the issuer will be reduced by the fees it must pay to the underwriters. The proceeds will be further reduced by additional flotation costs, such as printing and legal fees. These floatation costs increase the cost of capital to the issuer and must be considered when calculating the cost of issuing shares. To calculate the cost of capital for issuing new shares you will need the following data:

1. Annual growth rate
2. Annual dividend
3. Total flotation costs
4. Price of issuance

Current Stock Price	$60
Annual Dividend	$1.75
Assumed Annual Growth Rate	5%
Flotation Costs	3%

Using the information above, let's assume that the stock issued to the public at a price of $60 per share and that underwriter fees and other flotation costs total 3%.

The cost of capital = [Annual dividend / (Price - fees)] + growth Rate

[$1.75 / (60-$1.80)]+ 5% =

(1.75/ 58.2) +5% =

3% + 5 % = 8%

The cost of capital based on the issuance will be approximately 8%.

COST OF EQUITY BASED ON RETAINED EARNINGS

Investors who purchase common stock do so with the expectation that the price will appreciate and that they will receive an income stream in the form of dividends. Based on this expectation we can calculate the cost of equity capital. To determine the cost of equity capital using the dividend growth model a constant growth rate must be assigned to the dividend payments to be made by the company. In order to perform this calculation the following data must be obtained:

1. Annual growth rate
2. Annual dividend
3. Current market price of the stock

CHAPTER 7 Valuation

Using the dividend growth model lets calculate the cost of equity using the following data

Current Stock Price	$60
Annual Dividend	$1.75
Assumed Annual Growth Rate	5%

The formula is:

The cost of equity = (Annual dividend / Current market price) + growth rate

($1.75/ $60) + 5 =

2.91% + 5% = 7.91%

 TAKE NOTE!

The cost of equity using retained earnings will always be lower than the cost of equity from issuing securities because there are no flotation costs associated with the use of retained earnings.

The cost of equity capital is also the required rate of return when a company is investing its retained earnings into its business. If a company is able to invest its retained earnings at a rate which exceeds the required rate of return, the price of the company's stock should rise. Alternatively, If the return generated from investing the retained earnings does not meet the required rate of return, one would expect the stock price to fall. The estimated stock price can be found using the following formula:

Price = Annual dividend / (Required rate of return - actual return)

If the above company invested its retained earnings into a project that generated a 4% return the stock price would be estimated as follows:

$$\frac{\$1.75}{(7.91\% - 4\%)} = \frac{\$1.75}{3.91\%}$$

In this case the stock price would be estimated to be $44.75 after the retained earnings had been invested in a project that did not return the required rate.

The assumed annual growth rate is also used to calculate the future stock price. The future stock price in this example is $63. This is found by multiplying the current stock price by 1+ annual growth rate or in this case 60 x 1.05 = 63

Now that we have gone through the various costs of capital, let's take a look at calculating the weighted average cost of capital in a bit more detail. Below we have information about a company which we will use as the basis of our discussion.

On your exam you may be given either the debt / equity ratio or you may be provided with the debt / total capital ratio and the equity to total capital ratio and be asked to calculate the WACC. Keep in mind that the debt / equity ratio tells you how much debt was raised relative to equity, not how much of the company's total capitalization was raised by each.

If you are given the debt to equity ratio you must calculate both the debt to total capital ratio and the equity to total capital ratio to accurately determine the WACC. To calculate the these use the following formulas:

Debt to total capital ratio = Debt-to equity ratio / (100% + Debt-to equity ratio)

Taking the debt to equity ratio from the table below of 66.67 we get the following:

$$\frac{66.67}{(100\% + 66.67\%)}$$

$$\frac{66.67}{166.67\%}$$

The debt to total capitalization ratio is 40%

To find the equity to capital ratio use the following formula:

Equity to total capital ratio = 100% / (100% + Debt-to equity ratio)

$$\frac{100\%}{(100\% + 66.67\%)}$$

$$\frac{100\%}{166.67\%}$$

CHAPTER 7 Valuation

The equity to total capital ratio is 60%. Now that we have calculated the amount of capitalization coming from both debt and equity we are able to calculate the WACC.

SIA WACC Calculation	
Capital Structure	
Debt to Total Capitalization	40.00%
Equity to Total Capitalization	60.00%
Debt / Equity	**66.67%**
Cost of Equity	
Risk Free Rate	1.50%
Equity Risk Premium	7.00%
Levered Beta	1.20
Cost of Equity	**9.90%**
Cost of Debt	
Cost of Debt	7.00%
Tax Rate	28.00%
After Tax Cost of Debt	**5.04%**
WACC	7.96%

Once you have been able to calculate the contribution of debt and equity to the total capital structure, you must take the tax implications into account to calculate the WACC. Using a tax rate of 28% we see that the after tax cost of capital for the bonds issuance is much lower than the cost for equity capital. The following table shows how we calculated the WACC for SIA using the data above.

Source of Capital	Percent of Total Capital	After Tax Cost	Weighted Average
Debt	40%	5.04	2.016%
Equity	60%	9.90%	5.94%
WACC			7.96%

There are several important concepts that you need to know regarding how a company's cost of capital can change over time. As companies raise more capital their WACC can change as the debt to equity ratio changes. If a company issues more debt it's weighted average cost of capital will decline. Alternatively, if a company issues more equity its weighted average cost of capital will increase. Further, as interest rates rise and fall over time, the cost of borrowed capital changes and will impact the WACC. Another way to view the WACC is if market capitalization of the equity exceeds the market value of the debt, the WACC will be higher and vice versa.

DIVIDEND VALUATION MODELS

Investment bankers may use a dividend valuation model to determine a fair valuation for an equity security and to determine its estimated intrinsic value. Dividend discount models tend to take a long term approach to valuation and are less sensitive to short term changes when compared to other discount models. Dividend discount models are based on the value of the dividends paid from both current and retained earnings. However, like all models they are data dependent and selecting the appropriate inputs are crucial to arriving at a proper value. There are several dividend valuation models used by bankers including the dividend discount model, the dividend growth model and the gordon growth model.

The Dividend Discount Model: The dividend discount model takes the sum of all future dividends to be received and discounts them into a net present value. The model states that the market price of the stock should be equal to the net present value of all future cash flows. A simple way to estimate the value based on this method would be to take the annual dividend and divide it by the prevailing rate paid by other similar investments. If a utility stock is paying a $2 annual dividend and other similar utilities are yielding 5% the market price can be estimated to be $40. Found as follows:

$$\$2 / .05 = \$40$$

If the dividend remains constant it is assuming zero growth in the income generated to the owner. In theory the amount of the dividend should exceed the risk free rate by an amount equal to the risk to the investor, or saying this another way, the amount of the dividends should equal the risk free rate plus the risk premium. Another application of this model may be used to calculate the price of the stock based on the dividend relative to the discount rate as follows:

CHAPTER 7 Valuation

Price = Annual dividend / Discount rate

If SJI pays a $3.10 annual dividend and its cost of capital is 8 percent and we apply this as the discount rate we can calculate an estimated price for SJI as follows:

$$\frac{\$3.10}{.08}$$

Based on this data, the price of SJI should be $38.75

The dividend discount model may be used for issues that have both fixed and variable dividends over time.

The Dividend Growth Model: The dividend growth model values the stock based on the net present value of the cash flow to be generated by a dividend that is expected to grow over time. It is important to know that if all else is equal, the present value of a stock is significantly higher for an equity with a dividend that is predicted to grow. The higher the growth rate the higher the net present value. Because the dividend growth model calculates a higher net present value, this model will predict a higher stock price than the dividend discount model based on a constant dividend. For your exam it is important to note that you would never use the dividend growth model to value preferred stock, because the dividend is set at a fixed rate. Preferred stock should always be valued using a zero growth model. If we return to our example of SJI above and estimate a growth rate of 4% we would calculate the value as follows:

$$\frac{\text{Dividend}}{(\text{Discount rate - growth rate})}$$

$$\frac{\$3.10}{(.08-.04)}$$

$$\frac{\$3.10}{.04}$$

In this case we estimate the value of SJI to be $77.5, much higher than the previous estimate based on a dividend with zero growth.

The Gordon Growth Model: The gordon growth model can be used to calculate both the amount of the next dividend and to estimate a value for the stock. To calculate the next dividend use the following formula

Future dividend = current dividend X (1. + Growth rate):

If we use the data from above when given a growth rate of 4% we can calculate the future dividend as follows:

$$\$3.10 \times (1+.04)$$

$$\$3.1 \times 1.04 = \$3.22$$

In this example we now estimate the dividend to be $3.22 next year. Based on this information we can again calculate the price or intrinsic value of the stock based on its dividend by applying the following formula:

$$\frac{\textbf{Future Dividend}}{\textbf{(Discount rate - Growth rate)}}$$

Applying an 8 percent cost of capital as the discount rate and a 4 percent growth rate we get:

$$\frac{\$3.22}{(.08-.04)}$$

$$\frac{\$3.22}{.04}$$

Based on this model we arrive at an estimated intrinsic value of $80.50.

In the examples above we were provided with a growth rate for the company. On your exam you may be required to calculate the growth rate in order to perform the ultimate calculation. To calculate the growth rate for a company you will need the following data:

1. Earnings per share
2. Dividends
3. Cost of equity capital
4. Return on equity

Lets calculate the growth rate for QWER using the following data:

Earnings Per Share	$4.55
Dividends	$1.80
Cost of Equity Capital / Discount rate	9%
Return on Equity	10%

To calculate the growth rate multiply the earnings retention rate by the return on equity. The earnings retention rate is the percentage of EPS not paid out in dividends to shareholders. Saying this another way, it is the complement of the dividend payout ratio. The dividend payout ratio in this case is $1.80 /

$4.55 = 40\%$. Therefore, the earnings retention rate is 60 percent. Now that we have the earnings retention rate we can calculate the growth rate as follows

Growth rate = 60% X 10% = 6%

SUM OF THE PARTS (SOTP) VALUATION

When trying to assign a value to a business with different business units or segments, investment bankers may elect to employ a sum of the parts valuation. One of the key principles in SOTP analysis is that different business segments may be more valuable than others. Additionally, each segment's growth rate and contribution to the company's overall performance varies. Mature slow growing, low margin business units may be less valuable than a new business unit with a high growth rate and high margins. With this in mind bankers will value each business unit separately and add the values together to arrive at an ultimate value for the total company. There are three steps to performing a SOTP valuation. These are:

1. Identifying the business units
2. Performing valuation analysis on each unit
3. Adding the business values to arrive at the total value

When valuing each unit, the investment banker may elect to use one or more valuation models such as Discounted cash flow (discussed below) or comparative company analysis. In most cases the total value will be discounted to its net present value.

Let's take a look at QWER, a diversified holding company with 4 different business units. These business units are as follows:

1. Business unit A - A fast growing business operating in the ecommerce industry
2. Business unit B - A service business with a moderate growth rate
3. Business unit C - A mature capital intensive industrial company with stable earnings
4. Business unit D - A technology company with an above average growth rate

When looking at the business units above, with no other information, an analyst would assume that business unit A would be assigned the highest multiple, while business unit C would be assigned the lowest multiple. Using this concept, lets assign hypothetical earnings and multiples to each unit.

Business Unit	EBITDA	Multiple	Valuation
A	$2.4 million	14	$33.6 million
B	$6.1 million	11	$67.1 million
C	$8.4 million	9	$75.6 million
D	$5.1 milloin	12	$61.2 million
Total			$237.5 million

Based on the information above the total value for all business units is $237.5 million. It is interesting to note that even though business unit C was assigned the lowest multiple, it is still the most valuable unit because its EBITDA is the highest. We also see that the fastest growing business unit is the least valuable, but given the highest multiple due to its growth rate. If QWER had $40 million dollars in net debt the equity value would be $237.5 million - $40 million = $197.5 million. In addition to subtracting the net debt any non operating accounting adjustments would have to be considered to calculate the ultimate equity value of the company. Using sum of the parts analysis is appropriate for:

- Conglomerates
- Holding companies
- Companies who report results for different business units
- Companies with clearly identifiable assets
- Financial modeling for acquisitions

Sum of the parts analysis should not be used for companies who have a single operating unit nor for companies who do not disclose the operating profits of individual business units

DISCOUNTED CASH FLOW

When a business is contemplating making an investment in a new project, managers will often conduct a net present value calculation. The net present value measures the relationship between the expenses of a project or its cash

CHAPTER 7 Valuation

outflows and the income or cash inflows to be received from the project. All future cash flows are discounted to their net present value and evaluated. The discount rate applied to the cash flows is equal to the required rate of return. The internal rate of return for a project is the discount rate (required return) that results in the net present value being equal to zero. If the present value of the income to be generated is greater than the present value of the expenses, the project would have a positive net present value. A project with a positive net present value warrants an investment since the rate of return is greater than the required rate of return. One of the primary calculations investment bankers use to value a business is known as discounted cash flow analysis or DCF. Proponents of DCF analysis believe that the present value of a company is the discounted sum of all of its future cash flows. Unlike relative value calculations which are used to value one company relative to others (such as PE ratios and enterprise value ratios), DCF calculates an absolute or intrinsic value for the business based solely on its ability to generate a stream of cash flows. Discounted cash flow analysis is used to project cash flows generated by the business during future periods and to calculate the discounted current value of those future cash flows. One of the fundamental concepts of DCF is the fact that one dollar to be received in the future is not worth one dollar today. It is in fact worth less than one dollar. How much less, is contingent upon the amount of time until the dollar is received and the discount rate applied. The discount rate that is applied to the future cash flows may be based on a required rate of return, the weighted average cost of capital, or the cost of equity. When assigning the discount rate, bankers will take into consideration any risks associated with receiving the cash flow. While companies with steady and predictable cash flows will be assigned a lower discount rate, companies whose ability to maintain the cash flow is in doubt, will be assigned a higher discount rate. Using a higher discount rate results in a lower present value. For example, if an investor were to receive $10,000 1 year from now and applied a 5 percent discount rate to that payment, its present value would be found as follows:

$$\frac{\text{Future value}}{(1+ \text{discount rate})}$$

$$\frac{\$10,000}{(1+.05)}$$

In this case, the $10,000 payment to be received in 1 year would be $9,523.80. ($10,000 / 1.05). If we applied a discount rate of 10 percent, the $10,000 payment would be worth $9,090.90. ($10,000 / 1.10).

Bankers will often use DCF for a foreseeable period of time such as for 3 or 5 years. At the end of the forecasting period, the banker will assign a terminal value for the company. The terminal value may be used to calculate an estimated exit value for a private equity firm or to value the company as an ongoing business. If the business is to be valued as an ongoing concern, bankers will traditionally use either a perpetual growth rate or a terminal multiple to value the business. The perpetual growth rate assumes that the company will grow its earnings at an uninterrupted rate equal to the growth rate during the final year in the forecast period (in perpetuity). This method for calculating the terminal value clearly has its drawbacks as nothing remains constant forever. The terminal value using this method is the projected value of all future cash flows to be received starting at the end of the forecast period and continuing into the future forever. Another way of calculating the terminal value is by using a terminal multiple. A terminal multiple, which ironically is a relative value calculation, values the business based on the multiples assigned to other similar businesses. Valuing a business based on a terminal multiple is the more common way to assign a value to a business. The multiple traditionally uses an industry average of comparable companies such as a multiple of EBITDA. The terminal value based on cash flow and the assumed growth rate is found as follows:

$$\frac{\textbf{Expected Cash Flown X (1+Terminal Growth Rate)}}{\textbf{(Discount Rate - Terminal Growth Rate)}}$$

Investment bankers traditionally use DCF to assign a value to either the entire company or to the equity value of the company. This is an important distinction as it has a substantial impact on data that is used in the DCF calculation. When calculating the enterprise value, the cash flows that will be used are the FCFF and the discount rate will be calculated based on the weighted average cost of capital. The formula is:

$$EV = \sum \frac{(\text{Free Cash Flow To The Firm})_t}{(1+WACC)^t} + \frac{\text{Terminal Value}}{(1+WACC)^n}$$

Where t is the period and n is the number of periods. You will not be required to perform the above calculation, as you will not have a scientific calculator on the exam. It is included here for illustrative purposes. When calculating the equity value of the firm the FCFE is used and the discount rate will be calculated based on the cost of equity. The formula is:

CHAPTER 7 Valuation

Cash Flow To Equity
(1+ Cost of Equity)

The cost of equity will be calculated using either the capital asset pricing model (CAPM) or based on its cash flows using the dividend growth model.

Now let's calculate the value of a company based on the following information:

Growth Rate	5%
WACC (Discount Rate)	7%
Terminal Value	$4 million

Year	1	2	3	4	Terminal Value
FCFF	$320,000	$336,000	$352,800	$369,600	$4,000,000
Discount Rate	1.07	1.1449	1.225	1.31	1.402
Discounted Amount	$20,935	$42,525	$64,800	$87,462.6	$1,146,933
Present Value	$299,065	$293,475	$288,000	$282,137.4	$2,853,067

In the above table we see a 4 year estimate for the FCFF and the discounted present value for each. Notice how the present value of the cash flow is lower than the previous year even though the FCFF is growing by 5 % each year. This illustrates the time value of money. When we discounted the cash flow for each period, we used the following formula:

$$\frac{FCFF}{(1+WACC)^N}$$

The weighted average cost of capital for the example above was 7 percent. Resulting in a denominator of 1.07 raised to a power equal to the number of years until the discount period. Since you will not be given a scientific calculator on the exam, you must multiply the result by itself for each year until the discount period. For year three it would be as follows:

$$1.07 \times 1.07 \times 1.07 = 1.225$$

We then take the discount rate calculated above and use it to calculate the present value of the FCFF for year three as follow:

$$\frac{\$352,800}{1.225}$$

Completing the calculation we get a present value of $288,000. When we add the present value of all cash flows plus the discounted terminal value we get a total enterprise value of $4,015,744.

Now let's take our example one step further and calculate the implied equity value of the firm and the equity value per share. The implied equity value is often used as a basis for a fairness opinion rendered by investment bankers. Investment bankers who issue fairness opinions based on DCF analysis must include a disclosure regarding the DCF method used to value the company and that DCF analysis only works for companies with positive cash flows. You are likely to see a few questions on your exam requiring you to calculate the implied equity value. In order to do this we will need to know the following information:

1. The amount of cash the company has on hand
2. The amount of debt the company has on its balance sheet
3. The number of shares outstanding

Cash on Hand	$1.4 million
Debt	$1 million
Shares Outstanding	500,000

Now we are ready to calculate the implied equity value as follows:

Enterprise Value	$4,015,744
Plus Cash on Hand	$1,400,000
Minus Debt	$1,000,000
Equity Value	$4,415,744
Equity Value Per Share	$8.83

You may also use the implied equity value to calculate the IPO price and its proceeds if you are given the:

- Earnings
- The growth rate
- The multiple range
- The IPO Discount
- Percentage ownership to be offered
- Number of shares to be issued

Let's take a look at an example of a privately held company contemplating an IPO. The owners of SIA are planning to sell off part of their ownership in the company through an IPO. The details are as follows:

Net income	$2 million
Growth Rate	7%
Multiple Range	12-15
IPO Discount	10%
Percent Offered	40%

Using the above information we can now begin to work through a number of questions. The first step is to calculate the net income for the following period. In this case we get $2 million X 1.07 = $2.14 million. Based on the multiple range of 12-15 we get an estimated equity value range of $25.68 million-$32.1 million. This is found by multiplying the estimated net income by the multiple of 12 and 15 respectively. Taking into consideration the IPO discount of 10 percent we see the valuation range as $23.112 million - $28.89 million. Now we must account for the fact that only 40 percent of the stock will be issued to investors and we see that the likely proceeds are in the range of $9.244 million to $11.556 million before any floatation costs are incurred. If at the completion of the offering, SIA were to have 1 million shares issued the expected price range for the IPO would be between $9.24 and $11.55 per share.

Now that we have shown you how to calculate implied equity value, lets look at another way to calculate enterprise value. To calculate the enterprise value use the following formula:

$$\frac{\text{Cash Flow} \times (1 + G)}{(\text{Discount Rate} - \text{Growth Rate})}$$

The above formula estimates that the company will maintain a constant rate of growth in perpetuity. Let's take a look an example:

Cash Flow	$10 million
Growth Rate	5%
Discount Rate	9 %

Using the information and formula above we get:

$$\frac{\$10,000,000 \times (1+.05)}{(9\% - 5\%)}$$

$$\frac{\$10,500,000}{.04}$$

In this case we get an estimated enterprise value of $262,500,000. Finally we can estimate the value of an enterprise by taking the estimated cash flow to be generated in perpetuity and dividing it by the weighted average cost of capital. If we estimate that a company will generate $10 million in cash flow every year and has a WACC of 9%, we would estimate the net present value to be $10,000,00 / .09 = $111,111,111.

Now that we have reviewed discounted cash flow analysis, let's review the pros and cons of using DCF to value a business.

Pros	Cons
Very Detailed Analysis	Error Prone
Does Not Rely on Comparable Companies	Values Business in Isolation
Calculates Intrinsic Value of Business	No Relative Valuation
Contains All Major Assumptions about Business	Hard To Calculate Accurate Terminal Value
Includes Future Expectations	Very Sensitive to Changes in Data

It is important to note that DCF analysis is very sensitive to changes in the data and projections used to value the business. As such, a small change in the discount rate or projections can result in a large change in estimated value. The following table provides details on the impact of some changes in data:

Change in Data	Impact on Valuation
Cash flow declines	Value declines
Cash flow increases	Value increases
WACC (discount rate) declines	Value increases
WACC (discount rate) increase	Value declines
If CAPEX declines Cash flow increases	Value increases
If CAPEX increases cash flow decreases	Value declines
Taxes increase	Value declines
Taxes decrease	Value increases

Investment bankers will often use DCF analysis in conjunction with other valuation methods such as comparable company analysis and precedent transaction analysis to validate the results. By employing multiple valuation techniques, bankers can be more confident in their ultimate valuation range for the company. This is because each valuation method serves as a check on the others. Finally, DCF may be used as an evaluation tool as part of a leveraged buyout. The primary objective of an LBO is to use borrowed funds to

CHAPTER 7   Valuation

acquire a company. The target company's free cash flow is used to estimate the target's ability to service the new debt used to acquire the company. The discount rate used in an LBO analysis is the after tax cost of the debt. The discounted present value of the cash flows to be received during the term of the debt provides a good indication of the company's ability to service its debt obligations.

ECONOMIC VALUE ADDED

When making a decision to employ capital to expand a business, leaders must take into account the opportunity cost of using capital in line with the potential to add economic value or to generate an economic profit. The opportunity cost associated with employing capital to expand in one area is the foregone potential to use that same capital to expand in another area. For example, if a company has $10 million to invest in expansion and it is evaluating expansion choice A and B, each costing $10 million, the company may choose to expand in choice A or in choice B. There is no possibility of choosing to expand in both. A company's economic profit takes its explicit and implicit costs into account. A company's explicit costs are those associated with running the business. These costs may include wages, rent, COGS etc. A company's implicit costs are the opportunity costs associated with employing capital based on a business decision. These may be the interest the company could earn by purchasing Treasury securities or the expansion potential in other areas. In order to earn an economic profit the company must be able to employ its capital at a rate that exceeds the opportunity cost. An economic profit differs from an accounting profit in that an accounting profit only considers the company's explicit costs. As a result, it is possible for the same project to generate an accounting profit and an economic loss project based on the opportunity costs considered as part of the economic calculation. A project that generates an accounting profit but an economic loss is an inefficient use of capital. The money invested could have been invested more efficiently. The formula for the economic value added or economic profit is:

Economic Value Added = Accounting Profit - Opportunity Costs

More often than not, the opportunity cost associated with a project will be based on the weighted average cost of capital. Now let's take a look at an example of an investment made by QWER and evaluate the accounting profit and its economic profit. In order evaluate the project the following data is required:

1. Capital Investment
2. Tax Rate
3. EBIT
4. WACC

For our example let's assume that QWER invested in a new plant to expand its production and shows the following:

Capital Investment	$20,000,000
Tax Rate	28%
EBIT	$6,800,000
WACC	8.5%

The first step would be to use the data to calculate the accounting profit. The accounting profit is found by multiplying the EBIT by the complement of the tax rate. In this case:

$$\$6,800,000 \times (1-.28)$$

$$6,800,000 \times .72 = \$4,896,000$$

Now that we have calculated the accounting profit we can determine the economic profit using the following formula:

Accounting profit - (WACC X Capital Investment)

$$\$4,896,000 - (\$20,000,000 \times .085)$$

$$\$4,896,000 - \$1,700,00 = \$3,960,000$$

We see that the economic profit or economic value added is significantly lower than the accounting profit. Because the economic profit exceeds the WACC ($3.96 million vs $1.7 million respectively), the investment in the plant to increase production added shareholder value. You may also determine if a project added economic value using the following formula:

Return on invested capital
Capital Investment

Return on invested capital = EBIT X (1- Tax ate)

6,800,000 X .72 = $4,896,000

$4,896,000/ $20,000,000 = 24.4%

In this case the ROIC was substantially greater than the WACC so the expansion was a great use of capital.

Let's change our example and assume that the new plant production shows the following:

Capital Investment	$20,000,000
Tax Rate	28%
EBIT	$1,200,000
WACC	8.5%

Accounting profit = $1,200,000 X (1-.28)

$1,200,000 X .72 = $864,000

Economic profit = $864,000 - (.085 X $20,000,000)

$864,000 - $1,700,000 = ($836,000)

Here we see an example of a project that generated an accounting profit but incurred an economic loss. This expansion reduced shareholder value. When we look at the ROIC in relation to the capital invested we get:

$864,000/ $20,000,00 = 4.32%

In this case, the return on invested capital of 4.32% is significantly lower than the WACC of 8.5%. As a result, this project generated an economic loss and was a poor use of capital.

In this chapter, we have covered numerous valuation techniques and provided an understanding of the philosophy behind each. It is important to have mastered both the application of these valuation techniques and to be able to identify the main concepts for each valuation method. You will be required to perform many of these calculations on your exam and will be required to answer comprehension questions relating to the rationale behind each valuation method.

CHAPTER 7

Pretest

VALUATION

1. XYZ is a young technology company with a projected EPS growth rate of 22%. Its current EPS is $2.80. XYZ has been trading at a PE Ratio of 35. Based on this information, what is the projected stock price for XYZ?
   A. $119.56
   B. $98
   C. $85.40
   D. $143.43

2. An investment banker is working on the valuation of a large industrial company. Part of the valuation will be based on the company's normalized earnings. Which of the following statements best describes the concept of normalized earnings?
   A. Normalized earnings seek to project the impact the economic cycle will have on companies as part or the normal business cycle. while removing the impact of non recurring charges.
   B. Normalized earnings seek to project the earnings of a company midway through the economic cycle, while considering the impact of non recurring charges.
   C. Normalized earnings seek to project the impact the economic cycle will have on companies as part or the normal business cycle, while considering the impact of non recurring charges.
   D. Normalized earnings seek to project the earnings of a company midway through the economic cycle, while removing the impact of non recurring charges.

253

3. ZEP Manufacturing has earnings per share of $4.15 and its common stock is trading in the marketplace at $56. A manufacturing Index composed of companies in its peer group has a PE ratio of 15. When analyzing ZEP, it could be argued that:
   A. The common stock of ZEP is relatively undervalued to its peer group.
   B. The common stock of ZEP is fairly valued relative to its peer group.
   C. The common stock of ZEP is relatively overvalued to its peer group.
   D. The common stock of ZEP is priced based on the fundamentals of the company not related to its peer group.

4. SJI is a regulated utility company providing gas to a large number of residential and commercial customers. The company paid an annual dividend of $3.50 and had a dividend payout ratio of 40 percent. SJI is an attractive investment for income oriented investors due to its 5 percent dividend yield. Based on this information, SJI's PE ratio is:
   A. 11
   B. 10
   C. 9
   D. 8

5. An economically sensitive company has periods of substantial profits as well as times when the company records significant losses. Which of the following would be a useful valuation metric during times when the company is sustaining losses?
   A. PE ratio
   B. Dividend yield
   C. Earnings yield
   D. Dividend payout ratio

6. VTR reported net income for the previous year of $530 million. This year the company is expecting earnings to come in at $583 million. The stock is trading at $48 per share and the company has 200 million shares outstanding. What is the PEG ratio for this company?
   A. 1.8
   B. 10
   C. 18
   D. .81

CHAPTER 7 Pretest

7. Quantum Corporation is a fast growing company with earnings growth projected to be 24 percent. The company has a PEG ratio of .8. Using this information to calculate the PE ratio for Quantum Corporation, the PE is:
   A. 20
   B. 19.2
   C. 30
   D. 33

8. Kashmir Co. is a manufacturer of large industrial equipment. As such, its earnings are susceptible to economic trends. During the last 4 years the economic conditions have varied widely from peak to trough. Kashmir's earnings for the preceding periods are as follows:

Year	EPS
One	$2.84
Two	$3.60
Three	$4.91
Four	$3.19

   Given the information above, one would project normalized earnings for Kashmir to be:
   A. $3.34 with subsequent adjustments for non recurring items.
   B. $3.34 without subsequent adjustments for non recurring items.
   C. $3.63 with subsequent adjustments for non recurring items.
   D. $3.63 without subsequent adjustments for non recurring items.

9. You are an investment banking representative working for a client interested in making an acquisition of TRY. You are provided the following information:

Net Income	$400 million
Debt Outstanding	$190 million
Cash On hand	$50 million
PE Ratio	16
Stock Price	32
Outstanding Shares	200 million

   Given the above information, what is the enterprise value of TRY?
   A. $6.4 billion
   B. $7.04 billion
   C. $6.54 billion
   D. $6.59 billion

10. Accounting adjustments and other factors can make a company's valuations appear to be better than they actually are. Which of the following valuation metrics would be the least susceptible to manipulation?
    A. PE Ratio
    B. PEG Ratio
    C. EV / Sales Ratio
    D. Price / Book Ratio

CHAPTER **8**

M & A Analysis

INTRODUCTION

In this final chapter we will conclude our review by revisiting the concepts introduced detailing M & A transactions in chapter 3 and the valuation techniques described in chapter 7. We will further build upon these concepts and review how to use them to determine the value of an offer and to analyze the financial impact the transaction has upon the companies The content in this chapter is part of the data collection section of the series 79 exam.

HOW TO DETERMINE THE OFFERING PRICE IN M & A

When an acquirer is considering making an offer for a company, its management and bankers will work together to determine an appropriate valuation. The valuation of similar publicly traded companies (trading comps) and the prices of similar M & A transactions (transaction comps) are major considerations when calculating valuation. The economic theory known as "the law of one price" states that similar assets should all be priced (valued) the same. That is to say, that two companies that are similar in all or most respects should be trading / priced at the same multiple of financial performance i.e. PE, or EV/EBITDA. The first step when doing a comparable valuation analysis is to build the appropriate peer group of similar companies. In this case, bankers will look at the trading comps of publicly traded companies in the same industry. For example, QWER is in the tech sector and is seeking to acquire GMM Micro, a manufacturer of microprocessor chips. The bankers may build a list of trading comps for manufacturers of microprocessors as follows:

Company	EV/Sales	EV/ EBITDA	Price to Book
XTT Tech	1.2	12.4	12
DFG Micro	1.4	14.2	13
HHI Nano	1.5	17.3	15
Range	1.2-1.5	12.4-17.3	12-15
Median	1.35	14.85	13.5
Average	1.367	14.63	13.33

TAKE NOTE!

Private companies and companies in unique businesses may be difficult to value based on trading comps. In this situation bankers may look for a company who has a business unit that is similar to the company and use the business unit for valuation purposes.

Once the list of trading comps have been built, bankers would likely build a list of comparable transactions to determine how similar transactions were valued and what type of premium may be required to close a deal. The following lists valuation ranges for transactions completed in the tech space:

Company	EV/Sales	EV/ EBITDA	Price to Book
FDR Tech	2	14.1	14
DSW Inc.	2.4	15.9	16
SIA Co.	2.8	18.7	17
Range	2-2.8	14.1-18.7	14-17
Median	2.4	16.4	15.5
Average	2.4	16.23	15.66

When looking at the comparable transactions, it is important to take the type of buyer involved into consideration. For example, was the buyer a financial buyer or a strategic buyer? Remember that strategic buyers will usually pay a higher multiple than a financial buyer. Additionally, the currency used, the market conditions and whether the buyout was friendly or hostile all impact the multiple. Having created the data tables covering the trading and transaction comps, the bankers and the company are in a position to begin to formulate an offer. The first step would be to determine which valuation multiple to use. For your exam the EV/ EBITDA would be the most likely. The trading comps have an average multiple of 14.63 and we see that

CHAPTER 8 M & A Analysis

the average deal was done at a multiple of 16.23. Let's review the financial data for GMM Micro.

Stock Price	$31
Outstanding Stock	25 million shares
Market Cap	$775 million
EBITDA	$57 million
Cash	$15 million
Debt	$40 million

Since we are given the market capitalization of $775 million we can simply add the net debt to determine the enterprise value. In this case the net debt is found by subtracting the cash balance from the outstanding debt and we arrive at the net debt of $25 million. Therefore, the enterprise value is $800 million ($775 million + $25 million). The EV/ EBITDA for the target GMM Mirco is found as follows:

$800 million
$57 million

The EV/EBITDA for the company is 14.03. We can see that the ratio is slightly lower than both the median and the average for the trading comps of 14.85 and 14.63 respectively. Based on the average EV/EBITDA multiple for precedent transactions of 16.23. The value of the offer would be $925.11 million. Based on the multiple range of 14.1-18.7, the offer range would be $803.7 million - $1.0659 billion. Now that we have a range of valuations for the offer, we can calculate the implied equity value and the price per share. To do this we subtract the net debt from the enterprise value of the transaction and divide it by the number of shares outstanding. Based on the average EV multiple of the precedent transactions of 16.23 we get the following:

$925.11 million - $25 million = $900.11 million
$900.11 million / 25 million shares = $36

Using the same calculation we would see that the range of offers for the stock would be $31.14 - $41.63 based on the multiple range of 14.1-18.7.

Just beaucase the acquirer and its bankers have calculated price ranges for a proposed offer, there is no assurance that the shareholders of the target company will accept the offer. Though one could surmise that the greater the premium to the current stock price, the greater the likelihood that the deal will get done.

ACCRETIVE AND DILUTIVE TRANSACTIONS

In chapter 3 we introduced M & A transactions, the currency to be used for the transactions and provided an overview of the various types of analysis that may be performed as part of the due diligence process. In chapter 7 we provided a substantial amount of detail regarding the valuation process. Now in this section, we will review the transaction and its financial impact on the acquiring company. One of the primary concerns when a company seeks to make an acquisition is the financial impact it may have on performance. Of particular concern, is if the proposed transaction will be accretive or dilutive to shareholders. An accretive transaction is one that results in an increase in earnings per share. Alternatively, a dilutive translation is one that reduces the company's earnings per share. As part of the due diligence process, bankers will create pro forma financial statements. These pro forma financial statements will help bankers model the impact on the company's earnings. Remember that pro forma financial statements are hypothetical and are used to predict the future performance of the company in a post-deal world. These pro forma financial statements are created for the acquiring company and are used as an evaluation tool to determine if the transaction should move forward. For simplicity sake see the following:

Accretive	Pro Forma EPS	>	Acquirer's EPS
Dilutive	Pro Forma EPS	<	Acquirer's EPS
Breakeven	Pro Forma EPS	=	Acquirer's EPS

In chapter 3 we provided the following example of a takeover:

QWER Manufacturing Co. has agreed to acquire RTY Industries in an all-stock transaction and that QWER has offered to exchange 3 shares of QWER for each share of RTY. At the time the transaction is agreed to, QWER is trading at $40 per share and RTY is trading at $80. The current price of the offer values RTY Industries at $120 per share. Lets now examine the financial implications of the proposed takeover.

Company	QWER	RTY	QWER Post Deal
Stock Price	$40	$80	N/A
Shares Outstanding	10,000,000	5,000,000	25,000,000
Earnings	$30,000,000	$20,000,000	$50,000,000
EPS	$3	$4	$2

CHAPTER 8   M & A Analysis

In the above transaction, QWER was required to issue 15 million new shares to complete the acquisition of RTY based on an exchange ratio of 3:1 and based upon RTY's 5 million shares outstanding. After the completion of the acquisition QWER will have a total of 25 million shares outstanding and earnings of $50 million. This deal was dilutive to QWER's shareholders as the EPS post deal has dropped significantly. In this case, from $3 to $2 per share. Now let's change the terms of the offer and see how it impacts the accretion / dilution analysis.

EXAMPLE: QWER offers $60 per share and at the time the deal is agreed to, QWER is trading at $75 and RTY is trading at $50. Here, QWER is offering .8 shares for each share of RTY. The exchange ratio is found by dividing the offer price by the price of the acquirer's stock. In this case $60/$75 =.8 shares.

Company	QWER	RTY	QWER Post Deal
Stock Price	$75	$50	N/A
Shares Outstanding	10,000,000	5,000,000	14,000,000
Earnings	$30,000,000	$20,000,000	$50,000,000
EPS	$3	$4	$3.57

In this case, we see that the acquisition of RTY is accretive to QWER and its shareholders. QWER acquired RTY's $20 million in earnings in exchange for issuing only 4 million shares. As a result EPS increased from $3 to $3.57.

In the instances above, the stock price of QWER in the first transaction would likely fall in the market. The price decline would be in response to the substantial EPS dilution. In the second example, one would assume the price of QWER would increase given the accretive nature of transaction.

There are other ways you can anticipate the accretive / dilutive impact of a takeover. One way is by looking at the relative PE ratios of each company. When looking at a takeover using stock as currency the following may be anticipated though not guaranteed.

PE of Buyer	>	PE of Target	=	Accretive
PE of Buyer	<	PE of Target	=	Dilutive
PE of Buyer	>	PE of Offer	=	Accretive
PE of Buyer	<	PE of Offer	=	Dilutive

Another way to gauge the impact would be to look at the return on invested capital (ROIC) relative to the weighted average cost of capital (WACC).

ROIC	>	WACC	=	Accretive
ROIC	<	WACC	=	Dilutive
ROIC	=	WACC	=	Breakeven

There are a number of issues to keep in mind when analyzing the financial impact of the transaction. The first is, the pro forma income of the combined company is only a projection. The estimate will take into account any cost savings to be realized by combining the operations of the two companies. These synergies will increase the pro forma income estimate for the combined company. Further, an acquisition that is dilutive in the short run may turn accretive as the cost savings continue to enhance performance in future years. As a result 1+1 may equal more than 2. For example:.

QWER earnings	$30 million
RTY Earnings	$20 million
Cost Savings	$9 million
QWER Pro Forma Income Projection	$59 million

Ultimately, the impact on EPS can be determined by dividing the estimated income by the total number of shares of the acquiring company. The number of shares includes the additional shares issued to fund the acquisition. In our examples above the exchange ratio was provided. On your exam you may be required to determine the exchange ratio as follows:

<u>Offer Price</u>
<u>Market Price of the Acquirer</u>

Stock deals can be affected either through a share swap or the issuance of shares through a rights offering or another offering such as a private placement. With a stock swap, the acquirer should incur little to no floatation costs. If the shares are issued through a rights offering or private placement, the shares will likely be issued at a discount, raising the cost of the transaction for the buyer.

There are a number of ways that you may be required to evaluate acquisitions where the buyer is using its stock as currency in the transaction. Additionally, the series 79 exam is going to present you with questions where

CHAPTER 8   M & A Analysis

you must first calculate the required information in order to determine the ultimate answers. To illustrate this concept, here is another example;

EXAMPLE

RNR Industries is seeking to expand its steel production and offers to purchase LZ Steel for a price equal to a 30 percent premium to LZ's current stock price. The following information is observed regarding both companies:

Company	RNR Industries	LZ Steel
EPS	$4.20	$1.85
PE Ratio	18	12
Shares Outstanding	30 million	14 million

From the data above we can determine both the offer price for LZ and the number of shares that RNR would have to issue in order to complete the acquisition. In order to determine the offer price, we must first calculate the current stock price for LZ Steel as follows:

EPS X PE
1.85 X 12 = $22.20

By multiplying the EPS by the PE ratio we see that the stock is currently trading in the market at $22.20. RNR has offered a 30% premium for the company. Now we multiply the market price by 1.3 and we see that the offer price is $28.86 per share. Given this information we can calculate the exchange ratio to determine the number of shares RNR will have to issue to complete the transaction. First we must calculate the current market price for RNR as follows $4.20 X 18 = $75.60 . Now we can calculate the exchange ratio as follows:

<u>Offer Price</u>
Market Price of Acquirer

$28.86/ $75.60 = .3817

Based on the exchange ratio above we see that RNR would have to issue slightly more than 5.344 million shares to complete the acquisition of LZ Steel. Another way to calculate the number of shares would be to take the deal value of $404.04 million and divide it by the acquirers stock price of $75.6. In this case we get $404.04 million / $75.6 and again we see that RNR would have to issue slightly more than 5.344 million shares. There is a slight difference in the number of shares calculated under each method due to the rounding of the exchange ratio. Your exam will most likely round off answers and there will not be an answer that differs from the others based on the rounding application.

CASH AND STOCK TRANSACTIONS

Companies will often use a combination of cash and stock to pay for an acquisition. When performing an accretion / dilution analysis for a transaction to be completed on this basis, the calculation becomes a bit more complicated. Let's take a look at an example:

EXAMPLE

QWER offers to acquire RTY for $60 per share to be paid in 50% stock and 50% in cash. In order to finance the cash portion of the acquisition QWER will be issuing 10 year bonds. At the time the deal is agreed to, QWER is trading at $75 and RTY is trading at $50. We will keep the data constant from our previous example as follows:

Company	QWER	RTY
Stock Price	$75	$50
Shares Outstanding	10,000,000	5,000,000
Earnings	$30,000,000	$20,000,000
EPS	$3	$4
Tax Rate	28%	28%

In this case, to determine if the deal is accretive or dilutive to QWER shareholders we will need more information regarding the cash portion of the deal and will be using the following data:

Value of offer	$300 million
Value of stock payment @ 50%	$150 million
Value of cash payment @ 50%	$150 million
Interest rate on bonds	7%
Cost to issue debt	$2 million
QWER tax rate	28%

To determine how many shares QWER will have to issue to pay for the stock portion of the offer, use the following formula:

CHAPTER 8   M & A Analysis

<u>**Value of Stock Portion**</u>
Stock Price of the Acquirer

In this case:

<u>**$150 million**</u>
$75

In this example QWER will only be issuing 2 million shares to pay for the stock portion of the payment. Now we must take into consideration the tax implications of the added interest expense that will be incurred as a result of issuing the 7 percent bonds.

Annual interest expense = Principal X Rate

$150 million X 7% = $10,500,000

In order to calculate the pro forma earnings we need to determine the pretax income for both companies. To do this we use the following formula:

<u>**Net Income**</u>
(1- Tax Rate)

Using this formula based on a 28% tax rate, we see the pre tax earnings for both companies are as follows:

Company	QWER	RTY
Earnings	$30,000,000	$20,000,000
Pre Tax Earnings	$41,666,667	$27,777,778

Now that we have calculated the pre tax income for both companies, we can begin to build the model.

Pro Forma Pre Tax Income	$69,444,445
New Interest Expense	$10,500,000
Issuance Expense Amortized Over Life of Bonds	$200,000
Pre Tax Income	$58,744,445
Tax Expense @ 28%	$16,448,444
Net Income	$42,296,001

Notice how we amortized the $2 million issuance expense over the 10 year life of the bonds to arrive at an annual expense of $200,000. We are now ready to complete the accretion / dilution analysis.

Company	QWER	RTY	QWER Post Deal
Stock Price	$75	$50	N/A
Shares Outstanding	10,000,000	5,000,000	12,000,000
Earnings	$30,000,000	$20,000,000	$42,296,001
EPS	$3	$4	$3.52

Once again the deal is accretive to shareholders as the pro forma EPS have increased by approximately 52 cents per share or 17.3 %. This is found dividing the change in earnings per share by the pre deal earnings per share or in this case .52/3

There are a number of items that can impact the ultimate pro forma earnings. These include:

Cost synergies	Increase pro forma earnings
Amortization of asset write ups	Decrease pro forma earnings
Investment banking fees	Decrease pro forma earnings

Investment bankers will often evaluate the financial impact of an acquisition based on multiple offer prices and different stock and cash percentages. Traditionally, for cash and stock offers, the higher the offer price and the greater the percentage paid in the form of stock, the lower the EPS and the more dilutive the deal will be to stockholders of the acquiring company. Alternatively, the greater the percentage debt and the lower the interest rate, the less dilutive the deal will be to shareholders. Further, for aquirres who are making an offer based on a multiple of EBITDA, the above adjustments will be taken into consideration. Let's look at the same transaction but this time we will pay for the entire acquisition through the issuance of debt. QWER issues $300 million worth of 10 year 7 percent bonds. The cost to issue the bonds is $4 million.

Pro Forma Pre Tax Income	$69,444,445
New Interest Expense	$21,000,000
Issuance Expense Amortized Over Life of Bonds	$400,000
Pre Tax Income	$48,044,445
Tax Expense @ 28%	$13,452,444
Net Income	$34,592,001

Using the data above, we calculate the analysis as follows:

Company	QWER	RTY	QWER Post Deal
Stock Price	$75	$50	N/A
Shares Outstanding	10,000,000	5,000,000	10,000,000
Earnings	$30,000,000	$20,000,000	$34,592,001
EPS	$3	$4	$3.46

Here we see that the deal is accretive but that the increased interest cost has significantly impacted the pro forma EPS. The estimated EPS is approximately $3.46, a 6 cent reduction from the $3.52 estimated in the preceding stock and cash deal.

One question you may have to answer on the exam is what percentage of the combined company do existing shareholders of each company own. In cash transactions for the target company, the answer is zero, as the existing shareholders receive a cash payment in exchange for their shares and the shareholders of the acquiring company retain 100 percent ownership. When reviewing a stock deal, you must divide the new shares to be issued by the total number of shares outstanding after the deal is completed. To review this concept let's return to the following example:

QWER offers $60 per share for RTY and at the time the deal is agreed to, QWER is trading at $75 and RTY is trading at $50. Here, QWER is offering .8 shares for each share of RTY. The exchange ratio is found by dividing the offer price by the price of the acquirer's stock. In this case $60/$75 =.8 shares.

Company	QWER	RTY	QWER Post Deal
Stock Price	$75	$50	N/A
Shares Outstanding	10,000,000	5,000,000	14,000,000
Earnings	$30,000,000	$20,000,000	$50,000,000
EPS	$3	$4	$3.57

Once the transaction is completed, RTY shareholders own 4 million of the 14 million shares outstanding. Therefore, RTY shareholders will own approximately 28.5 percent of the combined company. We arrived at this by dividing the shares issued to RTY stockholders by the total number of shares outstanding at the completion of the deal. 4 million / 14 million = 28.5

percent. (rounded). Existing QWER shareholders will own approximately 71.5 percent of the combined company.

DETERMINING THE COMBINED ENTERPRISE VALUE

When one company acquires another, it is not only acquiring the ownership of the company but also all of its outstanding debt. As a result, the combined company's enterprise value will be the sum of all outstanding equity and debt. Let's once again return to one of our previous examples and introduce the respective market capitalization and outstanding debt.

QWER offers $60 purchase for RTY in an all stock transaction.

Company	QWER	RTY	QWER Post Deal
Stock Price	$75	$50	$77
Shares Outstanding	10,000,000	5,000,000	14,000,000
Market Cap	$750 million	$250 million	$1.078 billion
Debt Outstanding	$30 million	$20 million	$50 million
Enterprise Value	$780 million	$270 million	$1.128 billion

Here we see that the enterprise value of the combined company is greater than the enterprise value of each company separately. Because this was an all stock deal, QWER issued 4 million new shares to complete the purchase. The new market price is then multiplied by the total number of shares outstanding to determine the post deal market capitalization. The total debt is then added to market capitalization to determine the enterprise value. It is important to note, that if the question asks you to calculate the post-deal enterprise value and provides cash balances, you must remember to subtract the cash balances from the enterprise value. One way to do this would be to calculate the net debt of each company by subtracting the cash balances from the outstanding debt. Now we will add cash balances to QWER and RTY and review the change in enterprise value.

CHAPTER 8   M & A Analysis

Company	QWER	RTY	QWER Post Deal
Stock Price	$75	$50	$77
Shares Outstanding	10,000,000	5,000,000	14,000,000
Market Cap	$750 million	$250 million	$1.078 billion
Debt Outstanding	$30 million	$20 million	$50 million
Cash Balance	$20 million	$5 million	$25 million
Net Debt	$10 million	$15 million	$25 million
Enterprise Value	$760 million	$265 million	$1.03 billion

In this example, you can see that the debt load and enterprise value of each company was reduced by the cash balances. Additionally, the enterprise value of QWER post-deal was reduced by the combined cash balances of $25 million.

HOW TO BUILD AN LBO MODEL

As we mentioned earlier, a leveraged buyout employs a substantial amount of debt in an effort to gain control of a target company. In a leveraged buyout, the buyer seeks to acquire a company with the smallest down payment possible. In many transactions, the equity component is as little as 10 percent of the purchase price. Imagine an investor who wants to purchase a 2 family investment property and the investor purchases an $800,000 property by putting down $80,000 and obtaining a mortgage for $720,000. This investor would now own the property with the belief that the rental income will be able to not only cover the mortgage, but allow the investor to earn a profit each month. Additionally, as the rental payments are used to pay down the mortgage balance, the investor's equity in the property increases. In an LBO leveraging the target's balance sheet, if successful, will allow the buyer to earn a substantial return on the equity investment. As the cash flow generated by the acquired company is used to service the new debt, the buyer's equity increases as the debt is paid down. In order to accelerate the increase in equity, LBO financing is traditionally structured to be paid off in 5-10 years. Much of the financing will come from banks in the form of bank debt or senior debt. In many cases the assets of the target company are pledged as collateral for the loans. Thus putting the banks and other lenders in a secured position in the event of default. Larger more complex transactions may also include mezzanine financing which is senior to the claims of equity holders but subordinate to the claims of the senior creditors. Mezzanine financing traditionally comes from hedge funds and other large sophisticated investors. These lenders will often receive warrants to purchase stock in addition to a relatively high interest rate. When evaluating a leveraged buyout, financial sponsors such as LBO firms and private equity will build models designed to show the target's ability to support the debt service. The greater the target's free cash flow, the greater its ability to service and pay down debt. The following are some of the key ratios:

- Interest coverage ratio (EBIT/Interest payments)
- Debt service coverage ratio (EBIT- Capex)/ (interest + principal payments)
- Debt /EBITDA ratio
- Fixed coverage ratio (EBITDA- Capex - taxes) /(interest + principal payments)

It is important to note that the financial ratios used to evaluate the target's ability to service its debt must include any existing debt on the target's balance sheet. The financial sponsors will engage in an effort to improve the business's profitability and performance through restructuring and financial engineering. As the performance improves and the debt is paid down, the sponsor will seek to exit the business through a sale to the ultimate buyer or through an IPO. Let's now take a look at an example of a leveraged buyout.

TRY Private Equity Co. is looking to acquire BVC Manufacturing through a leveraged buyout. A deal for BVC shows the following financial data:

EBITDA	$100 million
Deal Multiple	9 X EBITDA
Deal Value	$900 million
Debt Financing	80% / $720 million
Equity Component	20% / $180 million

Through restructuring and financial engineering over a 4 year period, TRY has been able to grow BVC's EBITDA by 18% to $118 million. During the same period the company also paid down $300 million in debt. The financial sponsor (TRY Private Equity) is now looking to exit the business and sells BVC to the ultimate buyer for the industry average 9 X EBITDA. TRY's results are as follows:

CHAPTER 8   M & A Analysis

Exit Value	9 X $118 million EBITDA	$1.062 billon
Existing Debt	$720 million - $300 million	$420 million
Equity value	$180 million + $300 million + $162 million	$642 million
Exit Return	$462 million on $180 million invested	257 %

Notice how the equity value increased through both the repayment of debt and by the increase in value resulting from the increase in EBITDA. The $18 million increase in EBITDA increased the value of the company by $162 million. (9 X $18 million). In most cases, financial sponsors are looking for a substantial internal rate of return. In this example, $180 million grew to $642 million in 4 years. This represents a total return of 257%. The approximate internal rate of return is 37.42%. This is the rate at which the initial investment appreciated each year during the 4 year holding period. It will not be necessary to calculate the the internal rate of return on your exam, you will need to be familiar with the concept and how it will be used by financial sponsors to evaluate leveraged buyouts.

EMPLOYEE STOCK OPTIONS

The treatment of employee stock options during an M & A transaction is a complex topic. A recent study found that in 80 percent of the transactions, at least some, if not all of the out of the money stock options were canceled. In fact, unvested options that were in the money were canceled with no consideration paid to the employee. An option is in the money and has intrinsic value if the exercise price of the option is lower than the price of the stock (offer price). A vested option is an option fully owned by the employee. Employee stock options are usually granted with a vesting schedule, whereby the employee becomes the owner of the options over a period of years. Once vested, the employee may purchase the shares at the exercise price. The use of stock options as part of employee compensation packages has grown substantially and nearly all acquisitions of public companies require the buyer to factor these options into their strategy. When employees exercise their stock options, the exercise may increase the number of shares outstanding. If the number of shares outstanding increases, it causes the market cap to increase, thereby increasing the enterprise value of the company and the cost to the acquirer. This would be the case if the company issues shares to employees who exercise options. Another way a company can deliver shares to employees is to purchase the shares in the open market based on the number of options exployees exercise. While this will not cause an increase in the number of shares the company has outstanding, it will cause the company to incur potentially significant expenses. Let's take a look at how employee stock options may be handled.

EXAMPLE

At the time QWER offers to purchase RTY for $60 per share the company has the following options outstanding:

Vesting Status	Number of shares	Strike Price	Intrinsic Value
Unvested	75,0000	$45	$15
Vested	200,0000	$50	$10
Vested	100,000	$65	$0

Given the above information based on the offer price of $60, we can assume that the 75,000 unvested options with a strike price of $45 would be terminated. The 100,000 vested options with a strike of $65 have no intrinsic value as the exercise price is above the offer price and these options would also likely be canceled. Turning now to the vested options with a strike price of $50, these options are in the money and have $10 in intrinsic value. When the employees exercise the options RTY will receive $10 million (200,000 shares X $50). If RTY issues new shares to the employees who exercise the options, RTY will have 200,000 additional shares outstanding and it would increase the market cap and the enterprise value of RTY by $12 million based on the offering price of $60 per share. If RTY was trading in the market at $56, RTY could use the $10 million to repurchase shares in the open market. This would allow the company to purchase 178,571 shares ($10 million / 56). To provide the remaining 21,429 shares. RTY could issue new shares / reissue treasury shares or repurchase the additional shares using its own capital. If the company issued the 21,429 shares it would increase the market cap and enterprise value by $1,285,740. (based on the offer price of $60). If RTY used its own capital to purchase the shares at $56, RTY would incur a loss / expense of $1,200,024.

THE CREATION OF GOODWILL

In order to gain support of the target company's shareholders, buyers will have to offer a substantial premium. In most cases, the premium paid by the acquirer will value the company at a price that exceeds its net tangible assets. As a result, this premium will be carried on the balance sheet as goodwill. Because most companies have substantial assets carried on their balance sheets net of depreciation, the acquirer has an opportunity to write up the value of the assets to their fair market value at the time of purchase. For example:

If when QWER enters into the contract to acquire RTY, RTY has $50 million in fixed assets carried on its books net of depreciation and the fair market value of the assets are actually $75 million, QWER would write up the value of the assets by $25 million. The asset write up would reduce the amount of goodwill created by the purchase. Furthermore, asset write ups give the acquirer an opportunity to depreciate the assets from a higher value. Now lets look at how you may have to calculate goodwill.

KWFL enters into an agreement to acquire SIA for $50 per share. At the time the deal is announced SIA shows the following:

Stock price	$41
Offer Price	$50
Outstanding Stock	5 million shares
Total Assets Net of Depreciation	$190 million
Total Liabilities	$41 million
Intangible Assets	$35 million
Existing Goodwill	$60 million

The first step to calculating goodwill created by the transaction is to determine the total offer value. In this case it is $250 million ($50 X 5 million shares). Next we must determine the net tangible assets. We subtract total liabilities, intangibles and existing goodwill from the total assets. In this case net tangible assets are $54 million. (190 -41 -35 -60). The difference between the deal value and the target's net tangible assets is deemed to be goodwill. In this case it is $196 million (250-54). The goodwill created by the transaction is then added to the existing goodwill of the acquirer. Now lets say KWFL is reviewing the assets of SIA and determines their fair market value is actually substantially higher than the book value of the assets. If the actual market value of the assets was $275 million versus the $190 million book value, KWFL would mark up the assets to $275 million. KWFL would then take the $85 million write up and use it to reduce the amount of goodwill created by the transaction. In this case the goodwill would be $111 million. (196- 85).

CROSS BORDER COMPLICATIONS

When multinational companies merge or are acquired there are a number of factors that further complicate the transaction and impact its value. When engaging in a cross border transaction, the buyer, the target as well as their respective shareholders must keep in mind that:

- Currency exchange rates can have a substantial impact on valuation
- Multijurisdictional tax and regulatory issues may complicate the transaction
- Shareholders in other countries may not want to own shares of a foreign company

Acquirers want a strong domestic currency when seeking to purchase a forign company as this will reduce the cost of the acquisition to the buyer. A weak domestic currency makes a company more attractive and as a result more vulnerable to a takeover. The series 79 is a U. S. exam so most of the questions will deal with the relative value of the U.S. dollar. Let's look at the impact of the exchange rate on the following transaction:

EXAMPLE

ABC, a multinational corporation based in Dallas Texas enters into an agreement to acquire HGF a French conglomerate. At the time the deal is announced the Euro is trading at 1.25 and the offering price is 40 Euros per share. HGF has 4 million shares outstanding, making the total value of the deal 160 million Euros. ABC must now convert U.S. dollars into 160 million Euros. The total value of the deal in U.S. dollars is $200 million. (160 million Euros X 1.25). While the acquisition is being reviewed, the exchange rate between the U.S. dollar and the Euro is constantly changing. Assume that the deal clears all regulatory requirements and at the time of closing the Euro has increased to 1.30. In order to complete the acquisition, ABC must now go into the market and purchase 160 million Euros. Because the Euro increased in value to $1.30 the price to acquire HGF has increased to $208 million. In this case, the cost to acquire the company increased by $8 million based on the exchange rate at the time the transaction was completed. Alternatively, if the Euro fell in value and the Euro was trading at 1.20 when the deal closed, the total cost would be $192 million. In this case, the cost to acquire HGF would be less expensive. The exchange rate also impacts the value of stock transactions. For example, if ABC whose stock is trading at $75 offers to purchase HGF by paying HGF shareholders .8 shares of ABC, the deal is valued at $60 ($75 X.8). If at the time of the offer, the Euro is 1.25, HGF shareholders will receive stock worth 48 Euros. This is found by dividing the value of the stock in U. S. dollars by the value of the Euro, or $60 / 1.25 = 48. If again the Euro increases to 1.3, the value of the deal falls to 46.15 Euros. Additionally, just like we detailed in chapter 3, as the value of the stock the acquirer is using for currency changes in the market, the value of the offer changes.

CHAPTER 8

Pretest

M & A ANALYSIS

1. KNFL is seeking to acquire SIA to expand its portfolio and product mix. SIA's financials show the following information:

Stock price	$32
Shares Outstanding	10 million
Debt Outstanding	$70 million
Cash on hand	$50 million
EBITDA	$35 million

   KNFL is aware that there are limited companies in the space and will have to make an offer of at least 14 times EV/EBITDA. Given this, KNFL's offer would be closest to:
   A. $44.80 per share
   B. $49 per share
   C. $47 per share
   D. $41 per share

2. As an investment banking representative you are reviewing a group of potential takeover targets. As part of your analysis you are required to determine which of the target companies would allow the acquirer to most likely enhance its earnings. Which of the following would most be most likely to help the buyer achieve its goals?
    A. Purchase of a target company whose PE is less than that of the buyer.
    B. Purchase of a target company whose growth rate is greater than that of the buyer.
    C. Purchase of a target company whose EV is less than that of the buyer.
    D. Purchase of a target company whose EV is greater than that of the buyer.

3. Build Rite home builders is formulating an offer for SunnySide Builders. SunnySide shows the following:

EPS	$4.20
PE Ratio	15
Shares Outstanding	100 million

BuildRite plans to offer a 40 percent premium to acquire SunnySide. The offer values the stock of SunnySide at:
    A. $62
    B. $88.20
    C. $78.15
    D. $63

4. You have been asked to perform an analysis of the acquisition of GHG by PPLC. As a general rule which of the following circumstances would lead to the acquisition being accretive?
    A. The ROIC is greater than GHG's WACC.
    B. The ROIC is less than than GHG's WACC.
    C. The ROIC is greater than PPLC's WACC.
    D. The ROIC is less than PPLC's WACC.

5. ZXC has approached FHF Enterprises in an effort to acquire the company. You are provided with the following information:

Company	ZXC	FHF
EPS	$5.10	$2.65
PE Ratio	15	11
Shares Outstanding	40 million	20 million

ZXC Offers to acquire FHF in a stock deal and offers a 30 percent premium to the current price of FHF. How many shares will ZXC have to issue to complete the transaction?
   A. 9,908,496
   B. 7,620,091
   C. 7,908,496
   D. 9,620,091

6. JAW is contemplating the acquisition of ZOSO Inc. While drawing up a potential bid for the company, the investment banker evaluates stock and cash offers. Which of the following offers would be the least dilutive?
   A. 50 percent stock, 50 percent cash
   B. 30 percent stock, 70 percent cash
   C. 60 percent stock, 40 percent cash
   D. 70 percent stock, 30 percent cash

7. PIR Group has entered into a definitive agreement to acquire DSA Holdings for $60 per share in an all stock transaction. PIR Group is trading in the marketplace at $80, and DSA is quoted at $42. It is noted that PIR Group has 100 million shares outstanding, while DSA has only 30 million shares outstanding. How much of the combined company will the shareholders of DSA own upon completion of the transaction?
   A. 22.5 %
   B. 18.36%
   C. 30 %
   D. 25%

8. PLM Has agreed to be acquired by TYU. The terms of the deal required TYU to issue .7 shares for each share of PLM. The following data is observed:

Company	TYU	PLM
Stock Price	$100	$50
Shares Outstanding	20 million	10 million
Debt Outstanding	$75 million	$30 million
Cash On Hand	$40 million	$10 million

Upon completion of the transaction the stock price of TYU is trading in the market at $114. What is the enterprise value of TYU post transactions ?
   A. $3.133 billion
   B. $3.0885 billion
   C. $3.078 billion
   D. $2.85 billion

9. The internal rate of return would be most important to which of the following buyers?
   A. A strategic buyer, purchasing a target using cash to purchase a company.
   B. A strategic buyer, purchasing a target using stock to purchase a company.
   C. A strategic buyer, purchasing a target using cash and stock to purchase a company.
   D. A financial buyer using leverage to purchase a company.

10. GET is about to close on its acquisition of QWER. It is noted that at the time of acquisition GET has $324 million in goodwill carried on its balance sheet. QWER shows the following:

Total Assets Net of Depreciation	$200 million
Total Liabilities	$25 million
Intangible Assets	$20 million
Goodwill	$75 million

GET has offered $150 million to acquire GET. GET further notes that the market value of QWER's assets is $230 million. Once the transaction closes GET's balance sheet will show goodwill of:
   A. $404 million
   B. $394 million
   C. $364 million
   D. $399 million

Answer Keys

CHAPTER 1: EQUITY AND DEBT SECURITIES

1. B) A stockholder does not get to vote directly for executive compensation.
2. B) Each ADR represents from 1 to 10 shares of the foreign company. ADR holders do have the right to vote and receive dividends. Foreign governments put restrictions on the foreign ownership of stock from time to time.
3. B) The shareholders may vote to approve an increase in the number of authorized shares. All of the other choices are correct.
4. B) The Options Clearing Corporation (OCC) issues all standardized options.
5. D) Common stockholders do not have voting power in the matter of bankruptcy.
6. D) Bonds registered as to principal only will still require the investor to clip coupons and present them for payment.
7. D) Bearer bonds are issued without a name on them, meaning that whoever has possession of the bond may clip the coupons and claim the interest.
8. D) Raw land may never be depreciated because its useful life does not decline over time. The value or useful life of the other choices does decline over time and may be depreciated.
9. A) Choice I is incorrect in that an option is a contract between two parties, which determines the time and price at which a security may be bought or sold.
10. C) Call sellers and put buyers are both bearish. Both investors want the value of the stock to fall.

CHAPTER 2: SEC REPORTING, RULES AND REGULATIONS

1. D) XYZ industries is classified as a non accelerated filer because the market cap of its public float is less than $75 million. Non accelerated filers are required to file 10Ks within 90 days of its fiscal year end.

2. A) The question is asking which pieces of information are found in the 10K and not in the 10Q and each answer choice provides two pieces of information. In order for the choice to be correct both pieces of information must be correct. Of the choices listed the pair containing stockholder information and audited financial data is the only correct answer.

3. D) An asset write down qualifies as a non scheduled material event and the company would be required to file an 8K.

4. B) When a person or persons acting in concert acquire 5 percent or more of an issuer, certain negotiations such as standstill agreements must be disclosed in the filing of form 13 D.

5. D) Form 13 F must be filed within 45 days of the end of each quarter for all positions regardless of size. If the fund owns even a single share of stock, the ownership of that one share must be reported on form 13F.

6. A) Issuers may submit financial data and performance results using non GAAP methods such as free cash flow and core earnings so long as the non GAAP methods are compared to GAAP methods.

7. D) Regulation M-A sets forth a number of communication related rules for tender officers and offers to purchase securities. However, it does not require the issuance of a fairness opinion in connection with the offer.

8. C) A broker dealer may rely on the information provided by the party who is requesting a fairness opinion. The broker dealer is not responsible for verifying the accuracy of the information and will not be held liable for the issuance of the fairness opinion based on false information

9. B) the financial data may be used for 134 days and becomes "stale" on the 135th day and may no longer be used.

10. C) The exchanges where securities are listed, SARBOX and Regulation S-K all regulate the requirements for the audit committee. The exchanges require that at least one member of the audit committee be a financial expert. SARBOX requires each member of the audit committee serve as an independent member of the board of directors. Regulation S-K requires that the identity of the financial expert be reported to investors.

CHAPTER 3: MERGERS AND ACQUISITIONS

1. A) Form 8K is used to disclose a non scheduled material event and does not provide information regarding stock ownership. Forms 13 D, F and G are all used to report the ownership of 5 % or more of a company, Holdings by large asset managers and holdings of investment companies respectively.

2. C) A private equity firm wishing to withdraw money from a company that it owns without selling its stake would engage in a dividend recapitalization. In a dividend recapitalization, the private equity owners direct the company to issue bonds in order to pay the private equity owners a dividend. In this type of recapitalization the company has taken on debt for the purpose of paying dividends to its shareholders.

3. B) With a minority recapitalization the private equity or venture capital firm takes a minority stake in the business and the current owners retain the majority of the ownership. This is the best transaction for the owner who wants to take money out of the business yet retain control over the company.

4. B) Candidates for leverage buyouts must have a substantial balance sheet and predictable cash flows to obtain and service the debt. Only BuildCo would seem to be a possible candidate for an LBO.

5. C) The best option for the seller in this situation would be to enter into bilateral negotiations with a potential buyer. This will allow the owners to negotiate the transaction without altering the market to the fact that they are interested in selling.

6. B) In an acquisition, the target company ceases to exist and the target's shareholders will own a portion of the combined company, only if stock is used in whole or in part as currency. If an acquisition is paid for in cash the shareholders of the target company will not own any of the combined company.

7. B) While the above activities are only a few that will be taken during the auction process, the last that would be done is the creation of the data room. Of the choices listed, the order would be creation of confidentiality agreements, creation of the CIM, distribute the bidding procedure letter and creation of the data room.

8. C) A teaser would be sent to parties to gauge initial interest in potentially bidding on a company. The teaser provides a high level overview of the opportunity without disclosing the name of the company nor any identifying information.

9. C) The seller will seek to draft a confidentiality agreement that provides as much protection as possible. As the bankers represent the seller, it is their responsibility to provide information and to communicate with potential buyers. All of the other choices are activities the seller would want protection from.

10. A) Once a list of qualified interested parties has been compiled the seller will instruct the bankers to create an electronic data room where documents will be stored and access granted to interested parties for review.

CHAPTER 4: TENDER OFFERS, AND FINANCIAL RESTRUCTURING

1. D) All of the parties listed would be required to file either schedule 14D-9 or TO except a broker dealer who responds to shareholder requests for information or advice on the offer. Broker dealers who offer unsolicited advice and who are not a party to the offer are exempt from filing schedule 14D-9 or TO.

2. A) SEC Rule 14e-5 states that no covered person will be allowed to make open market purchases of the subject securities if the person is involved in the offer. The investment adviser in this question is not involved in the offer and may purchase shares in the open market without restriction.

3. C) Officers and directors may be paid a higher price for their stockholdings as part of a pay package so long as the payment has been approved by the compensation committee of the company offering the premium

4. B) An investor who is long call options, may not tender shares into the offer unless the investor has exercised the options. An investor who holds a company issued security that provides the right to acquire securities directly from the company may tender shares even though the security has not been exercised or converted.

5. C) If the number of shareholders falls below 300 the company will be required to file form 13e-3 with the SEC.

6. C) All of the choices listed are considered to be administrative expenses of the estate with the exception of back wages owed to employees prior to the filing of bankruptcy. Current wages are considered to be administrative expenses but back wages are not.

7. D) The bondholders have a secured claim on the building and are entitled to receive the principal amount due plus interest and certain expenses incurred by bondholders during the default.

8. C) When a group of secured creditors all possess a claim on the same asset, the creditors may enter into an intercreditor agreement or intercreditor deed in order to prioritize the respective claims on the asset.

9. B) In a chapter 7 bankruptcy, both secured and unsecured creditors are required to file a proof of claim within 90 days of the first creditors' meeting.

10. A) All of the choices listed are features of asset sales under securities 363 of the bankruptcy code except the choice that states all contract assignments must be approved. Asset sales under section 363 allows certain contracts to be assigned without consent.

CHAPTER 5: ISSUING CORPORATE SECURITIES

1. D) All of the items listed must appear in the tombstone ad.

2. D) All of the parties listed may be held liable to the purchasers of the new issue.

3. B) A syndicate may only enter a stabilizing bid at or below the offering price.

4. C) Companies who issue shares as part of a merger or acquisition will register the new shares with the SEC by filing form S-4. This is not a private placement so Rule 506D is not applicable. Form S-8 is used to register shares issued as part of an employee benefit plan. A shelf registration is traditionally used to issue debt securities.

5. D) Under Rule 147, 100 percent of the purchasers must be in the state.

6. C) A greenshoe provision allows the syndicate to purchase up to an additional 15 percent of the offering from the issuer.

7. C) In order to qualify as a public appearance, at least 15 members of the public must be in attendance. Attending a meeting with a company and two other analysts also does not constitute a public appearance. An exception to the 15 attendee rule, is if a member of the press is present. Therefore, the conference call with 5 members of the investing public and a reporter qualifies as a public appearance.

8. B) A business must first hire an underwriter to advise the issuer about the types of securities to issue.

9. C) The number of nonaccredited investors is limited to 35 in any 12-month period.

10. D) A company doing a rights offering will use a standby underwriting agreement whereby the underwriter will "standby" ready to purchase any shares not purchased by shareholders.

CHAPTER 6: FINANCIAL ANALYSIS

1. A) The three primary financial statements are, the balance sheet, the income statement and the statement of cash flows also known as the statement of sources and use of funds. These three statements will be included in the annual report.

2. B) An increase in accounts payable is credited as a source of cash and the company would expect the cash balance to increase.

3. A) In order to calculate the estimated retained earnings for the company you must first multiply the net income by the growth rate of 8 percent. $78 million X 1.08 = $84,240,000. The next step is to multiply the dividend payment by the increase of 5 percent. $15,000,000 X 1.05 = $15,750,000. Now subtract the dividends from the net income $84,240,000 - $15,750,000 = $68,490,000. To arrive at the estimated retained earnings we add this to the retained earnings carried on the balance sheet. $620,000,000 + $68,490,000 = $688,490,000

4. B) The best choice would be to provide pro forma financial statements showing what the performance of the company was without the write-down. Management should also discuss the impact of the writedown on the company's earnings call. The question is asking for the best choice to show performance, which would be to prepare the pro forma financial statements.

5. D) The company purchases finished goods directly from manufacturers. As a result the company does not have any work in progress as part of its inventory. GAAP requires that companies value the inventory at the lower of its historical cost or its market value.

6. C) When a company declares a 2:1 forward stock split, the par value of the stock will be reduced to half its par value and capital paid in excess of par will not be impacted.

7. C) During a period of increasing costs the oldest inventory would have the lowest COGS. As a result, the profit margin would be higher. Changing the inventory accounting method from LIFO to FIFO would increase the company's tax liability because it would increase the profit on each unit sold.

8. B) The question is asking about how efficiently a company generates earnings. The return on asset ratio tells an investor how efficiently a company uses its assets to generate earnings. The return on common equity only tells investors the return available to common stockholders.

9. A) The most likely cause of this is a difference in the interest and tax expenses between the two companies. With sales and net income being equal, the company who has higher COGS and SGA must be paying lower interest expenses and lower tax rates.

10. C) All of the choices listed create a deferred tax asset except rolling out profits to future reporting periods. When companies roll profits to future tax periods it creates a deferred tax liability.

CHAPTER 7: VALUATION

1. A) The first step in the question is to calculate the EPS for next year. In this case it is $2.80 X 1.22 =$3.416. Now we multiple the estimated EPS by the PE ratio and we get a price target of $119.56. Found as follows: $3.416 X 35.

2. D) Normalized earnings seek to project the earnings of a company midway through the economic cycle, while removing the impact of non recurring charges. The normalized earnings projection uses a mid cycle estimate and removes the impact of non recurring events to smooth out the earrings over time.

3. A) The common stock of ZEP is relatively undervalued. The PE of ZEP is 13.49, found by dividing the market price by its EPS. $56 / 4.15 = 13.49. The index has a PE of 15 and is therefore more expensive than the common stock of ZEP.

4. D) The PE ratio is 8. In order to calculate the PE given the information in the question, you must first calculate the EPS as follows: Annual dividend / Dividend payout ratio. In this case $3.5 / .4 = $8.75. Next we calculate the price of the stock by dividing the annual dividend by the dividend yield. In this case $3.50 / .05 = $70. Now that we have the stock price and the EPS. The PE ratio is Price / EPS. in this case 70/8.75 = 8

5. C) During times of losses the PE ratio is of little importance as the PE ratio would turn negative. The earnings yield tells an investor how much EPS is generated by the company for each dollar invested in the common stock.

6. A) To determine the PEG ratio we must first determine the company's earnings per share. In this case $530 million / 200 million shares = 2.65.

Now we must use the EPS to determine the PE ratio. $48 / 2.65 = 18.1$. Now we must determine the estimated growth in the company's earnings. $583 million / $530 million = 1.1. We must subtract the 1 to get the growth rate of 10%. Lastly we divide the PE ratio by the growth rate 18.1 / 10 = 1.81. Round to 1.8.

7. B) When you are given a projected growth rate and a PEG ratio you can calculate the PE ratio for the company by multiplying the growth rate by the PEG ratio. In this case 24X.8 = 19.2

8. C) The normalized EPS given the information is $3.63 (rounded), found by adding the EPS together for each period and dividing by the number of periods. In this case $14.54/ 4 =$3.63. (rounded). The average earnings are subsequently adjusted for non recurring and one time items.

9. C) Given the information we can calculate the enterprise value by determining the market capitalization for the company and adding the net debt. To determine the market capitalization simply multiply the stock price by the number of shares outstanding. In this case we get $32 X 200,000,000 = $6.4 billion. Next we calculate the net debt by subtracting the cash on hand from the amount of debt outstanding. $190 million - $50 million = $140 million. Now we add the net debt to the market capitalization $6.4 billion + $140 million = $6.54 billion.

10. C) The enterprise value to sales ratio is the least susceptible to manipulation as it measures the enterprise value in relation to raw sales numbers. Yes, there is always a chance that the sales numbers could be manipulated, but the question is asking for the least susceptible.

CHAPTER 8: M&A ANALYSIS

1. C) Based on the information provided the offer would have to be $47 per share. This is found by multiplying: the EBITDA by the offer multiple of 14 and subtracting the net debt as follows: $35 million X 14 = $490 million. From this we must subtract the net debt of $20 million. $490 million - $20 million = $470 million. Now to determine the implied equity value we divide by the number of shares outstanding $470 million / 10 million shares = $47 per share.

2. A) Of the choices listed, the purchase of a target company whose PE is less than that of the buyer is the only one that gives you an indication of the financial impact to the buyer's earnings. When a company purchases

a target whose PE is less than that of the buyer, the acquisition will most likely be accretive to earnings.

3. B) The first step in this question is to determine the current price of BuildRite's stock. To do this we multiply the EPS by the PE Ratio. In this case, $4.20 X 15 = $63. Now we multiply the current stock price by the premium of the offer. $63 X 1.4 = $88.20.

4. C) When the rerun on invested capital exceeds the weighted average cost of capital of the acquirer the acquisition will be accretive to the buyer's earnings.

5. A) The first step is to determine the current price of the target company. The current price of FHF is found by multiplying its EPS by the PE ratio. In this case $2.65 X 11 = $29.15. Now we must calculate the value of the offer at a 30 percent premium. $29.15 X 1.3 = $37.90. (rounded) . Next, to determine the number of shares we must calculate the current price of ZXC, again multiplying the EPS by the PE. In this case, $5.10 X 15 = $76.50. Now we determine the exchange ratio by dividing the offer price by the current stock price of the acquirer. $37.90/ $76.50 = .4954.(rounded). Now we can take the exchange ratio and multiply it by the number of shares the target company has outstanding and we see that ZXC would have to issue 9,908,496 shares (rounded).

6. B) As a general rule, the lower the amount of stock issued to make an acquisition, the less dilutive the transaction will be to the earnings of the acquirer.

7. B) Upon completion of the transaction, shareholders of DSA will own 18.36 percent of the combined company. The first step in solving this problem is calculating the exchange ratio found by dividing the acquisition price by the stock price of the acquirer. $60 / $80 = .75 shares. Each share of DSA will be exchanged for .75 shares of PIR Group. To determine how many shares PIR group will have to issue we multiply the number of shares DSA has outstanding by the exchange ratio. 30 million shares X .75 = 22.5 million shares. These 22.5 million shares will be owned by DSA shareholders. Now we divide the number of shares owned by DSA shareholders by the total number of shares outstanding upon completion of the transaction. 22.5 million / 122.5 million = 18.36 % (rounded).

8. A) In order to determine the enterprise value of the company after the transaction is completed, the first step would be to calculate the market capitalization of the company. TYU is issuing .7 shares to purchase PLM. As a result TYU will be issuing 7 million new shares. This brings the total number of outstanding shares to 27 million. We now multiply the

number of shares by the price per share. In this case 27 million shares X $114 = $3.078 billion. Now we must add the net debt of each company. In this case the total net debt is $55 million. The enterprise value is found by adding the net debt to the market capitalization as follows: $3.078 billion + $55 million = $3.133 billion.

9. D) A strategic buyer acquires a company to expand its business and for the synergies that may exist between the two companies. A leveraged buyout firm is a financial buyer who is seeking to exit the business and to generate the greatest internal rate of return.

10. C) The amount of goodwill is calculated by subtracting the net tangible assets of the acquired company from the value of the offer. The net tangible assets for QWER is $80 million. Found as follows $200 - 25 -20 -75 = 80 (in millions). The deal would create $70 in goodwill. However, the assets on the balance sheet are subject to a $30 million write up based on the market value of the assets. This reduces the amount of goodwill created by the transaction. As a result, the amount of goodwill created by the transaction is $40 million. Once added to the existing goodwill for GET, the total goodwill would be $364 million.

Made in the USA
Columbia, SC
05 December 2024